INTERNATIONAL RESEARCH FORUM 2007

INTERNATIONAL RESEARCH FORUM 2007

LUTZ HEUSER, CLAUDIA ALSDORF, AND DAN WOODS

Evolved
Technologist
Press
New York, NY

International Research Forum 2007
Lutz Heuser, Claudia Alsdorf, and Dan Woods

Published by Evolved Technologist Press, an imprint of Evolved Media Network, 242 West 30th Street, Suite 801, New York, New York 10001

This book may be purchased for educational, business, or sales promotional use. For more information contact:

Evolved Technologist Press
(646) 827-2196
info@EvolvedTechnologist.com
www.EvolvedTechnologist.com

Editor/Analyst: Dan Woods, Deb Cameron
Writers: John Verity, Dan Woods, Kermit Pattison, Richard Adhikari, Deb Cameron, Jonathan Berr
Copyeditor: Sara Kreisman
Production Editor: Deb Gabriel
Cover and Interior Design: 1106 Design
Illustrator: Tory Moore
First Edition: January 2008

ISBN: 978-0-9789218-3-5; 0-9789218-3-6

Contents

Preface

A Russian proverb says: repetition is the mother of learning. The meaning: If you want to get good at something, do it over and over. The team at SAP Research is happy to report that this proverb holds true for conferences and books that capture and extend the discussion and analysis. In May of 2007, SAP Research hosted the second International Research Forum in Eltville, Germany, and brought together leading thinkers from academia, business, and government to examine mega trends in Information Technology. This book, the second one we have created based on conference proceedings and subsequent research, shows we are starting to get good at all of this.

First of all, the conference was designed to cover four topics that built on each other in an evolutionary fashion. The conference attendees discussed the potential of Enterprise 2.0 in the first session, the service grid and the future of computing in the second. The third session covered user-driven innovation, a practice that should be accelerated by the trends discussed in the first two sessions. The final session focused on business model transformation, which should be made easier if all the prior trends take hold. The presentations and discussions, which included time for participants to analyze the issues and bring up new points and objections, provided a rich starting point for the chapters of the book.

It is hard to know exactly why, perhaps the quality of the program, perhaps the currency of the ideas, but for some reason this time around we attracted a star-studded collection of thinkers to help us build on the ideas collected at the Forum. We managed to talk to the leading researchers in the world in each of the topic areas: the people who coined the terms we discussed or whose research made the topics worthy of discussion. We are also pleased that our use of graphic illustrations has been more extensive.

All in all, we hope that you find this book as fun and exciting to read as it was to write. Please visit us at *http://international-research-forum.com* and let us know your thoughts.

Acknowledgments

The authors' first debt goes to the participants at the 2007 International Research Forum and the virtual participants who joined us afterward. They are the core of this book and we are grateful for their time and enthusiasm. Please see the Appendix for a full list of all those who are due our deepest thanks.

The team at SAP Research captured the conference expertly through video recordings, transcripts, and mind maps that provided an excellent start for the writing team. Dan Woods of Evolved Media and Claudia Heimer of Ashridge Consulting, who served as moderators of the forum, played an important role in keeping the discussion flowing and orderly, which helped us tremendously in the preparation of this book. We would also like to thank Henrike Paetz and her team at

SAP Research Communications for the enormous effort in organizing the event.

The writing team of Dan Woods, John Verity, Kermit Pattison, Richard Adhikari, Deb Cameron, and Jonathan Berr transformed raw transcripts and interviews into a pleasing narrative. The editorial team at Evolved Media was a pleasure to work with. Deb Cameron and Deb Gabriel were expert editors who squeezed every error out of the text and attacked the job of getting the manuscript approved and into its final form with extreme diligence. Deb Gabriel's work as Production Editor kept us on schedule. Tory Moore's illustrations and the cover and interior design work from Michelle DeFilippo and her team at 1106 Design make the book attractive and easy on the eyes.

No expression of gratitude would be complete without adding our thanks to Peter Zencke, the responsible board member for SAP Research at SAP AG, Henning Kagermann, the CEO of SAP, and the rest of the executive board for their vision and support of this project.

In May 2007, Lutz Heuser, Vice President of Corporate Research and Chief Development Architect at SAP AG, played host to the second International Research Forum. Like the first Forum a year before, the meeting, which took place in Germany, was a gathering of leading thinkers from academia, business, and government who were brought together to analyze pressing issues related to effective use of technology and to make forecasts about the future.

The 2006 International Research Forum led to the publication of a book that captured and distilled the ideas discussed at the Forum and then expanded on them through further research. The 2007 International Research Forum followed the same model and resulted in this book. But unlike the topics at the 2006 Forum, which were a

broad sampling of urgent issues, the program of the 2007 Forum followed a sequential thread.

The unifying idea which permeated each discussion was the concept of the Internet of Services. The Internet of Services is the larger
concept of a web-based service economy that ties together many trends
discussed in this book, such as the service grid, software as services,
social networking, and so on. In contrast to the first incarnation of the
web, Web 1.0 if you will, which was primarily a collection of pages, the
Internet of Services has emerged as a rich collection of content, functionality, and methods of interaction. Instant messaging, texting, viral
video, teleconferencing, voice over IP, social networking, blogs, wikis,
and virtual worlds all bring people together in ways never before possible. The digital means of production have been truly democratized,
not only because it is easy to create all of these forms of content, but
also because the moving parts, the services, are now available as
toolkits. Consumers have arrived en masse to enjoy the Internet of
Services, and the positive experience they get from many offerings is
putting pressure on business technology to follow suit. Indeed, it is
possible to see the phenomenon of software as a service as the application of consumer-friendly techniques applied to enterprise software.

In each of the Forum discussions, the potential of the Internet of
Services was revealed in new ways. Enterprise 2.0 explores the way
individuals, in their personal lives and in business, are empowered to
communicate and collaborate. The service grid, the idea of the Internet
of Services as a platform for computing, also enables user-driven innovation and business model transformation. The Internet of Services
provides the underlying global infrastructure to form flexible Business
Webs to provide value-added services. As we will see, the IOS is an
extended phenomenon that multiplies the potency of the trends and
tools discussed throughout this book.

The success of the first Forum and companion book smoothed the
way to engage with internationally known experts to become virtual
participants in the conference and extend and deepen the discussion
started at the Forum. During the follow-up research, the authors of

this book, Lutz Heuser, Claudia Alsdorf, and Dan Woods, were able to secure the participation of leaders in every field discussed.

- For Chapter 2, "Enterprise 2.0," Dr. Andrew McAfee, the Harvard professor who invented the concept of Enterprise 2.0, talked to us about how the collaborative technologies of Web 2.0 are transforming how work is done in the enterprise.

- For Chapter 3, "The Service Grid," Dr. John Seely Brown—who, along with his writing partner John Hagel III has been mapping out, in a series of books and white papers, the likely form that the ultimate service grid will take—helped the authors analyze the nascent elements of the service grid, the challenges that must be overcome, and the likely path forward.

- For Chapter 4, "User-Driven Innovation," Dr. Eric von Hippel, the leading researcher on the concept and author of two books on the subject, provided his ideas through an interview and his books.

- For Chapter 5, "Business Model Transformation," Mr. Navi Radjou, an analyst at Forrester, spoke to us about the idea of the Global Adaptive Organization and the way that companies are choosing different business models to suit the situation in each country and the needs of the strategy for each product.

Joining these thinkers in each chapter were other leading experts who provided even more valuable insights. Of course, the foundation for each chapter was the discussion at the Forum, which was lively and penetrating, as usual, and which is captured at the beginning of each chapter.

The Thread of the Forum Sessions

The 2006 International Research Forum covered a massive amount of ground. The four sessions covered Web 2.0, the semantic web, RFID

and real world awareness, and IT as a tool for growth and development. While these discussions were fascinating and resulted in an
interesting book, Lutz Heuser sought to focus the program for the 2007
International Research Forum so that discussions of each session lead
naturally into each other. Figure 1-1 shows the progression of the 2007
Forum program:

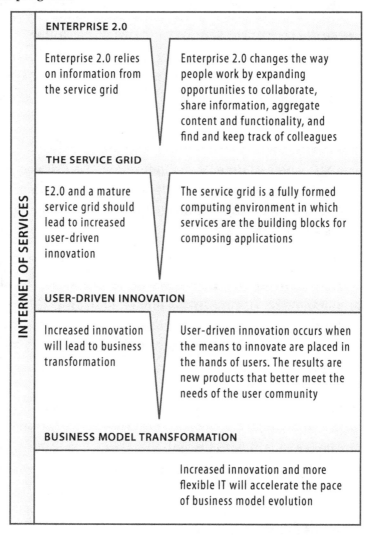

Figure 1-1. The Progression of Topics at the
2007 International Research Forum

As it turned out, this structure worked exactly as planned, both at the Forum and during the creation of this book. The ideas in each session raised questions relevant to the next session that needed to be discussed. The analysis built to a crescendo, which, at the Forum led to exciting dinner conversation and further research, and, in the book, led to a conclusion about how companies can best channel the energy driving the trends discussed to improve the way their organizations design and deploy technology.

Enterprise 2.0

The beginning session covered Enterprise 2.0, the idea of how Web 2.0 technologies and forms of collaboration that have emerged in the consumer space will be applied to enterprise computing.

In a sense, Enterprise 2.0 is another version of a familiar pattern in which the control and mechanisms of innovation slip out of the hands of corporate IT departments into the hands of users. It is as if the ball in some sort of sport were taken away from those in IT by users who are now playing their own game by their own rules.

This pattern first appeared when the personal computer was introduced into the enterprise computing environment and led to an explosion of do-it-yourself innovation based on the newly arrived word processing and spreadsheet programs. As the Internet rose in prominence, the same thing happened with web sites. In both cases, corporate IT departments found themselves watching an explosion of activity, some of it productive, some of it misguided, and wondering how to make sure that everything was managed according to prudent standards. The idea for most IT departments is not simply to lock down new forms of activity but to find out how to channel the energy in a productive fashion and manage the risks.

Enterprise 2.0 may be the most challenging explosion of do-it-yourself IT that has yet to arrive. The Forum session examined the different types of activity that are taking place under the moniker of Enterprise 2.0 and analyzed the patterns that are emerging and their implications. Individual publishing techniques such as blogs are bringing a wider awareness to the enterprise. Wikis are solving problems that knowledge management systems have long desired to address but were not able to. Social networking systems record the connections between people and allow applications to broadcast knowledge over a network of friends. Other techniques such as tagging and predictive markets help people find content and aggregate opinions.

The conference participants likened this to the sort of improvisation that emerges in a jazz band, but then quickly moved to the question of structure. How can all of this do-it-yourself activity be channeled in an orderly fashion? How can it be connected to the highly structured information in the enterprise? The first part of Chapter 2, "Enterprise 2.0," summarizes the discussion of the conference.

The authors looked at this discussion and decided that some basic deck clearing was in order. Many of the speakers seemed to use the terms like blogs and wikis in different ways. The technologies are deceptively simple and that simplicity can lull you into a false sense of understanding. The use and value of these technologies are different in an enterprise context than on the public Internet. Making Enterprise 2.0 work requires a new cultural mindset. With the help of participants Prof. Michael Rosemann and Dr. Mathias Kirchmer, and experts such as Dion Hinchcliffe, Phil Nelson, Denis Browne, and Dr. Peter Rip, the authors addressed these issues by asking and then answering a series of questions.

Service Grid

One of the key issues in the Enterprise 2.0 discussion involved the right way to incorporate structured information from enterprise applications into the free-form landscape of Enterprise 2.0. Services are the mechanisms by which that will happen. Services are also the raw material used to create mashups and widgets that are aggregated in role- and process-specific interfaces, frequently created by users themselves. And on the architectural front, perhaps the largest trend in computing right now is the movement toward service-oriented architecture, the idea of constructing computing solutions using services as fundamental building blocks. Software as a Service means delivering applications over the Internet instead of installing them in corporate data centers. Infrastructure as a Service means doing the same thing for infrastructure such as storage, databases, and computing resources of all kinds.

If services are sprouting up all over what will they eventually turn into? The answer to that question is another take on the Internet of Services called the service grid: the idea of a comprehensive, secure, reliable, and scalable collection of services that can meet the needs of enterprise solutions. The second session of the conference centered on analyzing the current and future states of how parts of the service grid that now exist will evolve and merge into a more complete form. The Forum discussion ranged widely, covering the use of service grids in research, the difference between creating services from scratch and creating them based on existing applications, the potential problems with managing the services at scale, ensuring semantic consistency, defining and meeting service level agreements, along with the advantages of using Software as a Service.

Looking back on this discussion, the authors were struck by how many different terms the word service showed up in and how many different meanings those terms had. So the analysis started by sorting out all of those terms. Then, with the help of Dr. John Seely Brown and his useful collection of writings, Dr. Peter Kürpick, Paul Butterworth, Anne Thomas Manes, and Patrick Grady, as well as participant Dr. Tony Hey, the authors analyzed the end state of the service grid from top to bottom. The questions asked and answered look at the current services that can be thought of as the service grid; define, using Seely Brown's vision, the ultimate form of the service grid; and examine the challenges to creating the grid and the benefits of getting there. The chapter then takes a close look at ways of automating the assembly of applications once a comprehensive service grid is in place.

The conclusion the authors draw is that Enterprise 2.0, along with the service grid, even in its embryonic form, will lower the barrier to making IT do what is needed. What this means is that more powerful tools will be in the hands of more people, solutions will be easier to create, and the result should be an increasing amount of experimentation and innovation, which leads us right to the topic of the third session of the Forum.

User-Driven Innovation

User-driven innovation is the idea that people who use products can play a valuable role in designing and modifying products to better suit their needs. What is needed to make this sort of innovation happen is to provide users the means to modify products. Then, amazing things can happen.

The Forum picked up this theme by looking at the way that IT is becoming more and more available to be improved by users through Enterprise 2.0, the rise of services, and other means. The discussion at the Forum then examined the institutional resistance to user-driven innovation, the ways that innovation might be encouraged, and other related issues.

The authors felt that Forum discussion was right on target and just needed to be expanded. To do that, the authors went right to the leading expert in the world on user-driven innovation, Dr. Eric von Hippel. Based on an interview with Dr. von Hippel, along with discussions with Mary Murphy-Hoye, Dr. Sonali Shah, Dr. Eric Kasper, and Prof. Nikolaus Franke, the rest of the chapter dives deeper into the topic, asking and answering questions about the definition and benefits of user-driven innovation. Barriers to user-driven innovation are analyzed and ways to encourage innovation are suggested.

Business Model Transformation

The last topic for the Forum was the idea of business model transformation. Business models are the way that the values, strategy, and capabilities of a corporation come to life. A business model is the identity of a company in action, translated into specific relationships between the company, customers, and suppliers, along with the processes that create value. The goal of this last Forum session was to examine emerging patterns in the shape of business models and to analyze the barriers that prevented change. The Forum discussion centered on how IBM manages its business models and how cultural orthodoxies represent the largest obstacle to transformation.

The authors picked up on the themes by speaking with Prof. Mathias Kaiserswerth about IBM and asking Claudia Funke to expand on the analysis of cultural barriers that she presented at the conference. The authors turned to Navi Radjou of Forrester to ask him to explain the emerging patterns in business models that he has captured in his idea of the Globally Adaptive Organization. To end their analysis, the authors summarize the idea of open business models that Henry Chesbrough has made popular in his recent writings.

What We Learned

At the end of writing this book, the authors came away with a renewed appreciation for the concepts discussed in this book. Each represents a massive opportunity for growth and creativity. Each could be the subject of a book in its own right.

In the Conclusion, the authors take a step back from the world of the future and instead focus on the near term. They gained insight by talking with Peter Thoeny, founder of TWIKI.NET. Given the discussions and the research we performed, what can we say about how to move forward in each of the areas discussed? What are the practical suggestions that fit into the world of the possible that most of us live in. With appropriate humility, the authors set forth a practical set of steps for making the most of the ideas set forth in the book to help make the organizations we all work in more productive and effective in achieving their goals.

Enterprise 2.0 is deceptively simple. Many people talk about Web 2.0 and Enterprise 2.0—with its collaborative technologies like social networking, blogs, and wikis—with only a partial understanding. Ask 10 people about the business value of social networking and you are likely to hear 10 different answers. What's the difference between a public blog on the Web and one inside a company? Most people working in companies can't distinguish between the values created in each context—and, consequently, can't reap the rewards.

When people think of the world known as Web 2.0, tools like blogs and wikis come to mind. One way of thinking of Web 2.0 is simply as all of the functions of the Internet of Services presented to individuals through a user interface. It's easy to imagine all that just drifting into the enterprise as business tools. But the business world already

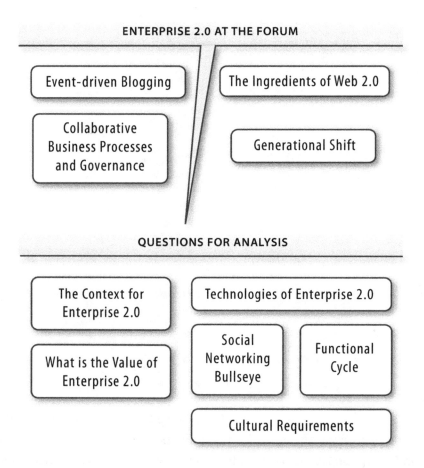

Figure 2-1. Enterprise 2.0 Chapter Map

was populated with computing infrastructure and established ways of working. New tools must be reconciled with existing ways of doing business. You can say what you want as an individual on Facebook and few people will care. But careless distribution of corporate information on a public blog or wiki could lead to violating regulations or breaking a law about disclosure.

This chapter challenges the oversimplified explanations of Enterprise 2.0 and shows that the truth is more complex. Building on the discussions of the 2007 International Research Forum, the chapter explores distinctions that haven't been fully explained in other venues. This chapter seeks to recap the latest developments of Enterprise 2.0 and point the way for further development.

Our tour will:

- Review the landscape from which Enterprise 2.0 evolved

- Summarize the proceedings of the conference

- Provide the analysis of the authors for further research based on the conference

- Examine fundamental questions about Enterprise 2.0:

  - What are the fundamental Web 2.0 concepts that set the context for Enterprise 2.0?

  - What are the technologies of Enterprise 2.0?

  - What is the value of Enterprise 2.0?

  - What are the cultural requirements for Enterprise 2.0 adoption?

  - How does Enterprise 2.0 relate to the remaining topics of the book?

From Web 2.0 to Enterprise 2.0

Almost as soon as that amorphous set of do-it-yourself technologies and software services known as Web 2.0 appeared as the latest consumer fad, attention shifted to the enterprise. Swarms of pundits, business theorists, venture capitalists, and entrepreneurs tried to sell corporations on blogs, wikis, software mashups, social networking, and other elements of Web 2.0.

The enthusiasm was immediate and palpable—although the optimism may not have been fully justified. Merely attaching the "2.0" suffix wasn't enough to prove that the Web actually had reached a new stage of evolution. Still, nobody could argue with the numbers. Tens of millions of people seized upon Web 2.0–style apps and services, sharing every aspect of their lives: political opinions, restaurant reviews, instant messages, multimedia web pages, photos, videos, and audio files. Suddenly, the Web was no longer just a one-way information channel but a giant stage with a cast of millions. Clearly, something big was afoot. Would the corporate enterprise benefit, too?

Soon enough, market research reports appeared, conferences were scheduled, and bloggers were trumpeting Web 2.0's technical and business possibilities. Terms like "social computing," "community," "collaboration," and "crowdsourcing" became all the rage, and Silicon Valley was abuzz with activity. Established software firms got in on the act too: Microsoft, for example, began promoting the Web 2.0 qualities of its SharePoint portal product, going so far as to add support for wikis, and promised lots more to come. SAP promoted the creation of widgets based on ERP that can fit into user-friendly environments like the home page-building systems offered by Yahoo! and Google.

It's Here

Blogs, wikis, and social networking appear to be the very antithesis of enterprise software. They're incredibly easy to deploy, use the Web as their execution platform, reach vast numbers of users, and require no training. Indeed, many of them explicitly invite remolding, even by non-technical users, because they have virtually no structure when launched. The task of defining the specific steps in a process is not done up front before the tools are put in the hands of users. The way people work emerges organically based on the needs of users. For most Enterprise 2.0 technologies, IT departments do not play the role of intermediaries who craft the solution. Enterprise 2.0 is a do-it-yourself phenomenon.

Certainly, enthusiasts argued, there must be ways for companies to exploit Web 2.0's lightweight, easy-going approach. Might not blogs and wikis help workers to collaborate and innovate more effectively? Didn't corporations, ostensibly organized around hierarchies, appear ripe for social-networking schemes that could locate talent and unite disparate individuals? Wasn't knowledge the main asset in many corporations— and one that IT had repeatedly failed to capture and manage? Might not these new schemes conquer the knowledge management problem once and for all?

Couldn't these new forms of electronic collaboration help the enterprise to work more efficiently with suppliers, channel partners, outsourcers, and customers? Might even hidebound back-office software applications improve their business value if recast in Web 2.0 style? And wouldn't these easy-to-master-and-remodel technologies amplify the intuitive, unstructured, spontaneous work patterns of today's knowledge workers?

Meanwhile, as these questions drew attention, bewildered CIOs were already wondering what to do about the blogs, wikis, and software mashups that had surreptitiously infiltrated their companies. Overnight, a vast "shadow IT" environment sprang up, threatening the corporate IT department's ideas of governance and data integrity. But, like the threats posed by initially uncontrollable personal computers and web sites, the value created by Enterprise 2.0 is too large to ignore.

CIOs were forced to confront a succession of serious questions: Would this wave of new technology help or hinder their companies? What standards and policies would be needed to make it as effective and least disruptive as possible? How would they ensure it didn't thwart existing policies and procedures or run afoul of regulations like Sarbanes-Oxley?

These same CIOs also confronted the limits of their own knowledge. Oftentimes their familiarity with this area was superficial. Enterprise 2.0 does not mean just throwing a blog at every problem, but it does mean using blogs. Enterprise 2.0 is not attempting to recreate Wikipedia, but it does mean using wikis.

To fully understand Enterprise 2.0, we must look at each technology in greater detail. But first, let's examine how the leading promoters of Web 2.0 have defined Enterprise 2.0.

The Ingredients of Web 2.0

What actually distinguishes a Web 2.0 app or service? Dale Dougherty, a co-founder of the publishing company O'Reilly Media, is credited with coining the term Web 2.0 as a catchall for the many new Web-based companies and ideas that sprang to life around the millennium. All shared a common theme: harnessing user-generated content. In a special O'Reilly Radar report on Web 2.0, *Web 2.0 Principles and Best Practices*, authored by John Musser, the company set forth the following eight "core patterns" that distinguish Web 2.0 from earlier generations of computing:

Harnessing collective intelligence. Web 2.0 services harness an "architecture of participation" that encourages masses of users to directly contribute content. Unique algorithms can analyze, restructure, and reorganize those contributions to improve function and utility.

Leveraging the long tail. The Internet's broad reach and low cost make it possible for businesses to serve many niche markets that previously were too small to bother with.

Software above the level of the device. Web 2.0 services accommodate the growing range of devices that, thanks to wireless access, are able to stay connected to the Internet almost anywhere on the planet. Many services, moreover, are able to provide much of their functionality even when a laptop or cell phone is offline, and later, when the Internet connection is reestablished, they seamlessly synch local data with that stored "in the cloud."

Lightweight and designed for scalability. By using lightweight business and software-development models, it's possible to jump on fleeting market opportunities, gain first-mover advantage, and scale a Web 2.0 business rapidly and at relatively low cost. Also contributing to rapid scalability is the emergence of hosted data storage and applications services supplied by some of the Web's largest providers, including Amazon.com and Google.

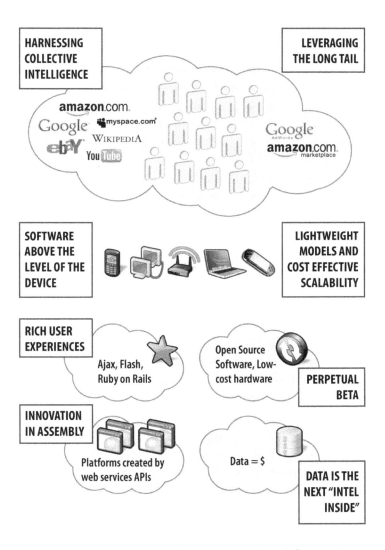

Figure 2-2. Eight core patterns of Web 2.0, as identified by John Musser in Web 2.0: Principles and Best Practices, *an O'Reilly Radar Report*

Rich user experiences. Increasingly, users expect to work with dynamic, interactive web content like videos. These capabilities rely on newer web design techniques including use of the Ajax scripting technique and Adobe's Flash multimedia authoring tools.

Perpetual beta. Because software runs online, not on users' own computers, and is delivered as a service, it can be updated almost continuously—with users invited to contribute ideas and even code. This approach trades quality of software against speed of development and time-to-market.

Innovation in assembly. Service platforms can be designed to enable the rapid remixing of data and services—so-called mashups—to help users customize services and seize business opportunities.

Data is the next Intel Inside. Unique, hard-to-duplicate collections of data may be more important to a service's success than its logical function. In many cases, this data is provided by users themselves: personal photos, web pages, restaurant and product reviews, and even—as proposed by a startup called 23andMe—personal genetic information.

Web 2.0 is decentralized and massively connected. Adoption tends to begin at the edge and grow inwards, not the other way around. Network effects create a true web of many-to-many connections that replace the one-to-many publishing and communication models of the past. Now, the edges become as important as the core, and old modes of communication are disrupted.

I Dub Thee ... Enterprise 2.0

Soon this trend moved from the free-for-all of the Web into the corporate world. Dr. Andrew P. McAfee, Associate Professor at Harvard Business School, popularized the term "Enterprise 2.0" to describe the use of Web 2.0 by corporations. Dr. McAfee was interviewed as part of the research for this book and his thoughts are incorporated throughout this chapter. In a widely read 2006 paper in the *MIT Sloan Management Review* titled "Enterprise 2.0: The Dawn of Emergent Collaboration," Dr. McAfee argued that this trend gave knowledge workers radically new ways of working together. As a whole, Dr. McAfee wrote, they could "usher in a new era by making both the practices of knowledge work and its outputs more visible."

Enterprise 2.0 at the International Research Forum

It was exactly this potential for new ways of harnessing and using knowledge through digital computing that prompted SAP to make Enterprise 2.0 the opening topic of discussion at the International Research Forum 2007. Conference organizers recognized the emergence of an entirely new genre of enterprise software. It was radically different from highly structured, transaction-oriented ERP systems, yet also entirely complementary to that software. Both will play a major role in corporate IT and each will benefit from the rich cross-fertilization. The following questions were distributed before the conference to start the discussion:

- How can collaboration and emergent structure and processes be encouraged?

- Is there any optimal lifecycle for harvesting and scaling processes that has been discovered through collaboration?

- How can we define boundaries between completely unstructured collaboration, partially structured collaboration, and the locked-down processes of hub systems?

- How can hub systems become self-improving based on data collected in use?

- How will a population of users accept systems that are rapidly evolving? When will the pace of change be accepted or rejected?

To kick off the discussion, Professor Dr. Michael Rosemann, Professor for Information Systems and Co-Leader of the Business Process Management (BPM) Group at Queensland University of Technology,

Michael Rosemann is Professor for Information Systems and Co-Leader of the Business Process Management (BPM) Group at Queensland University of Technology, Brisbane, Australia. His areas of interest are process-based management, process modeling, ontologies, and Enterprise Systems (ES). He is the Chief Investigator of a number of applied research projects funded by the Australian Research Council and industry partners including SAP. Prof. Rosemann has been teaching SAP solutions at universities since 1992.

On the educational side, he provided advice to a large number of universities about the design of an ES-related curriculum. He is the author/editor of 6 books and more than 130 refereed papers and is an Editorial Board member of 7 international journals. Prof. Rosemann chairs the Australian BPM Community of Practice (*www.bpm-roundtable.com*) and is a member of the ARC College of Experts. He was the Chair of the 5th International Business Process Management Conference in September 2007 (*http://bpm07.fit.qut.edu.au*).

Prof. Rosemann has intensive consulting experiences and provided BPM-related advice to organizations from various industries including telecommunications, banking, insurance, utility, logistics, and film.

Brisbane, Australia, provoked the audience by speculating how Web 2.0-style technologies might revamp existing enterprise software.

Technologies such as blogs, wikis, and social networking may appear highly appealing, but they won't enjoy much popularity in the enterprise if they remain so labor intensive. Although Generation Y—people in their 20s and thereabouts—has embraced Web 2.0, this cohort has yet to gain enough clout in the workplace to win acceptance for these technologies as enterprise tools.

But there's hope, Prof. Rosemann insisted. Until now, human-centered and system-centered workflows have been kept separate from each other. He suggested making blogs, wikis, and other Web 2.0 constructs "less curiosity-driven" and more able to support business collaboration. "Why don't we just open up the floodgates and combine

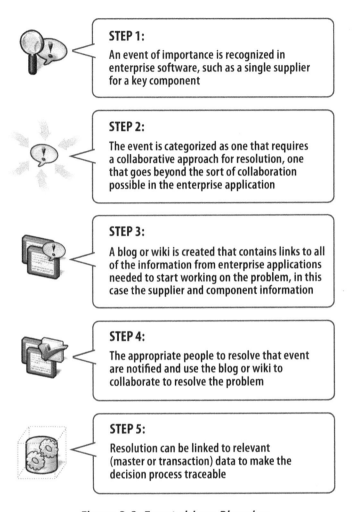

STEP 1:

An event of importance is recognized in enterprise software, such as a single supplier for a key component

STEP 2:

The event is categorized as one that requires a collaborative approach for resolution, one that goes beyond the sort of collaboration possible in the enterprise application

STEP 3:

A blog or wiki is created that contains links to all of the information from enterprise applications needed to start working on the problem, in this case the supplier and component information

STEP 4:

The appropriate people to resolve that event are notified and use the blog or wiki to collaborate to resolve the problem

STEP 5:

Resolution can be linked to relevant (master or transaction) data to make the decision process traceable

Figure 2-3. Event-driven Blogging

humanly entered data with quantitative, automatically derived data?" he asked.

Suppose a strike affects a manufacturer's key supplier. The manufacturer's IT system might automatically detect this disruption to the supply chain and initiate a blog that publishes relevant data from the ERP system. Managers and other internal and external stakeholders would be invited to visit the blog for updates about the crisis.

In Prof. Rosemann's view, this setup mixes human expertise with quantitative data pulled automatically from relevant supply-chain systems. Used properly, the blog could capture each exchange in an ongoing conversation—warts and all—and serve as a persistent hub where everyone could turn for the latest information.

"This kind of blog is not like today's—text heavy, labor intensive," Prof. Rosemann said. "It would be continuously enriched by selected ERP data and it would raise important questions: What products are purchased from this supplier, and where can we find replacements?"

This kind of resource represents an advance from traditional sources of communication like emails and conference calls. Emails tend to get lost in overfilled inboxes and therefore aren't so easy to review at a later date. Conference calls are difficult to conduct across a wide range of time zones. In such a system, all postings are kept in a central location and are traceable. If, at sometime in the future, someone wonders why the company stopped using a particular supplier, the record would show the thinking behind the decision. Indeed, the blog's contents might be linked to appropriate data in the ERP system and available at the click of a mouse. (Of course this example assumes that the data can be easily extracted from the ERP system, which implies a certain level of maturity in the availability of services and a service grid to support them, the topic of the next chapter.)

Collaborative Process Design

Prof. Rosemann said Web 2.0 technologies need hard, up-to-the-minute business data in order to become "less of a playground." The challenge is how to convert technologies into capabilities and thus allow Enterprise 2.0 to deliver maximum business value. So far, attention has centered primarily on knowledge workers. Indeed, it can be understood as simply the latest chapter in a long-running discussion about knowledge management—how to codify and share know-how to spur innovation or improve services.

But there are additional ways of deriving business value from these new techniques. It might be possible, Prof. Rosemann said, to collaborate online in the creation of new business processes. In one current research project, hospitals around the world will be invited to jointly rethink the processes of traumatology—treating serious multi-trauma injuries caused by violence or accidents. These cases involve specialists from several different institutions and locations who are engaged in processes such as first-aid at accident sites, intensive care, and rehabilitation.

Using software from IDS Scheer (a German company specializing in tools for modeling and managing business processes), the researchers have modeled a traumatology process that will be posted online for viewing and comment. Inspired by the collaboration of Wikipedia, a closed group of doctors, surgeons, and nurses will propose modifications.

Because those people are not familiar with modeling processes, Prof. Rosemann's team replaced the tool's usual process symbols with more familiar images such as ambulances, emergency rooms, and surgeries. A surgeon can log in and see a very intuitive environment, like Wikipedia's, and add her insight.

Could such an approach create better business processes? Probably, Rosemann said, but only in relatively uncompetitive markets. Airports and hospitals might make it work, but perhaps not banks, which are more competitive and reluctant to share process improvements. He also cited the example of eTOM (enhanced Telecom Operations Map), an industry-specific business process standard. Its development involved representatives from telecommunication companies from all over the world. They participated in weekly conference calls to share and consolidate business practices in order to jointly develop models for the main functions and processes in this industry.

"Can we speed up this kind of collaboration by using new technologies?" Prof. Rosemann asked. "Could I get hospitals around the world to work together, and within, say, three months, extend and rethink traumatology? Perhaps organizations like IDS shouldn't develop reference models as they now do, but instead host the communities and tools that develop reference models for different industries."

Prof. Rosemann pushed the Enterprise 2.0 idea even further, wondering if it might reshape the process of recruiting new employees. Imagine that a company identifies individuals with certain valuable talents such as technical skills or creativity. The company could tag the individuals' personnel records and, when needed, create consulting or contract jobs to fit these talents. Such a process might not work for every kind of job, but would be suited to projects requiring groups of specialists coming together, like filmmaking.

Prof. Rosemann cited an Australian computer gaming company that found a customer relationship manager by monitoring public blogs. The firm identified a young man in London who was blogging impressively about games, flew him to Brisbane, interviewed him, and hired him. "If the company had advertised in the Brisbane newspaper, they'd get hardly anyone suited to that job," he said. "Maybe the sort of people they were seeking are just not the ones who even read a newspaper on Saturday mornings."

He imagined an SAP HR solution that allowed users to specify terms or activity patterns and automatically search blogs for job candidates. One company called BuzzLogic has developed software that can analyze blog contents. "Perhaps I can set up employee master records of individuals who are not on my payroll," he continued. "I tag them in the SAP system, which gets continuous updates when changes occur in their work lives—as observed from monitoring a service like Facebook. This would lead to a more opportunity- than demand-driven recruitment approach."

Business Processes 2.0

Dr. Mathias Kirchmer was next to address the Forum. He envisioned using Enterprise 2.0-style collaborations to drive innovation. Why shouldn't companies exchange business process reference models, thus best practices, the same way people share videos on YouTube? He proposed an open-source environment in which companies contribute ideas about improving processes and share constructive criticism.

Mathias Kirchmer has been Senior Executive at Accenture since January 2008. He focuses on the development and delivery of the firm's business process management services. For almost 18 years, before joining Accenture, Dr. Kirchmer was with IDS Scheer, the leading provider of business process excellence solutions, last as Chief Innovation and Marketing Officer. Before that he managed IDS Scheer's Americas operations and its Japanese operations.

Dr. Kirchmer is an affiliated faculty member of the Program for Organizational Dynamics of the University of Pennsylvania as well as a faculty member of the Business School of Widener University, Philadelphia.

Dr. Kirchmer often hosts presentations and lectures at leading universities and conferences around the world. In 2004 he won a research fellowship from the Japan Society for the Promotion of Science. Dr. Kirchmer is member of the advisory board of the Business School of Widener University. He is the author of numerous publications.

Dr. Kirchmer suggested that such sharing might build bridges between disparate industries. In the biotech and machinery industries, seemingly quite different, the configuration of products during the final stages of production involves remarkably similar processes. In theory, companies working in these two industries might profitably share innovations with each other—especially if they had a mechanism that facilitated such exchanges.

Blogs, wikis, and most other Web 2.0 schemes may be extremely "user-friendly," but Dr. Kirchmer questioned how their loosely organized ways might perform in the structured, "procedure-based" enterprise. Can the technologies that delight gadget-happy teenagers be useful in corporations? What incentives are needed to encourage people to share knowledge on blogs and wikis? How can quality and trust in information be assured? Business process governance becomes a key topic so that information users add can be monitored for quality and usefulness.

Dr. Kirchmer asserted that Enterprise 2.0 techniques may indeed "improve the work process" for knowledge workers. He pointed out that transactional business processes have enjoyed tremendous improvement over the years as managers followed the advice of theorists such as August-Wilhelm Scheer and Dr. Michael Hammer. Their calls for applying heavy doses of IT and re-engineering business processes led

"Enterprise 2.0 will work like a jazz band. The bandleader calls a song, and because everybody knows its key, form, and chord changes, each player can safely improvise."
— Mathias Kirchmer

to the elimination of many jobs and increased cost efficiencies. In contrast, the knowledge worker, or symbolic analyst, has not experienced this kind of systematic attention to process. Dr. Kirchmer concluded that Web 2.0 technologies are just the thing to address this "huge opportunity."

Prof. Rosemann warned that Enterprise 2.0's "non-systematic approaches" might produce disappointing results. Companies also need more rigor, more structure, and more guidance, not simply more off-the-cuff comments from bloggers. "If we open up the floodgate for unmotivated conversations, we [will] potentially drown in the information."

Good point, said Dr. Kirchmer. But he argued that's precisely how "people who think for a living" actually do their work—in free-flowing, intuitive, relatively unstructured ways. By enhancing these activities, such workers could collaborate more effectively with colleagues.

The key issue, he continued, will be process governance. With their tighter degrees of freedom and flexibility, traditional policies and guidelines governing processes are no longer appropriate. "Enterprise 2.0 will work like a jazz band," he declared. "The bandleader calls a song, and because everybody knows its key, form, and chord changes, each player can safely improvise."

Governance Rules

At this point, the Forum's participants divided into four smaller discussion groups that met for a half-hour. Afterwards, a representative from each cluster presented his or her group's findings to the audience and the debate continued.

One of the main topics for the clusters was how enterprises might assure quality and usefulness in the information collected through free-form, Web 2.0 collaborations. Using techniques such as collaborative filtering, natural language processing, and analysis of dialogue structures, computers might actually help to organize and mine the low-density information that Web 2.0 schemes tend to accumulate.

But no amount of clever computing is likely to resolve a fundamental tension: the ease of use and freedom of Web 2.0 systems versus the rigor and efficiency of the enterprise. New governance mechanisms and incentives to encourage participation are needed. Ideally, a virtuous circle would emerge, with incentives driving contributions of content, rules of governance assuring the quality of that content, high-quality leading consumers to trust that content, and that, in turn, encouraging more people to participate.

Joachim Schaper, Vice President EMEA at SAP Research, characterized Enterprise 2.0 as the latest chapter in a long-running search for good knowledge management, or KM, techniques—using IT to capture and codify knowledge and make it readily available. Indeed, Enterprise 2.0's advocates argue that blogs, wikis, and social networking have the potential to foster collaboration and innovation. But will these innovations improve existing business processes? Or will they generate ideas for disruptive new products and services? The answer will depend on the incentives offered to potential contributors.

Why Bother?

One of the most compelling incentives, Forum members figured, is simply a sense of play. "Web 2.0 is all about fun and the flow that keeps our kids in front of these blogs and forums for hours and hours," said Prof. Max Mühlhäuser. "How do we transport this into the enterprise context? Usually, if we move things to business environments, they get boring."

Prof. Günter Müller said Cluster 2 offered the German word *Spassgesellschaft*, which he translated as "having fun in life," as an incentive for participation. "Maybe you don't want to talk to your boss or you don't want to talk at all," he said, "but this technology provides a tool for offering good ideas anyway."

While the jazz-band vs. symphony-orchestra analogy has its appeal, Prof. Müller argued that in his experience, many jazz bands aren't worth listening to. They play with too much creativity and not enough structure. Instead, businesses need a way to overlay the creativity of jazz onto the solid foundation of the symphony orchestra—to enable Web 2.0 to enhance traditional, well-proven business processes and structures. "We need this delta, this marginal addition of creativity, provided by the ones who have time, who have the talent."

Spassgesellschaft

Coined by German newspapers in the 1990s, Spassgesellschaft translates literally as "fun society." Writers in the feuilleton, or feature sections, used the neologism to describe the newly perceived lifestyle and attitude of a certain well-educated young crowd that was enjoying— and somewhat loudly, at that—the fruits of the "new economy": a flood of new technologies to play with, a booming stock market, and lots of disposable income to spend on what many observers saw as frivolities. Here, it seemed, was a new attitude to life: an emphasis on fun, almost to the point of hedonism.

Since then, and especially with the collapse of the dot-com boom, Spassgesellschaft has become loaded with irony. Today, the word connotes a class of Germans who live an intensely consumerist life and pay more attention to brand names than to politics or social problems. Critics see this crowd as somewhat ruthless: gladly willing to take advantage of and mocking others, fully embracing the self-interested morals and ethics of business, and living a fairly shallow life.

The term Spassgesellschaft captures an attitude to society that's also reflected in the rise of superficial talk and comedy shows on German TV, which stand in stark contrast to the tradition of quite political and cultured TV fare.

In short, Spassgesellschaft captures the latest layer of ultra-commercial American culture to find its way to Germany.

One powerful incentive could be social reputation, commented Dr. Schaper of SAP. Researchers feel rewarded when their work wins recognition from a peer group, he said. A researcher may take pride when her suggestion sparks a vigorous online discussion. "That's what researchers like," said Dr. Schaper. "They don't need to be offered extra money or other incentives. So, we need to find the sweet spot where pods inside the corporation get value out of contributing in a collaborative fashion."

Such efforts also could increase efficiency. In large companies like SAP, coding efforts often get duplicated by teams working in isolation from each other; the company must re-integrate code from disparate sources. "We're trying to mimic the open-source model inside the company, valuing that people are contributing to pools of code that can be easily re-used," said Dr. Schaper.

Another example is the SAP Developer Network (SDN), a lively online community where more than 1 million developers, analysts, and users pose questions and share technical know-how related to SAP software products. "SDN is a thriving blog and social networking community," Forum moderator Dan Woods, CEO of and Founder of Evolved Media, noted. "If you post a question on the SDN [bulletin] boards, you usually get an answer within 10 minutes of the posting."

When incentives are not compelling, the results can be extremely disappointing. The Web is littered with publicly accessible wikis that remain barren after some individual posts an initial concept with the expectation that others will provide the bulk of the data. Mr. Woods calls these "Tom Sawyer wikis," referring to the famous book by Mark Twain, in which the protagonist slyly persuades his pals to paint fences and thereby gets to relax while they do his chores. Unfortunately, wiki founders aren't as clever as Tom, and content fails to materialize because potential contributors perceive little reward.

Quality and Governance

Even with the right incentives and collaboration, there's still a need to maintain quality of content. Without rules and editing, an enterprise blog or wiki can quickly become unusable—or worse, a source of mistruths that disrupt on-going operations. Governance is critical to maintaining the quality and usefulness of content.

Forms of governance may emerge from the collaborative process itself. The showcase example is Wikipedia, the hugely successful Web-based encyclopedia that has grown through the efforts of many thousands of volunteers. As Forum moderator Dan Woods pointed out, rules governing Wikipedia entries have emerged from the community, not from a central committee. Mr. Woods said the rules are "quite strict, and in some cases, very ornate in terms of ideas." Yet the rules are generally heeded, even with divisive topics such as abortion.

Different Enterprise 2.0 technologies must be shielded from various kinds of "pollution." Public blogs, for instance, tend to attract spammers who post ads. YouTube must remain alert for copyrighted or offensive materials. Wikipedia must maintain accuracy and keep pages free from libelous statements. Social networks must protect individuals from identity theft.

The Generational Shift

How much use is Enterprise 2.0 actually getting? Despite all the talk, there are few good examples. "Who is really using social networking platforms in a corporate environment and who's doing that successfully?" asked Dr. Schaper. "I looked around my table here, and the set [of actual users] was pretty empty."

Then again, generational factors play into the equation. Asked how old the people at the table were, Dr. Schaper conceded that they were "all above 40, so I don't know if that's a good sample." According to many observers, generational issues are one of the biggest drivers that will compel enterprises to adopt wikis, social networking, and other staples of Enterprise 2.0. Younger workers, quite familiar with the technologies in their personal lives, are using them in the workplace, too. Unsanctioned wikis have popped up to organize company softball games, manage IT projects, and help dispersed workers create technical documentation.

Moreover, enterprises are realizing that if they don't implement social computing and other aspects of Enterprise 2.0 in a formal way, they risk being unable to attract the young talent they'll need in the future. A whole generation of young knowledge workers is taking Web 2.0 for granted. Looking for someone with like interests? Why not consult Facebook? They expect similar resources on the job.

While the discussions at the Forum ranged over many topics, most participants agreed in the end that Enterprise 2.0 adoption is increasing at an unstoppable pace and that the key question facing most companies is how to make this trend work for them.

Extending the Conversation: Questions for Analysis

The Forum's discussion of Enterprise 2.0 was all too short, but it stimulated much thought among the authors of this book, as many questions were raised as were answered. Each point of discussion seemed to start from a place of clarity, but then too often became shrouded in subtlety until everyone was a bit unsure of what was being discussed. The definitions of basic concepts such as blogs and wikis were not commonly understood. The importance of the topic of Enterprise 2.0 was acknowledged, but it was less clear *what* to do about it and *how* to succeed in making these new techniques work in a coordinated program.

After discussing the results of the conference and performing further research, the authors concluded that there was a need for a comprehensive tour through Enterprise 2.0. The authors sought out some of the leading thinkers in the Enterprise 2.0 field and discussed some central questions:

- What are the fundamentals of Web 2.0 that set the context for Enterprise 2.0?

- What are the technologies of Enterprise 2.0 and how will they change the computing environment inside companies?

- What is the value of Enterprise 2.0?

- What are the cultural requirements for Enterprise 2.0 adoption?

To answer these questions, the authors consulted with the following people who have been working on various aspects of Enterprise 2.0:

- Andrew McAfee, Associate Professor at Harvard Business School, who has written widely on Enterprise 2.0 and coined the term

- Dion Hinchcliffe, founder and Chief Technology Officer, Hinchcliffe & Company, a leading consultant who writes about Enterprise 2.0 and advises companies on adoption

- Denis Browne, Senior Vice President of SAP Imagineering in Palo Alto, who works on creating new kinds of solutions for the SAP platform that leverage Enterprise 2.0 techniques

- Phil Nelson, CTO and founder of several companies in the search and enterprise computing space, currently at thefind.com

The authors tried to capture and organize the insights from these thinkers to develop the threads of discussion started at the conference and make the resulting explanation of Enterprise 2.0 helpful to people who want to put these techniques to work.

What Fundamental Web 2.0 Concepts Set the Context for Enterprise 2.0?

Enterprise 2.0 is the collision of Web 2.0 technology and the existing infrastructure of enterprise computing. As such, Enterprise 2.0 is more complex than the world of Web 2.0, which filled a vacuum on the Internet in the consumer space. In the world of Enterprise 2.0, Web 2.0 technologies enter an environment with an array of existing elements: word processing documents, spreadsheets, and enterprise applications such as Enterprise Resource Planning (ERP), Customer Relationship Management (CRM), and Supply Chain Management (SCM). People are using these technologies to do their work and have been for years. Enterprise 2.0 is filling a vacuum of sorts in providing new, less structured ways to collaborate and work together, but existing forms of information must be incorporated into these new methods. The world of Information Technology has a long and complex history that must be understood before delving deeper into our main subject.

Enterprise Applications

The core of most companies—and indeed, the software that tracks most of the business activity in today's world—is found in traditional enterprise apps such as ERP, CRM, and SCM. In most cases, these systems are constructed around a highly structured central database that is kept up to date by applying well-defined updates, also called transactions, that record what is happening in a business. Enterprise applications are systems of record that represent the current state of a company in many dimensions. Financial information as well as information about products, customers, suppliers, staff, and regulations is all stored in enterprise applications.

For Enterprise 2.0 to work to maximum effect, the information in enterprise applications about customers, products, purchase orders, sales orders, inventory, warehouse levels, supplier, designs, contracts, and so on must be available. These existing elements must be incorporated and interwoven into the world of Enterprise 2.0 in order to really help people work on the core issues at a company. It has long been recognized that the highly structured world of enterprise applications could benefit from a more collaborative and flexible environment and there have been a number of attempts to make the structure of enterprise applications looser. Portals allowed users to assemble pieces of functionality from enterprise applications to meet special needs. Another attempt was knowledge management, a loose structure where information could be captured and managed. These efforts have helped but, unlike Enterprise 2.0 techniques, they have not opened the floodgates of collaboration. The key to making Enterprise 2.0 work is to allow the structured information to be available and incorporated into free-form collaborative processes. When this happens, organizations get the best of both worlds.

The Growth of Services

In order to use data from enterprise applications, you first have to have access to that data. In the past this was much more difficult because only proprietary and relatively difficult methods were available. Now, because of a standard known as web services, which allows people to use the Internet to publish pieces of functionality, the information inside enterprise applications is more available for all sorts of purposes, including incorporation in Enterprise 2.0 collaboration. Web services standards have also led to the development of Service-oriented Architecture (SOA), the idea of organizing enterprise computing by using services as building blocks. (The ultimate realization of SOA is known as the Service Grid, which is explored in detail in the next chapter of this book.)

Applications based on these "building block" services are called "composite applications." One example of a well-known form of composite application that is highly relevant to Enterprise 2.0 is known as "mashups." Mashups take their name from the world of music where the term refers to amalgamations created by sampling different songs. Mashups are applications combined in the same spirit.

While SOA frequently refers to services coming from enterprise applications, other services have emerged from outside enterprise applications for all sorts of purposes. They include Google's mapping services, Amazon's services for eCommerce and storage, and eBay's services for automatically interacting with their auction services, to name a very few.

The way services provide access to the data at the foundation of the enterprise, as well as other powerful functionality, sets the stage for amplifying the power of Enterprise 2.0 technology. Services bring information into collaborative environments and allow those collaborative environments to reach in and modify the structured world of enterprise applications.

The Rise of Web 2.0

After the dotcom bust in 2000, several forces converged. Blogging accelerated as a trend, and Wikipedia and Google search became widely adopted, standard reference tools. Open source infrastructure spawned an array of new technology. Google Ad Words delivered highly targeted ads that allowed companies to find new niche markets. This new technology gave rise to the "long tail business model," named by *Wired* Editor Chris Anderson in his book, *The Long Tail*, in which companies attempt to grow their market by serving the needs of many small, specialized niches rather than focus on the mass market with a smaller number of projects sold at large volumes.

Much of the new power of Web 2.0 was based on an innovation that made the browser a more powerful platform for building user interfaces. Ajax (Asynchronous JavaScript and XML) techniques change the role of a browser from a program that simply displays pages to a programming environment that could invoke many services, process the information gathered, display it, and interact with the user. This architecture allowed the creation of advanced web applications with better responsiveness and interactivity.

As the world economy recovered from the shock of 9/11, the progress made by Web 2.0 became more visible. Photos were shared and organized like never before on Flickr. Web sites were categorized by del.icio.us. Videos from YouTube became embedded everywhere. Mashups combined services from many places, especially Google Maps, to meet special needs. MySpace, Facebook, and LinkedIn showed the power of social networking. Tagging, crowd sourcing, and predictive markets all ballooned in importance as millions of people joined the party. In short, these developments demonstrated the power of connecting people. Soon this trend moved into the enterprise itself and started the Enterprise 2.0 ball rolling.

Edge Meets Hub

Enterprise 2.0 defies easy definition. As much as anything, it is a frame of mind, one that encourages solutions to emerge, as users do for themselves rather than have solutions designed for them by others. Users found that the goals that they had been trying to reach through more structured ways of working based on knowledge management tools were better served by blogs and wikis and other forms of collaboration.

Oftentimes these new tools entered the corporate world through the back door. First people grew accustomed to Web 2.0 in their personal lives. They blogged, used wikis, and sent text messages with their cell phones. But at work, they often found the technology lagged behind. In the workplace, the enterprise was a structured system that was designed to be a system of record and thus resisted change. People grew frustrated that they didn't have the same tools at work that they did at home.

A phenomenon known as shadow IT developed as individuals at the edge of the enterprise crafted their own solutions using available technology. Users are increasingly availing themselves of what have become known as "unstructured information systems." First, they began using email and word processing. Then they moved on to blogs, wikis, social networking schemes, desktop widgets, software mash-ups, and so on. These systems help knowledge workers to join forces in tasks that aren't easily automated. These technologies are the ones most commonly put under the umbrella of Enterprise 2.0. The hub of the corporation, the transactional ERP systems, was completely disconnected from these efforts.

The intersection between these hub-and-edge systems makes today's enterprise software landscape so fascinating and pregnant with potential. Slowly but surely, these two categories are taking on features of the other—pointing to a future synthesis of some sort.

One early form of convergence came in the form of the structured wiki. This began when Swiss software engineer Peter Thoeny created an engine for technical support in his company. The wiki was designed to capture and share knowledge among members of the tech support team. It worked extremely well, but eventually Mr. Thoeny realized that his wikis lacked sufficient flexibility to support many of the communication and collaboration tasks required in tech support. Thoeny added structured elements such as tables, grids, fill-in forms, and database queries that transformed his wiki engine, called TWiki, into a full-fledged environment for developing partially structured applications. In fact, his invention came into being in the late 1990s, years before the term Enterprise 2.0 was coined.

Meanwhile, ERP moved toward collaborative mechanisms. Probably the most widely used vehicle for text-based collaboration within large enterprises is the free-form text field that shows up in many ERP documents. Employees use these fields to communicate within the context of business processes—to indicate, say, special handling for a specific order or how to approach an important customer. These text fields have existed since the early days of ERP, but now, that reach has been extended and people are proposing new kinds of hybrid systems. For instance, an ERP system might be programmed to launch a blog or wiki whenever a certain type of problem condition arises, as previously explained. By automatically creating and populating the wiki with relevant data and inviting a pre-specified group of people to contribute their thoughts, this arrangement could get people off to a running start. The result: problems get solved faster than they might otherwise.

Now that we have covered the environment out of which Enterprise 2.0 emerged, the discussion can move to a more detailed level.

What Are the Technologies of Enterprise 2.0 and How Will They Change the Computing Environment Inside Companies?

When combined, the technologies of Enterprise 2.0 have a cumulative effect. The velocity of information increases. The connections between people and information expand and are recorded. The collective brain of an enterprise becomes stronger. Values change. Large organizations become more like startups: loose, unpredictable, emergent, and, best of all, highly productive.

When Web 2.0 techniques arrive in the enterprise, they have a different function and effect than they do in the outside world. The simplicity of these technologies sometimes obscures their larger significance—and the complications therein.

To answer the question of how each Enterprise 2.0 technology will create value, the authors will first present three concepts that help illustrate the value of a particular technology: the functional cycle, the dimensions of centrality and structure, and the social networking bull's-eye.

The Functional Cycle of Enterprise 2.0

Sufficient progress has been made in understanding the capabilities of Enterprise 2.0 for a new technology stack to be proposed, one that can help us understand the transformations that Enterprise 2.0 will initiate. Actually, the elements of this stack are better visualized as a cycle of activity. As shown below, this cycle describes the functions of Enterprise 2.0 and how they work together to create value.

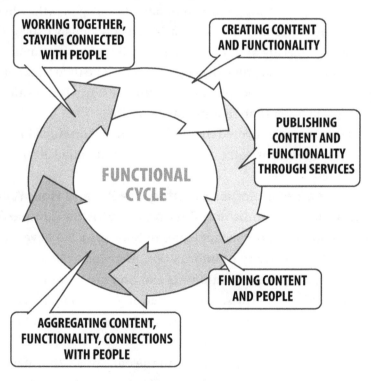

Figure 2-4. The Functional Cycle of Enterprise 2.0

The cycle starts with activities that get the ball rolling by creating content and functionality. Content could be everything from a short email to a thousand-page wiki. Functionality is created when someone writes a computer program and makes it available, usually as a service. In the context of Enterprise 2.0, this can mean services from traditional enterprise applications (via decomposition as described in the Forum discussion in Chapter 3, Service Grid) or from providers on the Web like Amazon or Google.

The next phase in the cycle is about finding content and people, which is often the same thing in Enterprise 2.0. Content can be found in many ways: searches, links, tagging, recommendations. In almost every case, one or more people are associated with the content.

Once people find each other, connections can be recorded in a social networking database, which becomes a giant network that shows who knows who. Informal individual connections between people are aggregated into a standard form. In many cases, the strength of the connection is recorded as well. These links can be mined for insight into the activities of individuals on both sides. Applications can use this network of friends to make further connections and broadcast content that may be of interest.

The same sort of aggregation happens with content and functionality. The bits and pieces that someone needs for a particular purpose are brought together to serve the needs of each individual.

The ultimate goal of the cycle is the idea of *using* all of this functionality and content to collaborate, increase productivity, and meet business goals, which can lead to the creation of more content and functionality to start the ball rolling over again.

Enterprise 2.0 seeks to increase the velocity of information and activity flowing through this cycle as well as to increase the connections made and recorded between both content and people. Activity that was ephemeral and took place only in transient browser sessions and discarded emails now leads to the creation of lasting content and connections that become a concrete asset.

Structure and Centralization

In addition to the functional cycle, there are two related dimensions that will help us understand the nature of each particular technology of

Enterprise 2.0 and the way that each technology fits into the cycle just described. Figure 2-5 shows the way that various technologies fit into a matrix defined by the dimensions of structure versus freeform content and centralized versus distributed.

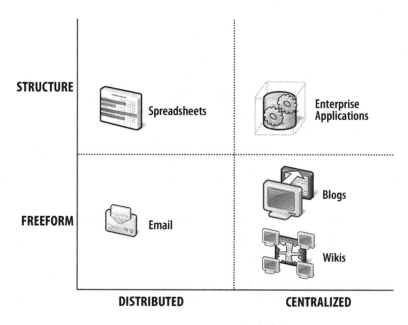

Figure 2-5. Structure and Centralization

The structure dimension runs from the most unstructured form of content, a page of text or an email that can just contain a string of words, to the most structured forms of content such as databases or enterprise applications that have a specific place on an entry form for every type of information, along with precise definitions of the relationships between them.

The dimension of centrality has at one end the most distributed forms of information, email, or word processing documents that are copied into many individual instances and shared by sending those copies around. Books and PDFs would fall into this category, and so would interactive forms built on those PDFs. At the other end of the spectrum are centralized forms of information such as blogs, wikis, and enterprise applications, which exist in one place and are shared.

These dimensions also help explain the role of various other artifacts of the enterprise-computing environment. For example, we can now see the role of a shared folder on a file system. A shared folder exists to provide some centrality for distributed documents that have no natural central home.

Dr. Andrew McAfee's Social Networking Bull's-eye

The third concept that helps us understand how Enterprise 2.0 technologies create value is the social networking bull's-eye, an idea created by Dr. Andrew McAfee. Dr. McAfee was interviewed for this chapter and provided more of his ideas through his published writings and his insightful blog.

Dr. McAfee has described the way that people work together with a bull's-eye diagram—a set of four concentric circles around a prototypical knowledge worker. This diagram provides a useful way to understand the relationship between social networking and Enterprise 2.0 technologies.

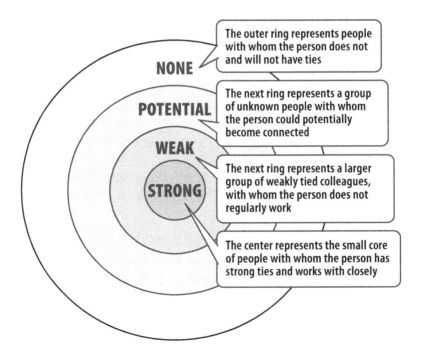

Figure 2-6. The Social Networking Bull's-eye

 **Andrew McAfee** joined the faculty of the Technology and Operations Management Unit at Harvard Business School in 1998. His research investigates how managers can most effectively select, implement, and use Information Technology (IT) to achieve business goals. He was the recipient of a US Department of Energy Integrated Manufacturing Fellowship for his doctoral research, which focused on the performance impact of enterprise information technologies such as SAP's R/3.

His current research falls into three categories. The first is an exploration of how Web 2.0 technologies can be used within the enterprise, and what their impact is likely to be. The second is an exploration of when IT leads to increased use of market mechanisms for coordinating activity, and when it instead leads to greater use of hierarchies. The third is a study of IT's impact over time on the structure of US industries.

He launched the first Harvard Business School faculty blog, which examines the impact of IT on businesses and their leaders.

Dr. McAfee teaches an MBA course called "Managing in the Information Age" and an Executive Education course, "Delivering Information Services." He also teaches in the Owner/President Manager Program, the General Manager Program, and the Senior Executive Program from the Middle East.

He continues to consult, primarily on helping companies formulate and execute IT strategies. He speaks frequently to industry and trade groups.

In the zone closest to the center are the people with whom this worker has particularly strong ties. Dr. McAfee describes them as long-term colleagues and work partners.

The next circle contains those who are "weakly tied" to the worker—people who she knows more casually, such as former colleagues.

The third circle consists of people who *could* potentially be valuable collaborators but remain unknown to the subject. "Inside any sizeable organization there are many people who would be very valuable colleagues, but we just don't have any good way to run across them," Dr. McAfee says.

In the outermost ring of the bull's eye are people with whom the worker has nothing in common, even if she were fully aware of them.

"Enterprise 2.0 technologies are valuable at each ring of that bull's eye," Dr. McAfee says. "But different technologies are more valuable in some zones than others, and there are different benefits at each ring. At the core, within the network of strong ties, a wiki is the prototypical technology because it helps you get your work done better, more responsively, with less redundancy. You're not emailing documents around all the time. It's a quick way to have the work part of the document emerge."

At the second level, Dr. McAfee sees social networking software, such as enterprise Facebook, as a valuable tool. "It's just a great technology for keeping on top of what your network of weak ties is up to and for exploiting that network," he says. "You can ask a question; you can pump it for information. You can reach out to a broad network of weak ties very easily using this software."

"Imagine a corporation in which people blog a lot—work teams, individuals. There's a culture that encourages everyone to narrate their work, to talk about what they're doing. Blogging is a great technology for that."

— Andrew McAfee

In the third circle, the corporate blogosphere offers the best means of turning potential ties into real ones. "Imagine a corporation in which people blog a lot—work teams, individuals," says Dr. McAfee. "There's a culture that encourages everyone to narrate their work, to talk about what they're doing. Blogging is a great technology for that."

At the outermost circle, Dr. McAfee sees prediction markets coming into play. He describes them as "an amazing tool for people who really don't have a lot in common with each other to come together and arrive at very accurate and decisive answers to important questions."

With these three concepts in mind, it is much easier to examine each particular technology of Enterprise 2.0 and determine its potential contribution.

Word Processing Documents, Spreadsheets, Email

Word processing documents, spreadsheets, and email are free-form and highly distributed. We all use them every day for creating and sharing content. In terms of the functional cycle, this category of document is primarily involved in content creation, although sending these documents around and the use of email lists is a form of distributed publishing. These documents represent part of the raw material for the rest of the process. The data in the systems of record are another source of fundamental information.

Enterprise 2.0 technologies help solve many of the familiar problems we have with distributed and unstructured forms of information, such as keeping track of the right versions of documents and consolidating changes made to multiple copies. Mechanisms such as shared folders attempt to solve some of these problems by providing a central location for distributed documents. On a wiki or a blog, which are centralized forms of content, there is only one version of a document, the one currently published, although a history of modifications may be recorded.

Unlike web pages, word processing documents, spreadsheets, and email lack accessible locations and cannot be easily linked to each other. This is a major problem.

Blogs

The term blog is a contraction of "web log." The main purpose of blogs is to enable individuals to communicate their thoughts to broad audiences. They are a "one-to-many" medium somewhat like broadcasting.

In the enterprise, a blog may help any sort of employee, from the CEO to a customer service representative, to reach out to fellow employees with thoughts about the company's current activities. It's the equivalent of a public-address system, amplifying one voice over others. Blogs can be set up to solicit feedback from readers about the items that the blog's owner posts there.

Originally, blogs were seen as a form of individual publishing, a way to share interesting Web pages with circles of known colleagues or, later, the broad, public audience. Bloggers would embed their posts with live hyperlinks and often write about the content of the pages at those links. Within the enterprise, similar use of blogs can help teams involved in scientific or engineering research to point out interesting content on the Web or share innovations.

Within the enterprise, blogs have a special value because their audiences are already pre-selected by working in the same organization. Trust amplifies the power of blogs to bring people together. On the Web, the audience is more fleeting and less interested in each other.

In terms of the functional cycle, the blog acts as a content creation and publishing mechanism when someone makes a post. When people comment on the post, they add to the content but are also able to find others who share an interest in the topic of the blog. Inside the enterprise these communities can form more easily than on the Web, where those who post a comment to a blog rarely contact and interact with other people who have commented. Colleagues in a company share a sense of trust and familiarity that is lacking on the Web. Once they hear what each other is saying, the urge to meet and talk can be stronger. Once a community of interest has formed, the collaboration may move to other venues for collaboration appropriate to the goals of the group, such as a mailing list or a wiki, and the connections formed can be recorded in a social networking database for future use. As a result, the connections made through enterprise blogging tend to have considerably more value than those made externally.

Dr. McAfee sees the "internal corporate blogosphere" as a "prototypical technology that's very useful for converting potential ties into actual ones." In this way, blogs help find people.

Imagine a corporation with a culture of blogging, he suggests, a company in which work teams and individuals narrate their work and talk about what they're doing. "With the search features that we have on blogs," Dr. McAfee says, "you can stay on top of that constantly changing blogosphere and realize when something of interest to you has been posted. That's a great way to find valuable colleagues and for a team to coalesce. There really wasn't a good way to do this prior to 2.0 technologies."

As an example of the benefits, he points to a company that builds resorts in the western part of North America. "One guy posted on his blog about a project that he'd worked on. He'd explained how he'd saved half a million dollars over what he thought a particular flooring system was going to cost." One of his colleagues wrote back to say he'd found this posting fascinating and that he was working on a similar project, and could he ask some follow-up questions? The blog costs virtually nothing to operate yet could generate huge savings. Says Dr. McAfee, "Now, what we might be witnessing there is a company saving half a million dollars."

Wikis

The wiki offers a method for groups of people to jointly construct web pages that are intended for sharing. Wikis tend to serve as permanent, constantly expanding repositories of knowledge. Users return to them again and again, unlike blogs, where postings quickly grow stale. Wiki pages may contain text, graphics, hyperlinks pointing to other web pages, and links to shared files. Wikis are free form but centralized. They help create content, find people, and collaborate.

The wiki's great breakthrough as a knowledge-sharing medium is that it harnessed the Web's global reach without requiring authors to master the intricacies of HTML. Only a few markup commands, or formatting tags, are needed to help organize text into paragraphs and sections and to highlight chunks of the text with bold or italicized fonts. Those who read the wiki's contents were also free to edit it—even to erase entire passages. (Revision mechanisms can help retrieve text deleted by vandals.) The wiki relies on its users to trust each other to be respectful as they make changes—indeed, its very openness may actually encourage trust.

Wikis have found much use by teams of researchers, software developers, technical support reps, and others who want to capture knowledge in a quick and easy way and share that knowledge. Without much overhead or pre-determined structure, wikis tend to quickly take on the shape and structure of thought that their users make use of, even if unconsciously. The process of joint editing acts as a sort of natural selection mechanism with useful structure—particularly helpful headings and subsections, for instance—being reinforced and less useful structure reworked and perhaps eliminated through a process of continual refinement.

While wikis are successful as general-purpose mechanisms for sharing information, their use within the enterprise falls into a few common patterns. To get the most from wikis, IT managers need to understand and employ the following patterns that were first published in *Wikis for Dummies*:

Content-based wikis enable communities of people to jointly create and refine content that's of interest to them. The prime example of this pattern is Wikipedia, the content of which has been contributed by people from all over the world.

Process-focused wikis help to track the progress of a project— the construction of a building, for instance, or the creation of a new piece of software.

Communities of interest can employ wikis to share information about and enthusiasm for a particular subject—a celebrity, TV show, sports team, or movie, for instance. Even before Thomas Pynchon's novel *Against the Day* was published in late 2006, a wiki devoted to it had appeared on the Web and ever since, readers have been able to consult this wiki for insights and observations—and to contribute their own thoughts, too. Within the enterprise, communities of interest may form around a specific revenue opportunity or risk.

Ease-of-use wikis take advantage of the simplicity of content creation of wikis to build web sites for almost any purpose.

Wikis Yearning for Structure

Peter Thoeny is credited with inventing the structured wiki, an attempt to explicitly create a new class of software that joins traditional structured applications with the new-fangled wiki. As such, the structured wiki is a precursor to much of what it is now referred to as Enterprise 2.0, and its development can be a useful pattern for how to introduce Enterprise 2.0 concepts into a company.

The structured wiki attempts to bridge the gap between hub and edge and provide the best of both worlds: methods for collecting and organizing data in well-ordered tables, which facilitates, among other things, transactional integrity and querying, and the open-to-all, easy-to-extend-hyperlink-and-annotate malleability of web pages. The structured wiki seems to appeal strongly to both IT departments and end-users. The former like the software because creating the application's logic is handed off to end-users; pretty much all IT has to do is run the server that hosts the software—or provide wiki dial-tone, as some advocates call it. End-users, meanwhile, relish the opportunity to build and maintain their own apps, which they can quickly pull together to meet fast-emerging needs and easily maintain over time as those needs change.

In short, the structured wiki offers a mirror image of how traditional enterprise apps are changing. The ultimate computing environment, it appears, is one that combines elements of Web 2.0 with those of structured enterprise apps.

In the conclusion we provide a detailed history of structured wikis, which the authors believe will be instructive to those attempting to understand and implement Enterprise 2.0 technologies.

These general patterns categorize most uses of wikis, but an even more diverse set of patterns has been described at WikiPatterns.com, a web site that lists dozens of successful wiki patterns—plus ones proven to be less than successful, referred to as negative patterns.

Search, Linking, Tagging, Folksonomies, and Predictive Markets

One of the most powerful and intriguing aspects of Enterprise 2.0 technologies is their ability to harness so-called "network effects." As more and more people contribute knowledge and add structure, their collective contributions make the knowledge more useful to everyone involved.

Search is at the core of this phenomenon. Without it, users have difficulty finding content, much less contributing. Search relies on links between content. Google's Page Rank algorithm uses the links between content to make inferences about which is most valuable. The difficulty or impossibility of linking is a large gap in Enterprise 2.0 capabilities, as we have noted.

Users can mark useful content they discover through a process known as tagging. Many Enterprise 2.0 schemes invite users to add short informational tags, or text labels, to shared items. Blog and wiki posts, photos from the Flickr photo-sharing site, and videos on YouTube can be tagged to indicate their significance. This kind of tagging is open to any individual. Others can search these tags to locate items that may contain information of interest—and locate other people with the same interests.

These tags function similarly to keyword search engines, but the openness of Enterprise 2.0 tagging creates a richer set of metadata. In the past, keywords generally were extracted from each document, or chosen from a pre-set taxonomy of information categories. Today's tags abide by no rules except the personal choice of each tagger. Two people tagging the same photograph may come up with entirely different descriptions.

Several web services harness this freeform tagging to better organize and search the public Web. One of these is del.icio.us, which enables individuals to tag web pages and share those tags to help others to find pages more quickly than a traditional Web search. Because tags are produced by an entirely human thinking process, they may be more valuable for searching than traditional keywords. Tags are a grassroots scheme for adding semantics to digital content—signifiers that indicate the meaning of documents, images, and other information, even if that meaning is entirely personal to a certain individual— no matter what the content creator might have originally intended.

Noted Enterprise 2.0 observer Dion Hinchcliffe says that initially he was skeptical about tagging, but real-world usage has convinced him that it is a powerful phenomenon. People will tag their content—

and this habit is especially visible in younger workers. "It's a behavior learned on the open Web," he says. "When they have an opportunity in the enterprise to tag as well, they use it because they know what it can do for them."

> *"You keep pushing the problem out to the network, imposing as little structure as you can. And what you get back is more structure than you ever imagined."*
> —Dion Hinchcliffe

Does tagging actually help? Mr. Hinchcliffe says it provides a new layer of metadata. It captures how users of IT systems think about their jobs and everything they do. It allows them to use their own language, and that enables some interesting scenarios. Mr. Hinchcliffe points to the example of a mutual fund client. Different teams began using the same wiki and were invited to tag content. Content has bylines, meaning finding content means finding people, and so groups and individuals with common interests find each other, Mr. Hinchcliffe reports, through random searching. They had two related sets of tags that didn't overlap, but users could find each other's material by searching. Even though the material was not theirs, they overlaid it with their own terminology and thinking. And this enabled them to find and use information that they would not have found otherwise because they didn't know the right words. "It is astonishing, and it happened over and over again," Mr. Hinchcliffe says.

This setup led to further gains. "You can search for things you didn't know you were looking for," Mr. Hinchcliffe says. "And it solved the problem of how to look up a word in the dictionary without knowing how it's spelled. How do you look for something on the Internet or on your wiki if you don't know what it's called? How do you find something that's close to what you want?"

Instead of relying on a few central experts with one way of thinking, the mutual fund invited all of its employees to contribute. This, adds Mr. Hinchcliffe, is the essence of Web 2.0. "When everyone gets to help organize information, we get the richest, most useful user-generated organization of that information," he says. "You keep pushing

 **Dion Hinchcliffe** is Founder and Chief Technology Officer for the Enterprise Web 2.0 advisory and consulting firm Hinchcliffe & Company, based in Alexandria, Virginia. A veteran of software development, Dion has been working for two decades with leading-edge methods to accelerate project schedules and raise the bar for software quality. He has extensive practical experience with enterprise technologies and he consults, speaks, and writes prolifically on IT and software architecture. Dion still works in the trenches with enterprise IT clients in the federal government and Fortune 1000. He also is the creator of Web 2.0 University, which provides the world's leading educational solutions in Web 2.0, Enterprise 2.0, and Ajax for private corporations and for the general public. He speaks and publishes about Web 2.0 and Enterprise 2.0 on a regular basis. Dion is working on a book about Web 2.0 for Addison-Wesley and is Editor-in-Chief of *Real World Ajax: Secrets of the Masters*. He is also currently Editor-in-Chief of the *Web 2.0 Journal* and *Social Computing* magazine.

the problem out to the network, imposing as little structure as you can. And what you get back is more structure than you ever imagined—more structure, more information, more meta data, and every possible point of view you have on the organization. And all this forms the richest fabric for knowledge management that you could possibly have."

Predictive markets can be viewed as another form of tagging. In predictive markets, choices are offered and a large number of people pick from the alternatives. The aggregate of these assertions provides information about the relative popularity or value of the alternatives.

UI Widget Frameworks

Arguably, the most important innovations in the success of Enterprise 2.0 are the new ways of melding web-based resources—data and computing—into systems whose value is greater than the sum of their parts. Specifically, software mashups and composite applications inject an invigorating dose of do-it-yourself into traditional software.

One often-missed implication of this do-it-yourself nature of Enterprise 2.0 is the way that, like the long tail model for products, user-created functionality serves the needs of niches of users. This do-it-yourself software is sometimes not of the same quality as the solutions that IT departments deliver, but it is good enough and it is suited to do just what a user wants. One of the lessons of Enterprise 2.0 is that good enough is good enough. Not every program must be scalable, robust, and bulletproof.

One simple example is UI Widget Frameworks, which lie at the easy end of the do-it-yourself spectrum. These user interface environments allow people to assemble many widgets and show a variety of information on a single page. A widget is a chunk of content or functionality gathered elsewhere, usually from a web service or some other mechanism, such as an RSS feed. Widgets are small panes in a graphical user-interface that are designed to display data extracted from selected applications. Widgets can display information about weather in a selected city, as supplied by a remote weather service such as Weather.com, or information about activities within the user's PC such as CPU activity or what's playing in a digital music player. Widgets are typically small—a rectangle only a few inches on a side—and unobtrusive. But they can present important information with greater simplicity than a traditional web portal page, which is graphically busy with many different pieces of information.

Of particular interest are Ajax-based user-interface frameworks, an example of the rapid assembly techniques described in O'Reilly's Web 2.0 framework. Building on the JavaScript language typically within a user's web browser, Ajax makes it possible to create web pages that do not have to be reloaded each time a user performs an action, thus allowing for greater responsiveness, speed, and interactive capability. That has enabled it to spawn a variety of environments for application assembly, some more enterprise-oriented than others. IBM, for instance, has brought out QEDWiki, a browser-based assembly canvas that allows people to create simple mashups using software components or services made available by content providers. Other services such as NetVibes and PageFlakes appeal mainly to consumers, but they may eventually serve enterprise purposes, too. All of them enable users, in typical drag-and-drop style, to pull together data and computational services from different sources on the Web and thereby create entirely new applications. Because many such apps are spawned to address unanticipated business problems almost immediately as they arise, software economist Clay Shirky has given them a fitting name: "situated apps." Similarly, IBM calls them "situational apps." Whatever the name, the technology has to be easy enough for users to create the applications on their own.

To build widgets, it helps to have some underlying programming available in an easy-to-consume form. Widget frameworks make it easy for programmers and non-programmers alike to configure them. Some widget frameworks operate within a particular desktop operating system such as the Dashboard framework in Apple's Mac OS X, while others are independent of any OS and rely solely on a web browser. A good example of the latter is the growing collection of Yahoo! widgets, which range from radio receivers to games to stock tickers.

Denis Browne of SAP is quite keen on the possibilities of widgets to provide lightweight alternatives to launching classic enterprise software, at least for simple tasks and for reading data. Data goes into these system-of-record environments and has a hard time coming out. "Users have to struggle to find their way to the information they care about," says Mr. Browne, who heads a West Coast Imagineering group at the company.

In other words, the user can't navigate efficiently and effectively to find answers. Mr. Browne suggests a rethinking of how to get information out of these systems from the end user's perspective. The idea is to cherry pick critical data, business processes, and transactions out of the enterprise system. SAP, like other software companies, has modeled many of the world's business processes and automated them "so that companies can close their books and the CEO doesn't go to jail." But in a way, the company has not spent much time "thinking about the end-user" and how he or she would interact with the ERP system.

Denis Browne, Senior Vice President, Business User Imagineering at SAP, has over 17 years of experience in the enterprise software market. His team explores and develops emerging technologies and business models which provide SAP customers with new solutions to improve their performance in the global marketplace. With innovative concepts and tools like Enterprise 2.0 and widgets, Mr. Browne's team points to the future of SAP solutions and the enterprise software market. Currently, he also consults with early-stage startup companies in the Bay Area, providing professional advice and guidance.

Before joining SAP, Mr. Browne spent 8 years working with numerous startups as a founder, chief technology officer, and product manager. For example, he led product strategy for Software as a Service, a web services platform company created by Marc Benioff, the Chairman and CEO of Salesforce.com. The solutions created by Software as a Service formed the basis of Salesforce.com's AppExchange offering. In addition, Mr. Browne spent several years at Oracle leading product development teams.

Mr. Browne graduated with an MA from the Institute of Technology in Carlow, Ireland. He is an avid traveler and spent a year and a half in 2002 exploring over 30 countries across North, Central and South America, Africa, Europe, Asia, and the South Pacific.

Widgets, Mr. Browne says, have the potential to give users easier access to relevant information. Widgets can present data from across the federated SAP landscape as well as third-party services and offerings. Consider a CRM example: An account executive is about to go on a series of customer calls. A widget mashes up the company's CRM data with Google Maps, thereby presenting a driving route. The widget might pull other contextual information about each client from Dun & Bradstreet, Hoover's, or Google News. The result is a system tailored to that person's particular job.

A project code-named Rooftop at SAP Research in Brisbane, Australia, is encouraging development of widgets in the standard widget runtime engines such as those provided by Yahoo, Google, Microsoft

(Vista Gadgets), Apple (Dashboard), and Adobe (Flash). Rooftop widgets are a created through a widget-building framework that gathers information using enterprise services, which bring information to the widget from enterprise applications. A widget can combine information from many services. Widgets also can be aware of each other. A stock price widget that looks up prices, for example, can be used alongside a widget that looks up news stories based on a ticker symbol. When the ticker symbol is changed in either widget, the information in the other widget is updated automatically. The Rooftop project makes creating widgets as easy as possible to encourage innovation by end-users. Using a drag and drop graphical interface, information from the enterprise services can be included and laid out on the widget and widgets can be linked.

Mr. Browne's team developed a widget for salespeople who previously had to click through 10 screens to get 5 pieces of data from a CRM system. "If they have 10 sales opportunities to monitor, that's 100 screens."

—Denis Browne

Mr. Browne is especially excited about the potential for Adobe Flash-based widgets that are independent of the underlying operating system. This means the widgets may port to mobile environments quite easily. Internally, SAP has launched some widgets for account executives that put critical information at their fingertips. This approach makes CRM more of an operational system, for use minute by minute, as opposed to being solely a traditional system of record.

Widget development depends on the existence of a critical mass of web services that adhere to well-described standards. Then those services can be combined into widgets. The goal of the development environments is to make this as easy as possible. The risk, of course, is that widgets are so easy to build that users may clutter their desktops with them. Mr. Browne says his group envisions employees having only one or two widgets—at most, five—that they use on a regular daily basis. "If you go beyond that, it breaks down," he says. Widgets, adds Mr. Browne, are best suited to consuming data, not adding to it. "You might do some very lightweight transactions—approving or rejecting a vacation request, for instance—but you don't want to overload that too much," he says. For more complicated transactions, widgets can be designed to take the user into the full app with the click of a mouse. Mr. Browne's team developed a widget for salespeople who previously had to click through 10 screens to get 5 pieces of data from a CRM system. "If they have 10 sales opportunities to monitor, that's 100 screens," he says.

Mashups

Mashups are one form of the innovation in assembly mentioned in the O'Reilly Web 2.0 framework. In terms of the Enterprise 2.0 functional cycle, mashups help aggregate content and functionality and create a working environment to solve a problem. Originally, mashups brought together mainly content with software that could display them as a single visual presentation. Unlike UI widget frameworks, which allow assembly of simple prefabricated chunks of content and functionality, mashups provide more process logic and perform new tasks.

The full vision of mashups is that they will enable full-fledged business applications, complete with data, business logic, and presentation functionality. So far, this vision has only been realized within limited environments, using pre-fabricated chunks of software. Over time, mashups may work with broader arrays of functionality, delivered in the form of web services and still assembled within a web browser using classic drag-and-drop principles.

The lower the barrier to assembly, the more value users will be able to extract from the data and logic in enterprise applications. As enterprises adopt the services paradigm, more of this data and functionality inevitably will be available for mashing up. What's not so easy to predict, however, is how well and how fast the assembly tools will evolve. For now, mashup environments are essentially fancy widget frameworks at the assembly level. They enable the assembly of existing parts and services; they aren't suited to creating new services or adding complex logic. To create advanced functionality, you end up using traditional programming techniques that users are not able to master. If mashups were easier to create, they'd bring more value to the enterprise.

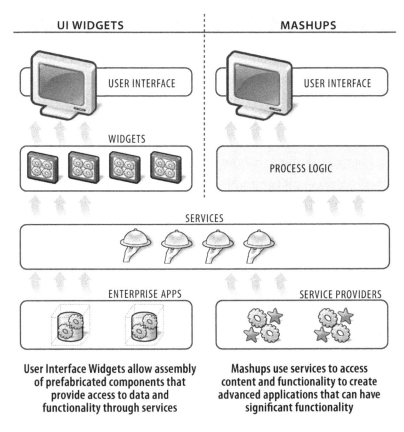

UI WIDGETS	MASHUPS
User Interface Widgets allow assembly of prefabricated components that provide access to data and functionality through services	Mashups use services to access content and functionality to create advanced applications that can have significant functionality

Figure 2-7. UI Widgets versus Mashups

"Now we're starting to see the rise of widgets, with millions of people remixing the Web essentially like paint: data from here, visuals from there, video from here, and I publish it, build on top of it, do all sorts of things," says Mr. Hinchcliffe. "This is not a small phenomenon, it's widespread. Some of the biggest web sites in the world, like YouTube, are driven by this kind of mashup."

BPM to the Rescue?

One of the challenges of expanding the power of mashups involves lowering the barrier to creating them. Most people have no trouble dragging and dropping widgets to make a page look the way they want. But to create a mashup, frequently the information from many services is combined into a new form and presented to users. The mashup may interact and process the information before using services to store it or send it for further processing. Right now, to perform this kind of programming requires complicated programming beyond the ability of most users. One question for the next phase of evolution of Enterprise 2.0 is how the world of do-it-yourself can be expanded. Is it possible to have a better Business Process Management (BPM) system that allows users to create better solutions without the help of IT?

"People with higher skills are needed to build anything more complicated," says Mr. Hinchcliffe. "What will it take to bring innovation in assembly to innovation in construction, with more logical complexity? Is that always going to require a programming language, or is there the possibility of a visual, easy-to-use BPM that gives users the power to actually build more complicated things?"

Right now, far too few people have enough expertise to design mashups for themselves. Developers are needed to reinterpret what users say, build something, and keep tinkering until users are satisfied. Change is happening, says Mr. Hinchcliffe, but slowly. "It's certainly coming, but it's going to be a while before that moves into the enterprise in a big way," he says.

There are some signs of progress. Now business analysts can just open Microsoft Visio and work with a business process, its complex conditional logic, and workflow. Developers tweak the diagram, pass it to testers, and send it into production. Still, it's not clear that businesses are aware of this kind of user-driven development or understand the benefits.

A few options already have appeared. According to Mr. Hinchcliffe, by fall 2007, enterprises could choose from 18 different visual mashup platforms. Most, he says, try to "make enterprise data mashable and give people a visual way of building the views they need."

Blogs and wikis can serve as mashup platforms, too, adds Mr. Hinchcliffe. They can host widgets of any kind and pull data from underlying sites. Mr. Hinchcliffe has worked with a government agency in Washington that had a problem communicating during fast-moving, crisis events. The organization put up a blog for each crisis situation. Anyone in the agency could visit the blog, find out what was going on, ask questions, and get answers from others. Soon, users started pasting widgets inside their posts, connecting satellite imagery widgets with MP3 audio widgets that could play back telephone calls that had been received at a call center. This enabled people at the scene of an incident to call in information from the field and have it appear on the blog. So, in effect, this agency built an ad hoc disaster management application.

History shows, however, that even when it's made relatively easy to do, customization doesn't necessarily win many users. There was much hype in the late 1990s about personalizing portal pages, and sites like Yahoo! and Excite spent heavily to make that possible. But, Mr. Browne points out, "the percentage of people that actually make a tweak or a modification is painfully low. If it's even about 1%, I would be impressed." It is an open question whether such a lack of uptake is due to lack of simplicity in the platform, lack of desire and education in the user population, or other factors. The advances made by users modifying and building products on their own, which we discuss in Chapter 3, User-Driven Innovation, suggests that there is an appetite for the ability to do it yourself. The question for mashups is, What technology will satisfy that appetite?

Social Networking

The rise of social networking has been widely perceived as a way for people—and especially young ones—to socialize digitally. But the idea of electronically mapping social networks offers great potential in the corporate world. While a blog may bring people together in an informal way, social networking formalizes and captures connections between people so they can be used in various ways. The database of connections shows who interacts with whom, how they do it and what they're talking about. By analyzing these networks, managers can gain valuable insights that Mr. Browne calls the "Marauder's Map" of the organization, referring to the fictional map in Harry Potter that shows the location and activities of individuals at a given moment. Because of the trust that exists between people in an enterprise, in some cases social networking may be even more powerful inside a company than on the public Internet.

Mr. Hinchcliffe believes the enterprise will seize upon social computing to take advantage of three powerful trends:

- Innovation is moving from a top-down to bottom-up model

- Value is shifting from ownership to experiences

- Power is moving from institutions to communities

Social networking strengthens personal connections and an overall sense of community. It leverages the social connections for knowledge and influence. Combined with UI frameworks and mashup platforms, social networking schemes may serve as the meeting ground where structured and unstructured tools finally converge. There are already

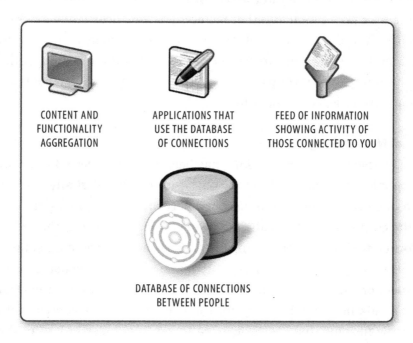

Figure 2-8. Basic Structure of Social Networking

early signs of this trend: Google launched an API called OpenSocial and Facebook is getting increasing attention from companies who are using it as an intranet.

Dr. McAfee recommends that companies that try to encourage social networking must pick the right tool for each ring of the social networking bull's-eye presented earlier. Companies must ask themselves a few basic questions: What are we trying to do? Are we trying to help strongly tied people collaborate better? Or create new connections between strangers? Only then will they effectively match each particular network with the appropriate technology.

Putting Social Networking to Work

How will social networking improve business productivity? The answer remains uncertain. There is increasing evidence that blogs and wikis genuinely provide benefits in the enterprise; they're not necessarily the time wasters some early skeptics feared. The question is *how* to apply them. Is MySpace suitable in the enterprise? Probably, says Mr. Hinchcliffe, but only if it's applied in a different way. Enterprise 2.0 suites combine many of the technologies mentioned in this chapter. The typical suite for Enterprise 2.0 includes social networking. It watches what individuals do with their Enterprise 2.0 tools and whom they connect with. It can show who is consuming the content produced by each employee, who is emailing, and so on. In short, it maps the enterprise's social network.

Once such linkages are in place between core enterprise apps and collaborative apps at the edge, some quite intriguing and promising possibilities arise. The many links that users start to create between core and edge become a new repository of information that's available for mining.

One major opportunity is mapping social networks and communities of interest within organizations. Say a large company has software development teams located in California, Germany, and India that, unbeknownst to each other, happen to be working on the same problem. Because they don't know of each other, there's no chance of collaboration. But with an internal social networking scheme, these three teams could find each other and start to share ideas. Each software developer would be encouraged to publish a profile and the system might create matches and alert everyone involved. For example, SAP has adapted some of these tools to create the SAP Research Net, or SRN. The SRN is a hybrid that borrows elements of the Semantic Web, social networking and mind mapping that allows employees to describe their current projects. This tool helps organize the knowledge and activity of the many employees and work teams. SRN provides a top-down perspective of everything happening within the organization.

Another useful model is Amazon.com, which tracks customer browsing and purchasing and analyzes the data for useful patterns and correlations. "The same thing can happen in the enterprise if you have a high level of participation," Mr. Browne says. Eventually, he predicts, "every single bit that changes on a disk or passes over a network is going to be tracked and traced, and it's going to be correlated and evaluated and assessed and have algorithms run against it to say what's actually happening."

Just as Google analyzes streams of search queries, corporations will be able to analyze these trends to learn more about their own internal activities. "They'll be able to look all the way down to the receptionist or the janitor and get more targeted, effective feedback and information about what's actually occurring right now so that they can action on it. This will be the Marauder's Map of your enterprise," says Mr. Browne.

The key to this is the feed that broadcasts what is happening. In Facebook the following control panel is used to express the type of information you want to see. You can ask for more information from specific people or specific applications. You can shut off information from specific people or applications as well.

It is easy to see how this might extend to the enterprise. You might ask for more information or less about what's going on with a project, in a department, or with a specific customer.

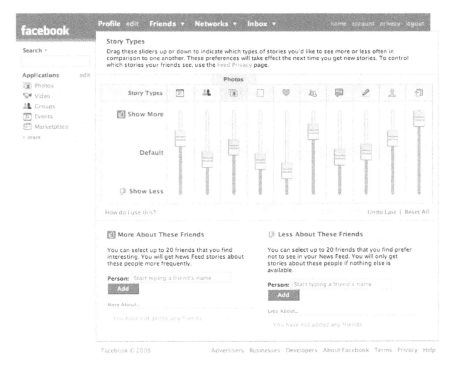

Figure 2-9. Facebook Feed Preferences

Can the Facebook Model Work?

The enterprise must clear a few hurdles before these capabilities can be brought into the corporation. Phil Nelson notes that the Web works so well because of a virtuous circle of participation. There are so many ways to retrieve information, such as searches, news feeds, or blogs, that people are motivated to add more. In an enterprise, he says, it's much harder to find information and thus people are more reluctant to contribute. "You're putting records in a document management system that no one is going to see and is hard to get at," says Mr. Nelson. "If I write a document, is anybody going to ever find it?"

On the Web, Google rose to success by brilliantly tapping link data and page ranks. Facebook built its success largely by tackling aggregation and searching. But it remains very difficult to get Google-like

Philip Nelson was an early innovator in search as the technical founder and CTO of Verity, the pioneering enterprise search company, from 1987 to 1997. Mr. Nelson also co-founded Impresse Corp, which offered a SaaS platform for marketing collaboration, and Anteros, which provides technology and services to enhance the user experience of enterprise software. He was also an Entrepreneur-In-Residence at Accel Partners, the CTO of Spark Networks (JDate), and has worked on diverse projects including gene sequencing, the design of artificial hip implants, XML file systems, and several DARPA efforts. He's currently working on the next generation of product search at thefind.com.

results within the enterprise because data is not linked in that manner. "Enterprise data isn't like Web data," says Mr. Nelson. "You don't have all that linking data, but you do have the linking through people."

Mr. Nelson predicts that Enterprise 2.0 will pick up speed when it attains Google-like search capabilities and a Facebook-like News Feed of what's going on within the company.

Still, Facebook offers only a partial model because it's still primarily based on social connections, not productivity. "The popular Facebook apps are the ones that make you look cool and the ones that make you look good," says Mr. Nelson. "It's not at all about getting work done. If you look around in Facebook, actual utility stuff like searching, shopping, buying a car, and all that kind of stuff gets almost no traction... The stuff that is successful is all performance art. It's all declaring what bands you like, poking each other, and drawing on each other's walls."

Ultimately, Enterprise 2.0 needs a platform with a data rich environment. Mr. Nelson expects the evolution of different types of networks, much as MySpace and Facebook both serve different roles. He points to two potential benefits: a database of connections between people and applications and an automated broadcast of news about colleagues and applications. This creates a productive cycle of push-pull. "You push stuff into the cloud, it gets organized by the cloud and then you can either find it by searching or have it pushed to you," he says. "And then, based on what you've learned from the cloud, you push new stuff in the cloud out the other side."

Mr. Nelson adds that, of course, such a scenario presents potential problems. Can corporations be truly open in the era of Sarbanes-Oxley? And does the company have the right to snoop on the interactions of, for example, a salesperson who might claim that contacts are personal property?

Facebook has done a remarkable job of linking information rich silos—people—into a network that alerts "friends" when something new is happening. Translate the model to the enterprise: Perhaps a network can tie together another information-rich silo—enterprise applications—and alert users to what their colleagues are doing and what's new.

"If there's a good way to get the data out, a News Feed equivalent of Enterprise 2.0, there will be that much more incentive for people to put data in," says Mr. Nelson. "And even if it's a pain to put it in, they'll put it in if they can get it back out again."

A Wider View

The authors hope that the survey of technologies sheds some light and provides a detailed illustration about how Enterprise 2.0 might work in practice. Before moving on to the next question, the authors want to take a step back and again consider the logic of the book as a whole.

Think of Enterprise as a brain. Enterprise 2.0 helps create connections akin to the neurons that link brain cells. Instead of just storing raw information, it stores connections between information and people. It's a meta-data layer that allows organizations to "think about thinking."

Enterprise applications like ERP are like cerebral regions with a specific role, like memory, hearing, or vision. But these cognitive capabilities have limited value if they're not connected. If you see something, you need to be able *think* about it and *do* something about it.

Essentially, this is the role of the services layer, and eventually the service grid that is discussed in the next chapter. It's the connective wiring that links the older infrastructure with the newer evolutions. As such, it turns the enterprise into something greater than the sum of its parts.

But if this brain functions properly, then it evolves. The key message of Enterprise 2.0 that we will explore further in the conclusion is that this evolution is not something that is planned. It emerges as users create more content and connections and change the systems to do what they want them to do. The patterns in the energy and logic behind this user-driven innovation is explored in the chapter following the service grid.

What Is the Value of Enterprise 2.0?

Enterprise 2.0 technologies create value when people put them to good use. There are countless opportunities to improve communication and collaboration in every company. Blogs and wikis are used in many different ways depending on the culture that emerges and the communication and working processes in play. So it is hard to list a set of bullet points about specific types of value that are created. We can say that people find information and other people faster in Enterprise 2.0 environments. When someone has a question, more people are aware of it. When someone creates some content, more people see it and can make use of it. The consciousness of wisdom and craft is expanded so general performance is improved. Connections between content and people are recorded and can be re-used. Users are empowered to create solutions for themselves.

Unlike groupware and knowledge management tools, which many users felt were inflicted on them, people usually have a positive reaction to Enterprise 2.0 technologies. They are generally not inflicted on users but are provided as a resource. People talk of creating a dial tone for Enterprise 2.0 technologies by installing reliable versions of the technologies. It is up to users to make use of that dial tone.

Now, Enterprise 2.0 offers a surprisingly rich and momentous alternative by exploiting network effects. The more people contribute content to these systems, the better they perform and the more people want to participate. They create content, search for other's content, add new content, and so on in a form of ongoing conversation. In short, it becomes a virtuous circle that continually adds value to the enterprise. Both Dr. McAfee and Mr. Hinchcliffe have come up with ways of explaining the mechanisms and value created by Enterprise 2.0.

Dr. McAfee summarizes these contributions with the acronym, SLATES (the acronym plays on the quality of wikis as blank slates). The list includes the following attributes:

Search—facilities that help users to find content

Links—encouraging users to make connections between different pieces of content

Authoring—ability to elicit input from users

Tags—accepting users' annotations concerning the meaning and topic of content items

Extensions—inferring interest and taste from past behavior

Signals—the ability to notify users of new content

Mr. Hinchcliffe has extended the SLATES acronym into his own, superset of key Enterprise 2.0 elements: FLATNESSES. The Web is flat, of course, but the acronym is built around the following terms:

Yet corporations don't always immediately recognize these values. Mr. Hinchcliffe says their response often goes something like this: "You're going to give my employees another set of tools to do more stuff? We already have tools to do that, like email, and we've got all the

Strengthening "weak ties"

According to Dr. McAfee, a growing raft of research demonstrates what's called "the strength of weak ties."

"If you can productively exploit your network of weak ties, you get non-redundant information, you are more innovative, and you can actually get your work done faster. So it's a pretty widely accepted conclusion from organizational research that being able to exploit weak ties is a very powerful thing."

At the next level, potential ties, there's other rigorous work that shows how important brokers are within organizations. Brokers, he explains, are people who introduce people who should know about each other. "They're kind of the human network formers. 'You're working on this? Oh, yeah, I heard about this going on over here. Let me make an introduction, and then you guys can figure out what to do about it.' Those people don't go away in a full Enterprise 2.0 world, but they're complemented by things like a robust enterprise blogosphere. And your human network of weak ties is complemented by social networking software. I've had good luck at communicating the value of Enterprise 2.0 when I frame it in those terms: These technologies can help you to exploit weak ties and they'll help you make connections that would not have formed otherwise."

structured tools. I don't need my employees spending more time on yet another set of tools to capture information. If someone is doing a lot of ERP work and they are given a wiki, they will start doing more of their ERP work in the wiki. How does that information not create yet another silo? They're going to copy and paste so much information from the highly structured system into the unstructured system and then which one is right?"

He predicts that these concerns will be answered by a new generation of much lighter web-oriented ERP tools. They will use RSS feeds to deliver information to individuals, obviating the need to copy and paste. When the data changes, the system automatically informs those who need to know. Thanks to RSS, people no longer have to visit 100 blogs each day to see if there's new information because new posts show up on a condensed list. And this, he says, is "what really made

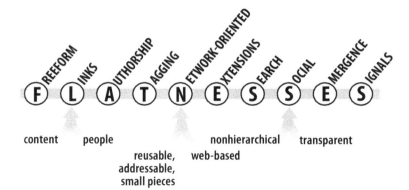

content   people   nonhierarchical   transparent
                    reusable,   web-based
                    addressable,
                    small pieces

the Enterprise 2.0 story start to happen. RSS made web-orientation work in a business setting. Information that people cared about could be pushed to them." In the future, Hinchcliffe suggests that ERP systems will push the information you are interested in at you rather than require you to go find it.

The Persistent Attraction between Free-form and Structure

Another way of understanding the value of Enterprise 2.0 is to examine the kind of environments people create for themselves. Enterprise 2.0 is helping resolve in many different ways a longstanding attraction between freedom and structure.

In almost every free-form environment, people have sought to increase structure to meet certain needs. Either structure is introduced in the tool or structured information is introduced into the free-form environment.

For example, in free-form tools like wikis, people tend to add structure like tables or forms just as Peter Thoeny did in creating the structured wikis. This sort of information can turn pages into database records that can be queried to create lightweight applications. In blogs people attempt to introduce or link to structured information from other sources so the free-form discussion can have a rich context that is immediately at hand.

Mindmaps and Structure

SAP Research has been using mindmaps to add structure to complex collections of information.

Presenting intricate systems of information—often involving text, numbers, and graphics—has always been a challenge. SAP, working with a software company called MindJet, has been exploring a new approach that combines the graphical presentation power of so-called mind mapping with the self-organizational power of wikis.

Mind mapping uses drawings to impose structure on difficult-to-grasp sets of ideas. The technique has mainly been used for brainstorming and project management. But SAP and MindJet see an opportunity for a live interface in back-end enterprise applications. SAP's Integrated Collaborative Map scheme allows users to prepare graphically friendly mind maps in lieu of the traditional methods of sharing information such as memos or slide presentations. ICMaps can take advantage of middleware to pull just the right data from an app and present it without any programming effort by end-users.

The ICMap tool has been developed to enhance Inspire, a process run by SAP's research division that collects ideas for new products. Each year, it culls more than 1,000 ideas from individuals, think tank exercises, and customer workshops. About 20 of these ideas are presented to the company's board to determine which should be developed into prototypes and shared with the organization.

As of late 2007, SAP had a prototype of ICMap running for the sake of a first few internal customers such as its patent department.

According to Gotthard Goetzinger, who heads the development project at SAP, there is always a single topic shown at the center of an ICMap document. Branches illustrate related topics and help reduce complexity. Colors can be used to categorize and comment on particular ideas, graphical lines may be drawn to show relationships, and so forth.

"The big advantage of this methodology is that if you paint a mind map and give it to me, I would normally have no problem in understanding it," Mr. Goetzinger says.

The ICMap tool has been designed to help make it easier to extract information stored in enterprise systems and present it in a user-friendly way. This tool reduces the inefficiency of the existing systems. "We have hundreds and thousands of services built in SAP applications, but in many cases information workers have problems that cannot be solved directly in a concrete way within a business process," Mr. Goetzinger says. "They end up grabbing information from their SAP system, copying it to an Excel spreadsheet, making some calculations, making a summary in Word or PowerPoint, and so forth."

Consider the problem of a machine breaking down on a factory floor. The company must provide a clear picture of the situation to those involved in fixing the machine and managing production. It must solicit their ideas for solutions. A mind map might show the broken machine, pending production orders, and so on. A manager might click on each order to show a bubble with names of customers.

This approach improves communications. The map can be shared quickly and allow users to grasp as much detail as they need—without having to bother accessing the underlying systems. If necessary, the users could click into a particular SAP application .

"The mind map provides a starting point," says Mr. Goetzinger. "It serves as a playing ground where information may be brought together and turned into a clear picture. People can view this information, make decisions, and report their decisions to this map, and then go away into other systems."

Mind maps offer some advantages over wikis. A wiki always shows the whole page with hyperlinks to other pages. A mind map allows users to hide branches and concentrate on one. As Mr. Goetzinger says, "This makes it easy to manage details and not get overwhelmed with information."

On the other hand, enterprise applications, which are highly structured, have long attempted to become more free-form. For a long time, in sales orders and other elements of ERP systems there have been text boxes that allow free-form information to be included. Now those text boxes at times contain links to blogs or wikis that support types of collaboration that are not possible in the enterprise application.

What is happening slowly is a gradual convergence of the domains of free-form and structured tools. Social media platforms can be applied to virtually any type of existing business process involving structured tools, says Mr. Hinchcliffe.

"All IT applications were making collaboration possible long before everyone else started on the Web," he says. "Data centers were the better models for doing it, then, but now the Web is offering much better models. Big, multi-user applications have had highly structured databases behind them, and they've been plugging workers into their businesses the entire time. Now, the Web has pulled way ahead of them in terms of providing better ways of collaborating. These are all the same class of problems."

What is happening now though is that structured wikis, UI widget frameworks, mashups, and social networking platforms are all offering, in various forms, environments that are friendly to both free-form and structured activities. It is not clear yet, but Enterprise 2.0 may end the search for the ultimate dashboard for working in business by providing a toolset to combine just as much free-form content and just as much structure as is needed for any particular task. The sidebar on "Mindmaps and Structure" provides an intriguing example of the combination of a free-form environment for organizing structured information.

A Flood of Startups

Another expression of the value of Enterprise 2.0 comes from venture capitalists. By fall 2007, they'd collectively invested more than $100 million into more than 2 dozen companies that aimed to turn Web 2.0 into the Next Big Thing for enterprises.

Still, venture capitalists haven't had to supply funding at the levels common before the first dot-com boom. This time around, web companies are less expensive to launch because they needn't be built much from scratch. They can take advantage of open-source software stacks, well-defined software interfaces, and pre-fab development frameworks like Ruby on Rails. As Chapter 3, Service Grid, will explain in detail, they're able to join a rich ecosystem of hosted computing and networking infrastructure. Amazon.com, for instance, is actively courting startups to use its hosted data storage, applications server, and payment services.

What Are the Cultural Requirements for Enterprise 2.0 Adoption?

While the functionality of Enterprise 2.0 is a compelling force for change, the wrong attitudes can shut down any potential benefits. Creating a functional dial tone for Enterprise 2.0 is only the first step.

But to ensure that the technology is used and the business benefits are created, the right sort of culture must emerge, and this rarely happens by accident.

Leadership

Enterprise 2.0 technologies are so compelling that their use can appear inevitable, but encouragement is needed. IT managers can help facilitate this transition; Dr. McAfee asserts that active involvement by managers is essential for success. Managers can foster a culture that's receptive to change and trust.

It can also encourage use of common platforms, instead of letting different departments and workgroups use different tools. The latter scenario produces the dreaded silos of information that plague other areas of IT.

"It's amazing how much traffic comes to my blog from people who were looking for something on a certain topic and found my blog in a search engine. We want that same effect in the organization."

— Dion Hinchcliffe

An informal rollout can help, too. Word of mouth within a company can serve as a form of viral marketing. Compelling content will draw users' attention, encourage their participation, and kick off a snowball effect.

Managers must walk a fine line between mandating use of the new tools and getting out of the way to permit 1,000 flowers to bloom. In many cases, it's only after managers endorse and use a new wiki that others will follow suit. Eventually, usage will become widespread and grow on its own.

What IT Can Do to Help

According to Mr. Hinchcliffe, grassroots technologies are more limited in the enterprise than they are on the Web. Who's securing this data? How can it be made searchable? If everyone sets up wikis and blogs, can the organization reuse and leverage this body of information? And how can this information be archived and searched?

IT can help by ensuring that all Enterprise 2.0 platforms have a consistent discoverability strategy. On the Web, that's automatic.

Companies are spending billions of dollars organizing information and making sure it's optimized for searching by Google. Without a similar phenomenon in enterprises, they won't get the same results.

"It's amazing how much traffic comes to my blog from people who were looking for something on a certain topic and found my blog in a search engine," says Mr. Hinchcliffe. "We want that same effect in the organization."

SAP through its TREX search engine, Google, Endeca, and many other companies are trying to solve this enterprise search problem. In a nutshell, the issue is that the internal landscape of business technology has not been oriented towards the Web; it's not composed of pages with links between them. This remains a major barrier for Enterprise 2.0—these billions of deep interconnections between the pages and content are the very things that make Internet searching work so well. The enterprise is missing those interconnections—the neurons that make up a vibrant, intelligent network.

In fact, Mr. Hinchcliffe continues, the enterprise lacks many point-to-point connections at all. These connections require three basic elements: searchability, links, and authorship. Absent everyone in the organization creating a hyperlink structure, we don't have strong search capabilities. "Right now, we have not solved the problem," says Mr. Hinchcliffe. "Enterprise search is in a terrible situation, and it's what everyone is consistently complaining about. Most companies are sitting on mountains of information that they're unable to leverage, never mind the stuff that's inside their employee's heads."

There are signs of limited advancement on this front. "I don't think most organizations are anywhere near the tipping point where all of a sudden they go, wow, these enterprise people and the tools coming in are really helping us," says Mr. Hinchcliffe. "They're getting some low-level improvements, no doubt, and that's why they're using these tools. But it's very departmental right now. I speak at a conference once a week, and I ask people, raise your hands if you have an easy way to post on a blog or wiki inside your organization. It is astonishing how few people raise their hands." Once again, generational issues and

institutional resistance come into play. Mr. Hinchcliffe says older organizations face greater challenges in adopting these strategies. Younger
organizations that grew up around the Web tend to adopt these strategies and tools with greater ease.

"I see older organizations as seriously challenged. They have 30 years
of infrastructure built up around these non-Web models that don't
support a lot of the outcomes they're looking for," says Mr. Hinchcliffe.
"Sit down at your local enterprise search engine, and chances are it's
searching one percent of the information in that organization, or less.
It can't find any information."

SAP's enterprise search solution is addressing this problem by creating a set of adapters that allow any set of repositories to be included
in the index scanned by the TREX search engine. This allows the index
scope to extend as far as possible and include documents, files, information in content management systems, databases, and any source
connected by an API. In addition, an API toolkit allows users to create
adapters other sources of information.

Resistance Is Futile

IT departments now have little choice but to embrace Enterprise 2.0.
It's much easier to swim with the tide than against it. Clearly, employees want ways of commenting in free-form text on information that's
stored in the structures of transactional applications. By enabling a
link in those applications that points to appropriate wiki pages, this
kind of unstructured commenting and collaboration can be encouraged without the data losing its link to an authoritative source.

Adding wiki-like functionality to enterprise applications retains
the ability to track and trace the usage of data records. Meanwhile,
users get the flexibility they want.

Eventually, it is likely that wikis, blogs, forums, and related capabilities will be available inside most enterprise applications that are now
on the structured end of the spectrum. This would invest Enterprise 2.0
constructs with the security, governance, risk management, and compliance that are so vital for managing the organization.

Generational Issues

Many companies are worried about the generational shift in their workforces. They're having problems attracting and retaining young talent and making those people productive and effective. And, as we saw above, these younger workers grew up with Web 2.0 and demand similar tools in their working lives. If enterprises and software companies don't heed these demands, they could face painful consequences in the years ahead.

Mr. Browne warns of a potential technological mutiny in which these younger end-users simply build their own IT systems using frameworks like Ruby on Rails. These workers, he says, might show up on Monday with a homemade mini app and tell the boss, "This is how I'm going to do my job. Take your enterprise system and do whatever you want with it."

This kind of revolt is already evident, Mr. Browne points out, in the growing use of wikis, blogs, chat rooms, and instant messaging. "A lot of these things come from the fringes into the enterprise, and the IT organizations are struggling to keep up with it all."

It must change with the times. In the past, IT created transactional models of what the enterprise was up to but now those methods are growing obsolete.

Indeed, one way to define Enterprise 2.0 is simply as a recognition that today's work environment is heavily shaped by the Net and increasingly populated by so-called digital natives. Unless IT adapts to this new way of working and living, there'll be a loss in productivity.

In addition, this disconnect gives rise to significant risks for the enterprise in terms of governance, risk, and compliance issues and the security and integrity of the business. Traditionally, IT has aimed to maintain the enterprise's integrity. IT is accountable and assures the CFO and CEO that it will secure and protect the enterprise by keeping it in compliance with various laws and regulations. IT's mission has not necessarily been to take care of end-users. But increasingly, managers and others on the edges of the enterprises have more freedom and choice than they ever did. They are no longer beholden to the edicts of the IT organization. They can take matters into their own hands if it helps them attain their business objectives of profit and growth. They will use whatever means at their disposal because they know the company will reward bottom-line performance.

This is not the first time that the enterprise has been infiltrated by information technologies that snuck in the backdoor. In the 1980s, the personal computer and electronic spreadsheet programs caught what was then called the data processing department by surprise. Today's Enterprise 2.0 technologies are more of a threat to IT, however, because they exist on the Net. On one hand, this increases their potential impact by reaching large numbers of people. On the other hand, it raises concerns about security. For example, someone with high-level access may take a large set of data out of the ERP system, post it to a wiki, and begin sharing it. This causes a loss of all traceability for that data and raises serious issues for governance, risk, and compliance.

"Will the relatively unstructured world of the Web be successful in the enterprise? I think that's starting to become a foregone conclusion," says Mr. Hinchcliffe. "The question is how do you do it, and how do you actually get results out of it?"

The question is not whether Enterprise 2.0 will infiltrate the organization, but *how* it will do so. One major topic of discussion in the Enterprise 2.0 community is how to slow it down enough to bring it under control. Mr. Hinchcliffe recounts the example of one energy company (whose name can't be disclosed) that rolled out some Enterprise 2.0 tools in early 2007 only to discover that about 40 of its 65 departments were already using such technologies. Employees were taking the initiative to buy these tools with departmental budgets or with corporate credit cards.

Mr. Hinchcliffe also cites the example of AOL, which rolled out a high-end document management system from a leading vendor. Two years ago, however, an AOL developer quietly installed MediaWiki, the software that powers Wikipedia. This underground software quickly spread to other teams and projects. "The entire company, every department, every project and technology, has an extensively used set of pages on that wiki," he says. "They call it AOL Office Wiki, and it's enormously popular. It's used 20 times more than Documentum is, even though Documentum is AOL's system of record."

Both audiences—end-users and IT—are trying to get their jobs done. The problem is that they're operating with different objectives. The challenge is how to create a synthesis that meets the goals of both.

Conclusion

Enterprise 2.0 offers the promise of a more highly developed "brain" of the enterprise. It makes the enterprise into more of a thinking, interconnected, interactive organic whole. It resolves many shortcomings that have bedeviled IT for years. It also faces a host of unique challenges.

For example, search on the Web is much better than search in the enterprise. The reason: links and accessibility. On the Web, content is created in a relatively accessible form and is replete with links to and from. In the enterprise, documents are not nearly as accessible and links are rare. Without links, search engines lack clues about what information is most valuable.

The success of Enterprise 2.0 depends not only on collaboration, but also on having something to collaborate about—namely the information at the heart of the enterprise applications. This, in turn, depends on a healthy service grid—the Internet of Services seen as a platform for computing—the subject of the next chapter.

If corporations can surmount the challenges described above, they will reap the rewards of more efficient teamwork and collective sharing of knowledge. Users would be empowered to create solutions as they see fit. In the ensuing chapters, we will take the next steps towards that vision.

The key question facing most enterprise users who have read this chapter is: What can or should I do about Enterprise 2.0? It turns out that this question involves so many questions that relate to the next three chapters that we have chosen to return to it in the final chapter of the book.

The concept of a service has taken over the world of computing. Everywhere you look you see it. The Internet of Services, web services, service-oriented architecture, software as a service, service-level agreements, and the topic of this chapter, the service grid, which is related to every one of the terms just mentioned.

In Chapter 2 we examined the role of services in providing a gateway to information that could provide more meat for the collaboration that is now accelerating in the enterprise. As Chapter 2 points out, services provide access to the transactional information and to functionality that can be combined and recombined, frequently by the end users themselves, to create personalized, highly collaborative computing environments that increase productivity.

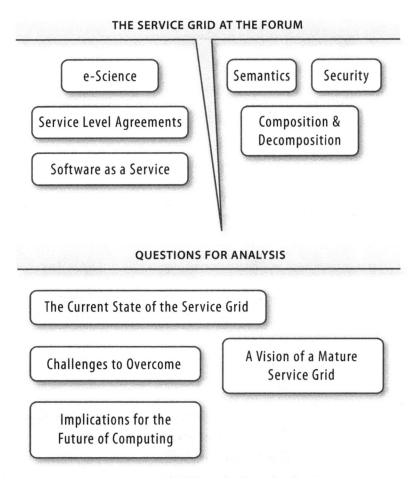

Figure 3-1. Service Grid Chapter Map

The consumer-facing Web 2.0 companies like Google, Amazon, eBay, and others have been leaders in providing robust services on the public network that provide access to functionality for maps, targeted stores, auctions, and raw computing functionality. These sorts of services join the more traditional services for credit card payments, shipping logistics, and other services that necessity forced into being before the Internet made things much easier.

This sliver of functionality based on services has sparked a huge amount of innovation. It is clear that there is a bigger transformation afoot. What if there was a general-purpose environment populated by all the services you need to run a business? This notion forms the basis of the service grid, a much larger world of services than any in place now. While there is no authoritative definition of the service grid, for the purpose of this chapter we understand it to mean the Internet of Services applied as a comprehensive platform for software development. If such a service grid came into being it would change the world of computing in many dramatic ways. It was this prospect that motivated the inclusion of the service grid at the second session in the 2007 International Research Forum.

This chapter introduces the concept of the service grid, summarizes the proceedings of the conference, and presents a set of questions about how the service grid will emerge and what its impact will be. Then, with the help of leading thinkers on this topic, these questions are analyzed to examine the short, medium, and long-term prospects for the creation of a universal service grid.

Conference Proceedings

Following the discussion of Enterprise 2.0, the Forum took up the notion of the service grid. Services consist of discrete software functions. They may be implemented in different languages. They may be governed by divergent business rules and policies. Without some kind of order being applied, the service grid could easily resemble the aftermath of the Tower of Babel rather than a solid foundation for computing.

For service grids to be useful, several questions need to be answered. The Forum session kicked off with a set of questions that included the following:

- How will applications handle the increased operational complexity that results from being composed of hundreds or thousands of services?

- How can services be made reliable and scalable?

- Who will fund the creation of reliable services?

A Service Grid Glossary

In this chapter we'll encounter the word service used in a number of different ways. Here are definitions for some of the key terms.

Services Software services, sometimes implemented as web services, though services can be delivered over any transport medium and may use standards such as REST instead of SOAP. Services are simple, granular applications delivered over a network.

Service grid A fully formed computing environment based on services that people access over the public Internet to assemble mission-critical applications. Portions of the service grid exist in areas such as the financial and manufacturing industries, but the service grids we refer to will be of far larger scope, being fully functional grid systems based on services.

Internet of Services A comprehensive delivery platform that covers all aspects of life from consumer purchases to business collaboration. This comprehensive "service ecosystem" rests on several building blocks: SOA, Web2.0, Semantics, novel business models, and user-driven innovation.

Grid computing A group of smaller computers, or clusters of computers, aggregated to provide a huge amount of computing power. Grid computing is not to be mistaken for service grids, where the grid is composed of services rather than computers.

Service-Oriented Architecture (SOA) The idea of constructing a computing environment based on services as the fundamental building blocks. It is gaining popularity and is being used by companies that are trying to make their IT environments more flexible and robust by exposing important functionality as services. They then create new solutions by combining and recombining these services.

Composite applications Applications that are built by assembling services together to create a new application. Mashups are another name for composite applications that has become current as part of Web 2.0 and Enterprise 2.0. Service orchestration, also synonymous with composite applications, relates to the coordinated execution of several services, supporting end-to-end flow of business processes of an organization and its partners.

Service Level Agreements (SLAs) Agreements about the quality of service drawn up between two parties. The SLA describes how the service will work, what minimal operational levels will be met, and sometimes what will have to be done if those levels are not met.

Software as a Service (SaaS) The offering of software for use over the Internet. Examples include Salesforce.com, Google Apps, and Workday.

Infrastructure as a Service (IaaS) Increasingly, companies are offering computing services, including storage and database access, over the Internet. Such offerings are referred to as IaaS. Examples include Amazon's S3, Elephant Drive, and others.

Governance Governance refers to the way you manage the creation, testing, deployment, design, and eventually the retirement of services. It is very important to service-oriented architectures and to service grids.

- Will the ability to run data centers and craft delivery architecture for reliable services be a competitive differentiator?

- How will dependencies between services be managed?

- How will services evolve and be versioned?

- How will the semantics of services be documented?

Some of these issues are easier to resolve than others, but users are not waiting for the perfect solution. The financial industry, for one, has long offered public services that are equivalent to the kinds of services that will eventually populate a fully realized service grid. The credit card payment system and the systems for interbank transfers operate just like a service grid. At a fundamental level, the Internet itself is a collection of services including name services (DNS), time services, and others, such as HTTP-based services. Some corporations have exposed business processes as services to enable them to work with their business partners; others have attempted to turn a profit by offering services publicly for a fee.

But these grids are miniscule compared to what will come about if the vision of service grids bears fruit: Giant grids that cross corporate and industry borders, and perhaps even national borders, some perhaps administered by a few large providers, others emerging as an agglomeration of smaller ones, or still others mediated by companies that Dr. John Seely Brown refers to as orchestrators. SAP has begun to plan for this future by launching projects that envision an Internet of Services, supported by enabling existing products with services (SOA by Evolution) and creating entirely new products based on services (SOA by Design).

The Forum discussion struck a good balance between optimism and sober consideration of the obstacles ahead. There was no talk of SOA or the service grid as a panacea. Instead, participants agreed that many long-standing technical issues and challenges in IT are not going away.

"Having software as a service in the cloud is important to researchers, because it will, for example, let them create mashups to enhance access to, and manipulation of, data by, for instance, plugging in a workflow to do bioinformatics into their application."
—Tony Hey

e-Science Shows the Way

Dr. Tony Hey, Corporate Vice President for Technical Computing at Microsoft Corp., kicked off the forum with his presentation, calling attention to the use of service grids and Web 2.0 technologies in the scientific community as well as in the R&D departments of pharmaceutical companies, engineering companies, and other firms.

Consuming information and services in a natural way is catching on in the field of scientific and technical exploration, where a new paradigm—a data-centric science or e-Science—is emerging. Researchers have huge amounts of data produced by sensor networks, RFID tags, high-throughput instruments, and computer simulations that scientists want to mine, combine, integrate, and federate, just as commercial businesses will want to do to their data in the future, Dr. Hey said. But, in order for scientists and engineers to annotate, share, explore, and learn from the masses of data available to them—often distributed on a global scale—and to collaborate more effectively, they have to add features such as blogs, wikis, videos, and face-to-face meetings, already common in social grids, to their technical grids. Scientists and engineers are *prosumers*, being both *producers* and *consumers* of information, he said.

Tony Hey, Corporate Vice President for Technical Computing at Microsoft Corp., coordinates efforts across Microsoft Corp. to collaborate with the global scientific community. He is a well-known researcher in the field of parallel computing, and his experience in applying computing technologies to scientific research helps Microsoft work with researchers worldwide in various fields of science and engineering.

Before joining Microsoft, Dr. Hey worked as head of the School of Electronics and Computer Science at the University of Southampton, where he helped build the department into one of the top five computer science research institutions in England. From 2001 to 2005, he has served as director of the United Kingdom's e-Science Initiative, managing the government's efforts to provide scientists and researchers with access to key computing technologies.

Dr. Hey is a fellow of the U.K.'s Royal Academy of Engineering and has been a member of the European Union's Information Society Technology Advisory Group. He also has served on several national committees in the U.K., including committees of the U.K. Department of Trade and Industry and the Office of Science and Technology. Dr. Hey received the award of Commander of the Order of the British Empire honor for services to science in the 2005 U.K. New Year's Honours List.

Dr. Hey is a graduate of Oxford University, with both an undergraduate degree in physics and a doctorate in theoretical physics.

Such grids consist of cloud services, social networking, mashups, and semantics, using existing simple technologies people can experiment with. The IT industry is already talking about services in the cloud, Dr. Hey said. Users can invoke these services from the Web and create new applications by incorporating them into their applications without having to own the services themselves. Having software as a service in the cloud is important to researchers, Dr. Hey said, because it will, for example, let them create mashups to enhance access to, and manipulation of, data by, for instance, plugging in a workflow to do bioinformatics into their application. These mashups are easy to create using tools like Yahoo Pipes or Microsoft's Popfly.

The Use of Social Grids in The Cloud

They may have begun as sources of entertainment, but social grid services in the cloud offer features that make them useful for web-based collaboration.

Del.icio.us

Owned by Yahoo, del.icio.us is a social bookmarking web service for storing, sharing, and discovering bookmarks. It uses a nonhierarchical categorization system where users can tag each of their bookmarks with a one-word descriptor.

Tags are similar to keywords, but they are nonhierarchical. Users can assign as many tags to a bookmark as they want, and can rename or delete the tags at will. This lets users fit information into categories they select instead of preconceived categories. When another user posts related content to del.icio.us using the same tags, that begins building a collaborative repository of related information. For example, the repository on del.icio.us titled "10 Ways to Make Your iPod a Better Learning Gadget" carries the tags iPod, learning, tools, howto and tips.

Connotea

You can think of Connotea as del.icio.us for scientists and clinicians. While it has extra features for some web sites, including PubMed and many journals, which are specific to its target audience, it lets users bookmark any URLs. In most cases, Connotea automatically collects the bibliographic information—the author and the name of the journal—for web pages saved. Where it does not, the user can manually save and share links to those pages.

Users can import references in batches from the Firefox browser to Connotea. Or, if they can export references from their reference manager in RIS format, which is supported by most desktop reference managers, they can upload all the references to Connotea, either using the existing keywords associated with each reference or selecting new tags for them.

Other services in the cloud will enable blogging, data processing, transformation, uploads, and storage. Some of these are already in use. For example, Dr. Hey said, a chemistry research group maintains a members-only blog to record the results of failed experiments. This blog helps capture a repository of useful knowledge about what not to do, which is as important as what to do. This knowledge might otherwise be lost as members of the group move on to new jobs.

Repositories of knowledge such as that captured by the chemistry blog could be stored in the cloud. Storage services in the cloud let users access and interrogate data when they want to without having to care where the data is stored and who stores it, according to Dr. Hey. Major platform companies such as Amazon are experimenting with this, offering storage as a low-cost service accessible over the Web. That data can be used with computing on demand services to create a global scale research environment in the cloud, he said.

Just having text and data repositories in the cloud is not enough; researchers also want context-aware services so they can put together workflows that actually understand what is going on and can automatically bring in information, RSS feeds, and anything else that is relevant to what they are doing at the time, Dr. Hey said. Again, this is where mashups can be created to automatically pull in relevant services from the cloud as and when needed. In essence, increasingly users want to use the service grid "to program without doing programming by, in effect, just connecting boxes," said Dr. Hey. In other words, they want to combine services into interesting applications that meet their needs, without having to know how the code works.

The Discussion

The discussion during the service grid session ranged over two key areas: matters relating to the service grid, which is largely a future concept, and those relating to software as a service (SaaS).

The Service Grid Concept

Things got lively after the presentations as participants discussed the points raised. Although there was agreement on some points, views varied widely overall. A couple of the participants said that business, not the technology, was the real driver for service grids.

Prof. Dr. Wolfgang Wahlster, Director and CEO of DFKI and a Professor of Computer Science at Saarland University, said that service grids are an exciting concept but must tackle key issues: ensuring interoperability based on semantic technologies and guaranteeing the

Wolfgang Wahlster is the Director and CEO of DFKI, the German Research Center for Artificial Intelligence and a Professor of Computer Science at Saarland University. In 2001, the President of the Federal Republic of Germany presented the German Future Prize to Prof. Wahlster for his work on language technology and intelligent user interfaces. He has also been elected to four international academies and learned societies. He was the first German computer scientist elected foreign member of the Royal Swedish Nobel Prize Academy of Sciences. He has published more than 170 technical papers and 7 books on semantic web technologies, user modeling, and intelligent user interfaces. He serves on a number of international advisory boards, and is a member of the supervisory boards of various IT and VC companies. Prof. Wahlster is an AAAI Fellow, an ECCAI Fellow, and a GI Fellow. He is a member of the executive committee of the International Institute of Computer Science at Berkeley.

In 2006, he was appointed Chief Scientific Advisor of the German government on ICT innovations in the research union "Business – Science" and he has been awarded the Federal Cross of Merit, First Class, the Officer's Cross of the Order of Merit of the Federal Republic of Germany. Since 2007 he serves as Chairman of the Steering Committee of the Deutsche Telekom Laboratories.

correctness and security of service compositions. The emerging business webs are positive examples of how these problems can be solved.

However, these community-based service grids form only part of the picture; the kind of service grids being envisioned are far larger and more wide-ranging in scope. Still, the problem of intercommunication between grids needs to be resolved.

Semantics

The question of semantics will be a major sticking point for the service grid. The semantics of a service grid will likely consist of common terminology about business rules and processes, tied together with the Semantic Web. But each enterprise has its own business processes, business rules, and definitions of business terms. How will these be rationalized so that hundreds, or even thousands, of different enterprises can use a service? Will an external body determine the semantics of a service grid? Will that external body determine the semantics of all service grids? What kind of organization will that be, and who will set it up? How will it enforce compliance? Is it even possible, given the large number of users—possibly up to 10,000, as stated earlier—that could be on a service grid, to have an external body determine the semantics on a service grid? Or will things degenerate into a Tower of Babel? And why will semantics be important, anyway?

Prof. Wahlster said there is a strong need for semantic web services because spontaneous, automatic, plan-based composition of services are only possible when machine-understandable semantics are available for services. While much research has been done in this area, we are still a long way from having a general system that provides automatic service matchmatching and composition that manages itself during service execution and that never requires human interaction to search for services and compose them by hand.

Relatively simple or not, the problem is that at least part of the raw data of business blocks—business rules—has not been codified. And, while there is agreement on basic business and legal requirements—any high-level corporate compliance executive can tell you what the Sarbanes-Oxley Act pertains to, for example—there is plenty of variation in the specifics of how they apply to any one corporation. The raw data of genetics, on the other hand, has been semantically codified, Dr. Hey pointed out. A genome is a genome, and everyone in the genetics field agrees on the definition of chromosomes, DNA, RNA, nucleotides, the structure of DNA, amino acids, and the function of proteins, to pick a few examples.

"There is a strong need for semantic web services because spontaneous, automatic, plan-based composition of services is only possible when machine-understandable semantics are available for services."
—Wolfgang Wahlster

Composition and Decomposition

Prof. Lutz Heuser rounded off the discussion by raising important points related to the service grid. He highlighted two ways services can be created: by composition or decomposition. Decomposition consists of service-enabling legacy systems, while composition consists of taking business objects that expose simple services and composing them to create more complex services from scratch. SAP calls the latter SOA by Design.

Several problems accompany the process of decomposition. The obvious one is security, which poses the biggest challenge, Prof. Heuser said; next is side effects. Others are: the issue of trust; service level agreements or SLAs; the need for a combination of decomposed and composed services; and rising user expectations triggered by the use of cloud services.

Side effects are actions that were useful in the past when there was no concept of a service being exposed, and there was a holistic view inside an organization to run the whole transaction inside the corporate firewall, Prof. Heuser said. Look at it this way: Enterprise applications hosted in-house are often set up so that, when a transaction is executed, various other applications are automatically notified and create linked transactions of their own. So, if a corporation's administration department places an order for 100 new desktops, a copy of that order will be sent to systems in HR, accounting, and IT support, for example.

The automated performance of ancillary transactions is useful when the legacy application is controlled end-to-end by IT, which has a holistic view of the entire process. But, when that legacy application is service-enabled, does the person invoking the service want the same automatic consequences as someone using the user interface? For example, if creating a sales order automatically initiates a credit check from the user interface, should a service creating a sales order also initiate a credit check?

Thus, when an enterprise decomposes and exposes a service provided by a comprehensive application engine, like an SAP ERP, it has to figure out how to ensure that only that service gets executed,

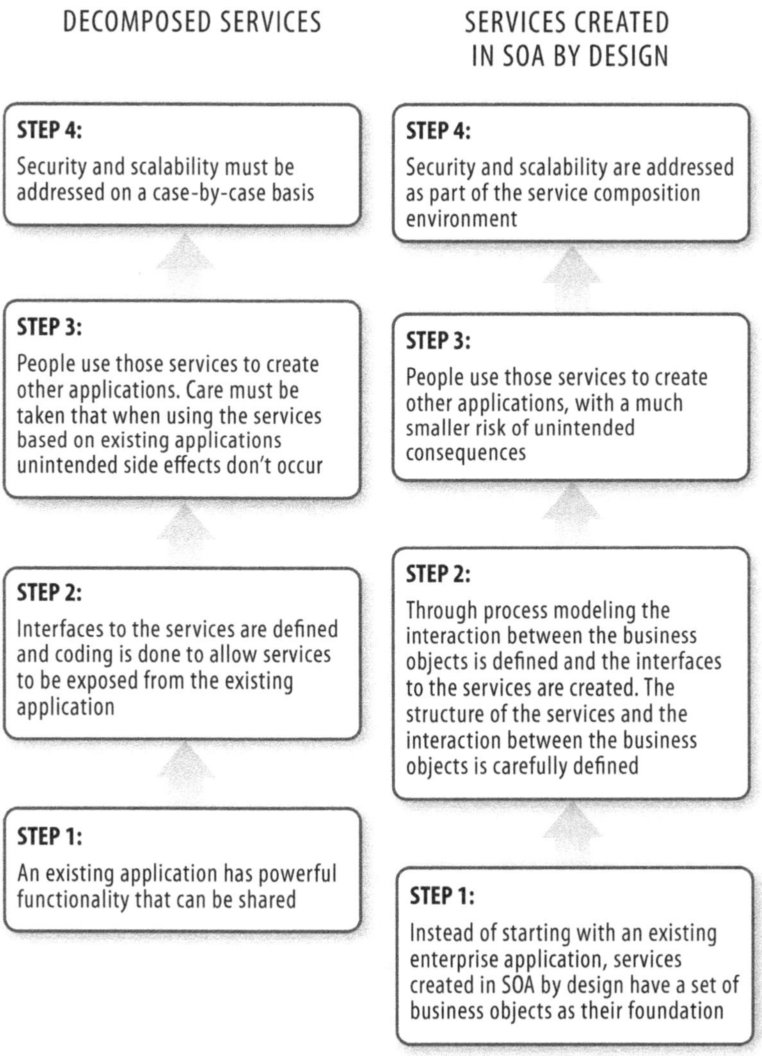

DECOMPOSED SERVICES

SERVICES CREATED
IN SOA BY DESIGN

STEP 4:

Security and scalability must be
addressed on a case-by-case basis

STEP 4:

Security and scalability are addressed
as part of the service composition
environment

STEP 3:

People use those services to create
other applications. Care must be
taken that when using the services
based on existing applications
unintended side effects don't occur

STEP 3:

People use those services to create
other applications, with a much
smaller risk of unintended
consequences

STEP 2:

Interfaces to the services are defined
and coding is done to allow services
to be exposed from the existing
application

STEP 2:

Through process modeling the
interaction between the business
objects is defined and the interfaces
to the services are created. The
structure of the services and the
interaction between the business
objects is carefully defined

STEP 1:

An existing application has powerful
functionality that can be shared

STEP 1:

Instead of starting with an existing
enterprise application, services
created in SOA by design have a set of
business objects as their foundation

Figure 3-2. Decomposed Services Versus Services by Design

without all the ancillary transactions being launched automatically.
Further, the service provider must offer some sort of guarantee that
the software offered as a service will not trigger side effects, and this
is a big challenge, especially when legacy systems are involved, Prof.
Heuser said.

The Question of Trust in the Service Grid

Then there is the question of trust. This has several aspects. On the one hand, there is the user's trust in the service provider. How can the user trust that the service will perform as claimed? When something goes wrong, will the service provider take corrective action as soon as possible? Will the service provider ensure that there are as few problems, and hence as little downtime, as possible? Will the service provider provide some sort of compensation for business lost during downtime? On the other hand, the service provider has to trust that the customer will use the application to do what it supposed to do; that the customer will not use the service as a back door into other customers' applications; and that the customer controls access to the application so that unauthorized personnel will not access it.

The Role of Service-Level Agreements in the Service Grid

When a service or data is not available, the business of the enterprise, and the bottom line, are impacted. Prof. Heuser said availability issues can, and must, be solved, so availability services are needed. It has long been common practice to resolve issues of trust and availability with service-level agreements (SLAs). But, while they may have been effective when applied to transactions between an enterprise and its suppliers, they may not be adequate in a world where multiple services may be offered by one provider to hundreds, perhaps thousands, of customers. Customers will only sign SLAs if they trust their SLA partners, Prof. Heuser pointed out.

Dr. Pradeep K. Khosla, Dean of the College of Engineering at Carnegie Mellon, also raised the issue of SLAs between services. "How are they going to be negotiated? How are they going to be enforced?" he asked. These issues map into liability and performance, and many questions are still unanswered, Dr. Khosla said, adding that, if services are aggregated from multiple suppliers, the question of who should bear the liability will arise.

But, because service providers may aggregate services from hundreds of suppliers, the question of whether they have obtained

Pradeep Khosla is Dean of the College of Engineering, Philip and Marsha Dowd Professor of Engineering, and Founding Director of CyLab at Carnegie Mellon. Dr. Khosla is a recipient of several awards including the ASEE George Westinghouse Award for Education (1999), Siliconindia Leadership award for Excellence in Academics and Technology (2000), the W. Wallace McDowell Award from IEEE (2001), and Cyber Education Award from the Business Software Alliance (2007). He currently serves on editorial boards of IEEE Spectrum, IEEE Security and Privacy, and Oxford University Press Series in Electrical and Computer Engineering. Professor Khosla's research has resulted in 3 books and more than 300 articles.

Dr. Khosla is a consultant who serves on many advisory boards at a national and international level. He is a member of the Board of Directors of Quantapoint Inc., BitAromor Inc., the Children's Institute, the IIT Foundation, Mellon-Pitt (MPC) Corporation, and Pittsburgh Technology Council. He also serves on advisory boards of Institute for Systems Research (Univ of Maryland), College of Engineering (Univ of Waterloo), and the College of Engineering at the Illinois Institute of Technology.

assurances about the quality of services from their suppliers arises. And, even if a service provider has SLAs with its partners, what is its track record in terms of offering these aggregated services? Can it be trusted?

Security

The issues of security and reliability will, however, take a new turn when service providers have to aggregate services from several suppliers and offer these services to multiple users. Multiple levels of security may need to be implemented, and security will have to be applied to the suppliers, service providers, and client companies using aggregated services. And, apart from the question of trust, the issues of who will sign SLAs with whom, how parameters will be set, lines of responsibility, and a mechanism to resolve disputes will need to be considered.

The issues of trust and security came up during the discussion. Dr. Khosla pointed out that users might fear that small developers have embedded spyware or other malware in their services that they then supply to service providers. That will not be a concern with large service providers such as Google, whom users are more likely to trust. "Security is going to be a really important issue," he said.

Dr. Khosla raised the related question of data privacy. If, for example, a company using software as a service had its software processes audited, the audit could extend to the service provider as well. That might happen, although the auditing of a service provider would require work on a much larger scale than the auditing of one of its customers. Can a service provider protect itself from this problem? Would legal agreements similar to the end user licensing agreements (EULAs) now used by software companies suffice? In EULAs, the user agrees that the software is supplied as is, and that the supplier is not responsible for any problems caused by the software.

Scalability and Reliability in the Service Grid

Another key issue with the service grid is scalability. Because services will be delivered over the Web, traffic flow will fluctuate wildly. Businesses may see their scale skyrocket from one to 1 million users within a day, and if they fail to service those users, they will lose them. Should some sort of load balancing be implemented? If so, who should provide the load balancing—the service provider, or the supplier it sources the service from, or the customer? How will the hardware and software requirements for load balancing be calculated? Will SLAs have to be renegotiated if traffic flow spikes or plunges beyond the parameters set in the SLA? How will service providers and customers accurately track consumption of services and the charges thereof?

Life Cycle Management

Another issue for the service grid is life cycle management. Implementing this will give rise to questions of how to turn an application into a service, how to design, configure, deploy and adapt it, and how to tear it down. Some of the issues to be addressed will include: What exactly should be automated? To what degree? What kind of automated monitors must be in place to ensure the systems are running smoothly? How often should reports be generated? What thresholds should be set for exception reports? Where will exception reports be filed? What actions should be taken when exception reports are filed? Will there be a manual override if exception reports exceed a certain level or exceptions pass a predetermined threshold? What should that level be?

Service Delivery and Service Consumption

The third, and highest, level will be service delivery and service consumption. Here, Prof. Heuser discussed payment for services. How will companies impose tariffs, or measurements of users' consumption of services so that they can charge them appropriately? Consumption may fluctuate wildly from day to day because the services are on the Web, so how should it be measured? What checks and balances should be put in place to make sure the measurements are accurate? Should provision be made for dispute resolution if disputes arise? Will charges be imposed on a sliding scale?

Still, thought can be given to adapting this model to the needs of service providers aggregating services from several suppliers. Could the service provider work out what a unit from each of its suppliers means, in mutually acceptable terms? Could it then get its customers to agree to that definition of a unit?

Perhaps the service provider could agree with its suppliers to charge only for the actual amount or measure of services used, once a common unit for each service has been defined. If so, its billing and payment systems might have to interface tightly. The billing system will calculate usage by customers and base its charges on that, and the payments system will calculate how much of its suppliers' services it is using and calculate the amount due to them.

Despite the buzz around the service grid, little is being done right now because of the difficulty and complexity of the issues involved,

Prof. Heuser said. There are many unanswered questions, in the areas of infrastructure, service life cycle, and delivery of services.

Even if these questions are answered, the layers then need to be put together to create a top-to-bottom stack. This will give rise to other issues: How do we achieve this top-to-bottom stack? What standards will be used? Will new standards have to be worked out? Will security and reliability issues have to be tackled again for the stack as a whole? How can we ensure the reliability and robustness of the stack? Can the stack talk to other stacks? How can this be ensured? What protocols need to be put in place to enable communication between stacks? What additional security measures and access controls will be needed if communication between stacks is possible?

However, Prof. Heuser is optimistic that the service grid will overcome these obstacles. When the Web was launched 16 years ago, nobody could have imagined all the different functionalities and capabilities it enabled, nor can we imagine what it will let us do 20 years into the future. Enabled by the service grid, utility computing is potentially an order of magnitude more powerful than the Web, Prof. Heuser said, and that means its capabilities could be equally mind-boggling in a much shorter time—maybe only a decade. Perhaps we shall not have to wait that long; solutions to some of the problems brought up have already been developed.

Software as a Service (SaaS)

Another topic discussed by Forum participants was software as a service (SaaS). Prof. Wahlster said the term is misleading because the service is actually the transaction executed at the end, while software itself is only a piece of code, whose correct execution on an input provides a service. SaaS is mainly a business model, rather than a technology per se, and previous approaches taken in an attempt to sell the concept of SaaS as a technology, such as utility computing and Sun Microsystems' claim that the network is the computer, failed.

INSTALLED SOFTWARE MODEL

Software is installed and running under company's
control in its own data center

SAAS MODEL

Application runs at a centrally located server not operated by
the vendor of the application

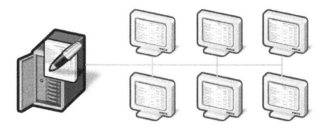

Figure 3-3. Installed Software Model Versus SaaS Model

When software is hosted in this way, the infrastructure is a shared fabric, with perhaps tens of thousands of competitors using it all at once, and that will make security considerations paramount. How will the providers ensure that users do not ride the service to hack into competitors' systems? How will providers ensure that the correct service is delivered to the correct user? How will providers ensure that unauthorized users do not get onto the system from the client's side? Perhaps the answer is to have a combination of service agreements, tracking systems to see what is being delivered to whom, and anti-hacking measures or some sort of monitoring to prevent unauthorized access.

Service providers may also want to require clients to sign agreements pledging that they will implement tight security on their side to prevent unauthorized access to the service.

Dr. Khosla said that software as a service eliminates the cost of managing and maintaining infrastructure, which every year amounts to 10 times the cost of purchasing that infrastructure. The considerable savings realized by opting for SaaS create an economic argument for going that route. However, one key piece to enabling computing and data in the cloud is missing: An SLA that guarantees users access to their data and service no matter where they are. Once that guarantee is in place, infrastructure costs will be further lowered, because, instead of using PCs, enterprises can install simple access devices. Amazon appears to have solved that problem through its S3 and EC2 services.

The economic argument did not convince Prof. Wahlster, who contended that, rather than lowering costs, SaaS would increase them in many cases. Owning anything permanently, including software, often is cheaper than renting or leasing it. While enterprises would want to lease software as a service under certain circumstances, claiming that all software will eventually be leased or rented by users and not owned by them is hype. For mission-critical applications, users want to own the software in order to retain complete internal control over its usage. Another reason for this is that 80% of the software written worldwide gets embedded, and this limits the market for SaaS. It does not make technical sense for embedded systems such as, for example, the antilock braking system in a car, to download their software from the Web.

Agreeing with Prof. Wahlster, Dr. Hey said there will never be a total switchover to software downloads. Microsoft, for example, believes that software for clients and for the server will coexist with software for services in the cloud, but they will be targeted at different markets. Embedded systems, such as those found in cars, will pull down information and updates from cloud services as and when needed.

Another participant agreed with Dr. Hey that SaaS would coexist with installed software. People will want some software on their PCs and other software downloaded as a service. For Prof. Heuser, the question of SaaS boils down to one of convenience in that users can get anything they want whenever they want. Getting service from the cloud is better for users than having the service or instances of different software installed on their PCs and managing them.

> *"IT people are hung up in this space of services when the business guys could care less; technology is not what's going to drive SaaS."*
>
> —Mary Murphy-Hoye

Dan Woods asked whether an operational barrier exists that will stymie the delivery of SaaS, pointing out that there have been several attempts to deliver SaaS. One is Hailstorm. Then there is SAP, which plans to increasingly create software as a service on the scale required by the customer. Is this more difficult than it looks, and will the operational problems of delivering services such as Gmail, for instance, stop big companies from getting there?

Dr. Hey acknowledged that there have been some spectacularly unsuccessful attempts at launching SaaS, and that there is uncertainty about whether services like Amazon's S3 and EC2 will be commercially successful. However, early attempts, such as those to provide service grids for the scientific and technical computing community, where the information and data demands are rather extreme, will help companies understand what cloud services should be developed for, and provided to, industry. The research community can be useful to industry by allowing a period of experimentation with complexities and volumes of data not yet faced by the commercial sector.

Technical issues are not what will drive the adoption of SaaS; business requirements will. "IT people are hung up in this space of services when the business guys could care less; technology is not what's going to drive SaaS," said Mary Murphy-Hoye, Intel's Director of IT Industry Research and IT Senior Principal Engineer.

Analysis

Clearly, the coming of the service grid represents a transition for computing. The beginnings of the service grid are with us, and in the near term, many companies appear to be pursuing the creation of internal service grids organized around the concept of service-oriented architecture. A compelling vision for the ultimate end state of the service grid has been set forth by Dr. John Seely Brown, whom we interviewed for this chapter, and his writing partner John Hagel III.

The analysis section of this chapter examines where we are now and the barriers that must be overcome on the way to achieve a fully realized service grid. To help us navigate this territory we also interviewed the following people:

- Dr. Peter Kürpick, Chief Product Officer (CPO) webMethods Business Division, member of the Executive Board of Software AG

- Anne Thomas Manes, Vice President and Research Director of Burton Group

- Paul Butterworth, Chief Technology Officer of AmberPoint

- Patrick Grady, Founder, Chairman and CEO of Rearden Commerce

- Alister Barros, SAP Research

The questions we seek to answer are:

- What is the current state of the service grid?

- What will the fully realized service grid look like?

- What are the key challenges to be overcome to create a fully realized service grid?

- How will barriers to the service grid be overcome?

- How will composite services be orchestrated through the service grid?

- How will the world of computing develop from the current state toward a fully formed service grid?

- How will the service grid reshape the environment for enterprise computing?

What Is the Current State of the Service Grid?

The service grid is largely a future concept, but we can see evidence today that it is sprouting in a limited way in many areas.

We see evidence of the service grid in the following areas:

- The Internet's own service-based infrastructure

- Grids in existing industries, such as the banking industry

- Internal corporate service grids

- Service grids with partners and suppliers

- Application vendor service grids (SAP, Oracle, IBM, and others)

- Public services being used in mashups, such as those from Google and Amazon

Existing Service Grids

The first and most established example of a service grid is the Internet itself. While these are not services in the SOA sense, the Internet is run based on a wide variety of interoperable and established services that arguably form a service grid encompassing DNS, time services, HTTP-based services, and so on.

Service grids, like the ones the financial community has, such as the SWIFT bank payment network and the credit card processing network, are early examples of service grids to do specific things for a targeted group of users.

Early parts of the public service grid came into being when FedEx and UPS realized that people wanted to be able to track their packages themselves and provided publicly available services to enable this.

The Corporation and Service Grids

Many companies are pursuing SOA inside their companies, creating internal service grids that suit their particular needs and computing environments. In this case, services are often being created to integrate multiple systems and sometimes to expose internally used services to partners.

From this internal service grid, it's a relatively small step to create a service grid that helps companies, particularly manufacturing companies, create mini service grids with their suppliers. By integrating with partners at the level of services, faster integration can be achieved and more data can be moved from application to application, speeding up the way business is conducted.

Application Vendor Service Grids

Application vendors such as SAP are service-enabling their entire massive software base and in the process have created a productized version of a service grid. SAP's approach illustrates the systematic process required to create services at scale.

SAP's general approach toward providing services is called enterprise SOA. The specific set of services that are delivered as part of SAP's product are described in what is called the Enterprise Services Repository. Because SAP has thousands of developers working on hundreds of services at time, the company has a process for design-time governance that ensures all the services created will not overlap in their duties, will interoperate, will use the same standards in particular for data definitions naming conventions, and will meet the needs of those who will be using the services.

The ideas for services come from SAP customers, systems integrators, vendors of related products, as well as developers and product managers inside SAP. Each of these groups are inspired to better meet customer needs by creating sets of services to provide access to application data and functionality. SAP also gathers input through a variety of touch points but most of the suggestions from outside of SAP pass through an initiative called the Enterprise Services Community, which runs a formal process for collaboration on gathering requirements and designing services.

The design time governance process looks at every proposed service from two perspectives. First, the process examines the role the service will play in the portfolio of services in the Enterprise Services Repository. Each service added must serve a useful purpose and not overlap with existing services. The second part of the governance process focuses on the actual design of services and addresses issues such as naming, structure of data elements, use of standards like those for global data types, application of common patterns, and so forth. In this way the services both fit into the big picture and also work with each other seamlessly. Redundant definitions of data elements and other design problems are avoided which makes the services as easy as possible to use in combination with other services. SAP believes that customers that rely on this productized collection of services will be able to leapfrog others who attempt to build collections of services on their own or integrate diverse collections of services.

Customers who adopt SAP's service grid will have to build services that are unique to their business needs. SAP is now in the process of teaching interested customers how to run this design-time governance process internally so they can develop custom services that will interoperate smoothly with the services in the Enterprise Services Repository.

SAP is delivering services created through this process as groups of functionality along with usage descriptions called enterprise service bundles (ES bundles). These bundles, details of which are available to the public on the Enterprise Services Wiki (*https://wiki.sdn.sap.com/wiki/x/LQ0*), typically follow one of several patterns:

- Providing an interface with a third-party network. The Insurance Claims Investigation ES bundle allows insurers to integrate with networks that help insurers detect fraudulent claims.

- Interfacing with third-party software. The Information System Integration ES bundle allows geospatial information systems to be integrated tightly with SAP ERP, allowing tracking of human resources and equipment in a geographic area to coordinate efforts such as emergency management.

- Enabling collaboration with partners. The Outsourced Manufacturing ES bundle enables brand owners to work with manufacturers. The Batch Traceability and Analytics ES bundle enables companies who find a problem in a batch of materials to trace that defect back through their supply chain and forward to customers as needed.

- Extending the software interface to nontraditional SAP users. The Inventory Lookup ES bundle allows a manager on a golf course to view real-time inventory information using his Blackberry. The Project System ES bundle allows subcontractors to update project status in SAP ERP via a composite application. The Advertising Management ES bundle allows publications to offer a composite through which the public can place classified ads.

This is just a sampling of the ES bundles SAP has created to date, but it provides an overview of the patterns being used to enable robust, standards-based integration with its software base.

Public Service Grids

Google, Amazon, and others point the way that public services are going. Google has opened up APIs for selected portions of its SaaS offerings and for its other services such as Maps. Google Maps APIs are used in about half of the mashups being created in any two-week period, according to Programmable Web.com's Dashboard (*http://www.programmableweb.com/apis*). Some SaaS companies create internal service grids for their users. SaaS companies, such as Salesforce.com, open up their APIs so that services will be available to construct solutions in their application domain. Table 3.1 shows the relative impact of services on a few prominent market players.

Company	Impact of services APIs
Salesforce.com	40% of traffic comes from APIs
Amazon	28% of sales come from 3rd parties; some percentage of these are via APIs
eBay	Number of transactions coming through APIs rises 84% annually

Table 3-1. Revenues from APIs (Source: ProgrammableWeb.com)

Some 140,000 developers have registered to use Amazon Web Services (AWS). Amazon has also begun leading a charge in the area of Infrastructure as a Service (IaaS) by offering storage services and a database offering.

SaaS providers like Salesforce.com are building applications that are available over the public Internet. Salesforce.com has an environment called App Exchange in which it provides developers tools to build applications that extend Salesforce.com. Workday is another SaaS provider that offers online versions of HR, financials, and other software. Although Workday offers SaaS, it is not a software provider *per se* but rather an aggregator for providers who are willing to have their offerings available as SaaS. For example, Workday uses ADP for payroll and Chronos for time management.

Bottom Line on the Current State of Services

Although none of these efforts really illuminate the ultimate state of the service grid, they highlight important movement in this area. Now let's explore a vision for the fully formed service grid.

What Will the Fully Realized Service Grid Look Like?

A fully formed service grid will enable users to orchestrate an end-to-end business process, according to Dr. Peter Kürpick, Chief Product Officer (CPO) webMethods Business Division, Software AG. Users should

Peter Kürpick is the Chief Product Officer (CPO) webMethods Business Division and Member of the Executive Board of Software AG. Dr. Kürpick, joined Software AG in April 2005, and in his role is responsible for the company's webMethods business line, which holds all products related to Service-Oriented Architecture (SOA).

Before coming to Software AG, he was Senior Vice President Server Technology at SAP and as such was responsible for major parts of the SAP NetWeaver stack, which is the foundation of all SAP applications. At the beginning of 2000 he acted as Executive Board Assistant, during which time he worked out of Palo Alto, New York, and Germany for Prof. Dr. Hasso Plattner, former CEO and co-founder of SAP. Dr. Kürpick started his career in IT in 1998, joining SAP as a software developer.

Dr. Kürpick earned a Diploma in Physics focusing on theoretical physics/supercomputer topics in 1989 and a Ph.D. in theoretical physics in 1993. From 1995–1997 he did his post doctorate in the U.S., working at the University of California at Berkeley, the University of Illinois at Urbana-Champaign, the Kansas State University, and the Oak Ridge National Laboratories, Tennessee.

be able to pick and choose what they need to dynamically assemble services to execute new business processes. And this is more than business process management; it means orchestrating a business process that calls heterogeneous systems, taking into account all the tasks that normally have to be performed inside an enterprise, such as authorizations, security, compliance with rules, and auditing.

In order to provide these features, the fully realized service grid would consist of:

- A critical mass of services with a wide range of functionality

- Services that are trusted, with features like security, reliability, authorizations, security, transaction support, ACID compliance, performance metrics, and auditing

Supporting the Service Grid: Managed Services

How will service grids do that? In their paper, "Service Grids: The Missing Link in Web Services," John Hagel III and Dr. John Seely Brown say that service grids will provide managed services. Standards alone are not enough, they say; the standards will need to be harnessed in the form of managed services so that their full value can be realized.

Service grids will perform four broad categories of managed services, Mr. Hagel and Dr. Seely Brown say. These managed services are needed to provide robust support for the services used in the composition of applications.

These managed service categories are:

- Shared utilities, which provide services that support the application services as well as other utilities within the services grid—security utilities, performance auditing and assessment utilities, and billing and payment utilities

- Transport management utilities. These include messaging services to facilitate reliable and flexible communication among application services, and orchestration utilities that help companies assemble sets of application services from different providers

- Resource knowledge management utilities. These include services directories, brokers, and common registries that describe available application services and determine correct ways of interacting with them. They also include specialized services for converting data between formats

"I would expect that you're going to eventually find maybe a half a dozen or a dozen fundamental service grids, and ecologies of services that have been carefully tuned for that. And each one of those ecologies may be a brand."

—Dr. John Seely Brown

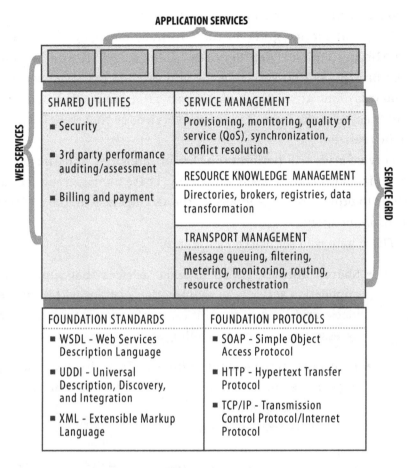

Figure 3-4. The Service Grid (adapted from "Service Grids: The Missing Link in Web Services" by John Hagel III and John Seely Brown)

- Service management utilities. These ensure reliable provisioning of services. They also manage sessions and monitor performance to ascertain conformance to service quality specifications and SLAs

In essence, service grids will offer the following capabilities as a managed service: security, message routing, data transformation, and interoperability; performance monitoring; and exception resolution,

Anne Thomas Manes is a renowned technologist in service-oriented architecture with a 28-year industry background. In 2002, *Network World* named Ms. Manes one of the "50 Most Powerful People in Networking," and in 2001 she was one *of Enterprise Systems Journal*'s "Power 100 IT Leaders."

Prior to coming to Burton Group, Ms. Manes was CTO at Systinet, and Director of Market Innovation in Sun Microsystems's software group. Her industry background also includes field service and education at IBM Corporation, customer education at Cullinet Software, product management at Digital Equipment Corporation, chief architect at Open Environment Corporation, and research analyst with the Patricia Seybold Group.

Ms. Manes' areas of technology expertise include service-oriented architecture, web services, XML, governance, superplatforms, application servers, Java, J2EE, .NET, application security, and data management. She is a frequent speaker at trade shows and at InfoWorld, JavaOne, and RSA conferences. A member of the *Web Services Journal* editorial board, she authored *Web Services: A Manager's Guide* (Addison-Wesley 2003) and has participated in web services standards development efforts at W3C, OASIS, WS-I, and JCP.

Mr. Hagel and Dr. Seely Brown say. They will sit on top of a services architecture that consists of standards such as TCP/IP and HTTP underlying XML, SOAP, WSDL, REST, and UDDI.

It's important to note that these capabilities are all essentially infrastructure, what Anne Thomas Manes, Vice President and Research Director of Burton Group, refers to as "nonfunctional requirements," in other words, capabilities that are needed but that developers need not code themselves, instead relying on code provided as part of the infrastructure itself to handle features such as security and load-balancing.

In this way, we can see the benefit of service grids to enterprise IT. Grids will take over the handling of communications complexity, thus shielding the enterprise from technology infrastructure issues by moving the communications complexity from the enterprise edge to the network, say Mr. Hagel and Dr. Seely Brown.

Ms. Manes takes the same view. In service grids, all communications are mediated through the infrastructure itself, so when a message is sent from one end point in an application to another, the message will automatically be routed through the infrastructure, which will ensure that the message is properly delivered.

Service Grids: One or Many?

Although in this chapter we refer frequently to "the service grid," in practice, a single, unified service grid is unlikely. While the service grid will provide far more functionality than we see today, it's not likely to be singular, according to Dr. Seely Brown. "I would expect that you're going to eventually find maybe a half a dozen or a dozen fundamental service grids, and ecologies of services that have been carefully tuned for that. And each one of those ecologies may be a brand."

While service grids will provide flexibility and choice, there will be no fixed requirement to use them. They and their utilities will be optional overlays on existing networks and both providers and consumers of services can choose whether or not to use their functionalities, Mr. Hagel and Dr. Seely Brown say. And they will not be fixed bundles of services; instead, they will be loosely coupled federations of utilities that users in different application environments will be able to tailor to their needs by pulling down only the services they require.

As you can see, there are a lot of moving parts to this vision of the service grid. SAP Research is pursuing two major initiatives in this area: The THESEUS Program in Germany and the Smart Services Cooperative Research Center (CRC) in Australia. Technologies coming out of these programs will be enablers of the service oriented business model.

Clearly the service grid is not going to create itself. A variety of technological barriers stand in the way. We examine these challenges next.

**John Seely Brown** is the independent co-chair of Deloitte's new Center for Edge Innovation, a visiting scholar at USC, and advisor to the Provost. Prior to that he was the Chief Scientist of Xerox Corporation and the director of its Palo Alto Research Center (PARC). While head of PARC, Dr. Seely Brown expanded the role of corporate research to include such topics as organizational learning, knowledge management, complex adaptive systems, and nano/mems technologies. He was a co-founder of the Institute for Research on Learning (IRL). His personal research interests include the management of radical innovation, digital youth culture, digital media, and new forms of communication and learning.

Dr. Seely Brown—or, as he is often called, JSB—is a member of the National Academy of Education, a Fellow of the American Association for Artificial Intelligence and of AAAS, and a Trustee of Brown University and the MacArthur Foundation. He has published over 100 papers in scientific journals and was awarded the Harvard Business Review's 1991 McKinsey Award for his article, "Research that Reinvents the Corporation" and again in 2002 for his article, "Your Next IT Strategy." In 2004 he was inducted in the Industry Hall of Fame. With Paul Duguid, he coauthored the acclaimed book *The Social Life of Information* (HBS Press, 2000), and with John Hagel he co-authored *The Only Sustainable Edge* (HBS Press, 2005) a book about new forms of collaborative innovation. This book also provides a novel framework for understanding what is really happening in off-shoring in India and China and how each country is inventing powerful new ways to innovate, learn, and accelerate capability building.

What Are the Key Challenges That Must Be Overcome to Create a Fully Realized Service Grid?

Many of the challenges that were brought up during the International Research Forum were echoed by the experts interviewed for this chapter. Here we examine these challenges in more depth.

At a high level, the following graphic captures the distance that must be travelled to move from the current Internet to the fully realized service grid:

	INTERNET - TODAY	SERVICE GRID - TOMORROW
Infrastructure	Webserver, Browser	Services Delivery Platform
Content	Web Pages	Services and Multimedia Content
Content Description	html	Semantic Descriptions
Focus	Consumers	Enterprise and Consumers
Connections / Interfaces	Hyperlinks between Web pages	Composition of Services and Information Mash-ups

Figure 3-5. IoS Versus the Existing Web

Each of the areas mentioned, from infrastructure to interfaces, represents significant challenges, as the following analysis brings to light.

Semantics

A service grid implies communication across many, many services. But without a common set of semantics, it's difficult to see how this would work. Ecosystems, like that of Salesforce.com, SAP, or Amazon, can define their own semantics. But as service grids mature and cross industry boundaries, the issue of semantics becomes more of a problem. For example, take the term partner. Depending on your vocabulary, a partner could be a customer, supplier, peer, or employee. How will the semantics of services be defined in a way that enables them to interoperate? How can you compose applications from the buffet of services in the service grid if you're not sure exactly what the services do?

Ms. Manes agrees that "the bigger impedance to the service grid is really semantics, the definition of what is the information that has to be exchanged. And then you have to start defining standard data types, standard ways to represent purchase orders or delivery requirements or invoices, things like that." Although some of this is being done by industries, the job is far from complete.

Beyond semantics is the concept of taxonomy. In a taxonomy, everything is uniquely identified. Taxonomies are important because we need precision in terms. The definition of X must be only X and not X but sometimes also Y. Human beings can interpolate meaning (a door might be a door to a house or the gate of a castle and still be a door) but computers, with their binary way of thinking, cannot.

But while semantics represent a huge problem to overcome, Dr. Seely Brown believes that semantic problems will be—and in fact are even today being—solved through computing power, which handles transformations between different systems. Rather than getting all services to use the same vocabulary, which could be onerous, computing resources could be dedicated to performing transformations from one vocabulary to another. Nonetheless, this does not obviate the problem of semantic consistency. Whether vocabularies, semantics, and taxonomies are reconciled before a service is published or on the fly in the service grid via computational transformation, this consistency must be achieved.

In addition to the semantics from one application to another, there is the issue of semantic documentation. What does the service do? How does that compare or contrast with other services in the service grid? Are they complementary or alternatives? How do they fit into various processes? This is another level of semantics that must be addressed for the service grid to realize its potential.

Security and Privacy

Security is another important barrier to the service grid. The issue of security is paramount on the Internet, and service-based applications only raise the bar on security. Who has access to the service? Is data encrypted? What protections are needed on a given service? Are services interconnected in a way that compromises their security? Could Trojan services be introduced?

Data privacy is another concern, and a bigger one than most people realize, according to Dr. Seely Brown. Who has access to monitor the traffic in the service grid? A great deal of information can be inferred from traffic patterns and sometimes from the services themselves: "If I use this particular subservice, the mere fact that I've called it up, I don't know who they may use as sub-subservices two or three tiers down. And the mere fact that a sub-subservice has been activated may actually reveal to somebody that I'm doing something I don't want them to know." Even though no one may have unauthorized access to all the traffic data, information about particular services being invoked can lead to compromises as well.

Reliability and Service-Level Agreements

Assuring reliability of applications within the corporate network is not easy, but it is definitely a circumscribed problem. As Paul Butterworth, CTO of AmberPoint, explains, "If you're building a traditional application, using libraries and APIs, you can assume that everything is going to be in one big execution space. Then, the simple model is that either everything works or everything has failed, because the application is either up or it's down. And so the calculation of how reliable the application is going to be is very simple. It's what is the mean time to failure and the mean time to repair for this executable that represents my application."

Adopting a distributed architecture like SOA changes the game: "As soon as you go distributed, however, the problem becomes much more complex. Let's assume you use the same model for building it. Now, the probability that your application is running is the product of the probability of each component being up and running. Clearly, reliability goes downhill pretty quickly, unless you take some sort of overt action to make the overall system more reliable." Furthermore, there are many other questions related to services. Mr. Butterworth says, "Another problem that arises is how to gain confidence in services. How does one know that a service truly provides the level of service that's needed and expected of it? Are services always going to be

**Paul Butterworth** is the Chief Technology Officer at AmberPoint, a leading provider of SOA runtime governance solutions. Prior to AmberPoint, he was the Chief Technology Officer for Forte Tools at Sun, where he was responsible for the technical strategy for the Sun developer tools products. As a founder of Forte Software, Mr. Butterworth was the Chief Architect and Senior Vice President of Engineering and Customer Services. Before founding Forte, he served as chief architect and director of Product Engineering at Ingres Corporation. He holds a B.S. and M.S. in Information and Computer Science from the University of California at Irvine.

performing as you expect them to? Are they going to be reliable and secure enough for what you're trying to do?" To overcome such issues a transparent SLA management is required which allows for precise tracking between the perspectives of various stakeholders (service providers, software providers, infrastructure providers, customers) as well as the various levels of a business/IT stack (from business-level SLAs down to infrastructure level).

Scalability

Scalability is yet another issue for service-based applications. Significant engineering effort is required to make applications like those of Google, Amazon, and eBay scale.

Stateful applications require even more attention when it comes to scalability. Additionally, many current applications require that state be maintained. Scaling such applications, according to Dr. Seely Brown, requires a dramatic increase in cost, engineering work, and brainpower, and many enterprise applications will require the same type of treatment. "But it can be done. On the other hand, correctly designed services are stateless and thus much easier to scale with the right kind of infrastructure."

A specific scalability aspect enters the scene for multi-tenancy environments. Here, the same or highly similar service-based applications are to be provided to thousands or even millions of customers/ tenants. Looking at each tenant in isolation will not allow for a truly overall scalable solution. Instead, resource sharing between different customers while maintaining full logical isolation is key for implementing scalable and thus affordable solutions.

Operational Complexity

Why is operational complexity such an important issue for the service grid? Although monolithic applications have their own internal complexity, services, which are far more granular and loosely coupled, increase that complexity by an exponential factor.

With traditional applications, the many moving parts are frozen at design time and their interactions can be tested before an application is released. With composite applications, the moving parts are never frozen, and a new version or element could be introduced at any time. Load testing, functional testing, and life cycle management all become more complex problems, as illustrated in Figure 3-6.

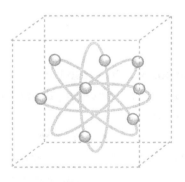 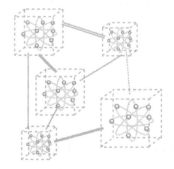

**TRADITIONAL
ENTERPRISE APPLICATIONS**

Complex web of connections
between business objects that are
frozen at the design time

**COMPOSITE
APPLICATIONS**

Connections are not frozen at design
time and can be changed. Provides
flexibility but more operational risk

Figure 3-6. Operational Complexity in the Service Grid

Composite applications are flexible, but now the operational risk, rather than being a single point of failure, has many, many potential points of failure that are hard to monitor. The interdependencies are hard to track, changes are hard to test, and the entire application is hard to audit. Measuring performance is another challenge inherent in the service grid.

How Will Barriers to the Service Grid Be Overcome?

Though the move to aggregators may not follow the precise evolutionary course that Mr. Hagel and Dr. Seely Brown describe, the previous discussion of barriers makes it clear that the distributed nature of the service grid is going to require brokers to facilitate service grids.

The Need for Aggregators

Dr. Kürpick states that aggregators will be needed, in part because of the numbers of participants in the service grid: "You will have hundreds and hundreds of companies providing services. An enterprise will have dozens, maybe hundreds of individual service agreements with those providers, which is a nightmare. So, as much as we have the MasterCards and the Visas of this world, there will be another company that is going to be the interface between all providers and all consumers. We're going to see these mega orchestrators, companies that provide thousands and thousands of different services across hundreds of different providers and then deliver them back to millions of enterprises, and they manage all the SLAs. In a logistics supply chain you always have these tier one, tier two, tier three, because otherwise—as a car supplier you don't want to deal with 15,000 suppliers, right? You want to deal with 100. And that's going to happen in the service world as well."

The service grid provider could become an aggregator in the same way the Li & Fung Group, a Hong Kong company active in the retail and fashion goods industries, operates, Dr. Seely Brown said. Li & Fung does not own manufacturing plants, but coordinates the activities of thousands of manufacturers, suppliers of materials, and business services in several countries to achieve rapid mass production of new products for customers. Although clients see it as one centrally managed company, Li & Fung is really putting together the services of about 10,000 specialist factories and other companies on four continents at the back end.

> *"We're going to see these mega orchestrators, companies that provide thousands and thousands of different services across hundreds of different providers and then deliver them back to millions of enterprises, and they manage all the SLAs."*
> —Peter Kürpick

Loosely coupled services that will be called as needed will constitute the service grid. Again, look at Li & Fung: It does not use all of the 10,000 companies it works with on every project; some will be brought in on certain jobs and not on others, depending on what they can bring to each project. "Nobody's captive in the Li & Fung network," Dr. Seely Brown said. Of course, a customer will probably not use all the services available in a service grid; only those that have a bearing on a project will be used for that project.

Surmounting Operational Challenges

Some of the challenges service grids face will be met through the evolution of platforms targeted for this purpose, such as Amberpoint. AmberPoint provides policy enforcement points, monitors interactions, tracks service-level agreements, and can automatically reconfigure an environment in response to observed anomalies.

According to Mr. Butterworth, the service grid presents three kinds of operational problems, each of which requires new approaches and best practices.

- How do you build these applications?

- How do you test them?

- How do you operate them once they're rolled out?

A key challenge underlying all these problem areas is the transparent reconciliation of different stakeholders' perspectives, such as software

Supporting Nonfunctional Requirements

Before an application is developed (and remember that a service is essentially a granular application), requirements are defined.

You can separate application requirements into functional requirements, what the application should do, and nonfunctional requirements, other characteristics the application should have.

Functional requirements for a currency conversion application, for example, might include how many types of currency conversions it would handle, what data will be used to determine exchange rates, and how large or small the amounts converted would be.

Nonfunctional requirements include a whole host of capabilities that are critical to the application, and yet auxiliary to its basic functionality. Nonfunctional requirements include:

- Response time
- Latency
- Load balancing
- Support for a certain number of concurrent users
- Security measures, such as authentication types supported
- Privacy, including encryption of the data stream
- Support for various client types (browsers, PDAs, cell phones)
- Support for ACID database transactions

Developers for certain types of products are typically experts in their functional areas, but not experts in the nonfunctional areas, which are nonetheless requirements.

These nonfunctional requirements are essentially infrastructure, which could be provided by an in-house intermediary platform such as Amberpoint, or by the platform of an aggregator. For example, Rearden Commerce, discussed later in this chapter, includes SMS messaging as an input option in its API. In this way, developers need not write SMS support into their applications; they can simply leverage the framework created by Rearden.

providers, infrastructure providers, service providers, and service consumers. Lifecycle models and associated operations have to clearly support those perspectives, still allowing individual stakeholders to implement their specific strategy while also mediating transfer of operational knowledge as much as needed for a successful end-to-end operation.

Changes are inevitable with services. And, as Mr. Butterworth points out, "The services making up the app are not all in one's control. And if they were, there's a good chance one or more of them will change underneath the app and make it fail. So, a scheme is needed for confirming changes in the environment and enabling the roll-out of those changes so that they can be adopted in an incremental fashion." AmberPoint offers versioning to help ease the transition of upgrading services in a gradual way. "The IT department might start by letting, say, only a certain set of 10 users use the new version. Then, over time, more users could be added. If anything goes wrong, the IT department can roll back fairly quickly to the older version of a service and not shut down all the users of the system."

Barriers as Nonfunctional Requirements

In fact, upon examination, many of the barriers to the service grid, including the operational challenges just described, fall into the category of what Ms. Manes refers to as nonfunctional requirements, such as the type of security that the application requires. Supporting nonfunctional requirements—without writing the code again and again—is essential.

The Role of Declarative Policies

How do loosely coupled services state their nonfunctional requirements? One answer is through declarative policies, which are being addressed in standards such as WS-Policy.

Essentially, a service can, through declarative policies, state that it can only be invoked over a secure connection or that it requires two-factor authentication. By separating the service from its nonfunctional requirements, it makes it easier to change those requirements over time. For example, if the banking industry must now require three-factor authentication by law, the declarative policy can be changed, rather than having to modify the services themselves.

How does this work in practice? When a consuming application tries to invoke a service, it reaches a policy enforcement point called an intermediary. The intermediary is like a gatekeeper or proxy that says, "Wait, if you want to get to that service, you'll have to have this type of authentication." Depending on the way the intermediary is set up, it could provide the additional service rather than refuse access to the calling application. These intermediaries intercept calls to ensure that they conform to the policies that have been defined or declared.

Intermediaries can also help with semantics. If a calling application uses the ACORD XML standard and the service uses another XML dialect, the intermediary could perform the semantic transformation on behalf of both parties. In this way, semantics, which is the biggest difficulty faced by the service grid, could become less of an issue. However, notice that the mapping between semantic entities must still be established so that the intermediary can handle the translation. On the positive side, however, by having the intermediary handle semantic transformations, such transformations can always be handled going forward. This is easier than making everyone speak the same language, which is, in practice, never going to happen.

According to Ms. Manes, Burton Group refers to the implementation of nonfunctional capabilities as services as the "infrastructure services model" (ISM), that is modeling infrastructure capabilities as services. "Once the capabilities are modeled this way, you enable a policy-driven environment," says Ms. Manes. The developer or administrator can use declarative policies to configure (as opposed to code) support for nonfunctional requirements. For example, you can configure a security policy and attach it to an application or service interaction to specify that it requires authentication and supports a particular set of authentication mechanisms. The policy is enforced automatically at runtime by a policy enforcement point (which is a component of the runtime infrastructure).

Rearden Commerce: A Glimpse at an Aggregator

In the example of Li & Fung, we see a company without a product, a company that serves as an aggregator of the business services of thousands of other companies. Taking these ideas into the realm of technology services rather than purely business services is Rearden Commerce. Rearden Commerce takes the idea of declarative policies and uses it in its role as an aggregator. Focused initially on the travel and business services space, the company provides an on-demand personal assistant that helps people find and buy what they need based on who they are, what they like, where they are, the context of what they're doing, and their company's purchasing policies. Based on a pure service-oriented architecture, Rearden Commerce's technology platform instantly connects users with a network of 137,000 merchants and third-party application providers. As the user searches for a particular service—for example, dining—the Rearden Personal Assistant mashes up content from multiple sources (e.g., OpenTable, Google Maps, Zagat Ratings, and so on) to inform the user's purchase decision and completes the reservation online. The personal assistant then automatically populates the user's calendar with reservation details, forwards guest notifications, and sends updates to whatever device the user has designated, such as a cell phone or PDA.

A closer look at Rearden Commerce reveals that the company is seeking to create a rich service grid, and has more than a thousand business customers and their employees up and running on it today. According to Patrick Grady, CEO and Chairman of Rearden Commerce, "Fundamentally the entire systems architecture is designed around the notion of a computing service. At the lowest level of our architecture we have operational services—things like provisioning, multi-tenant support, profile loading, monitoring, and analytics. Upon this foundation we have built an ever-growing portfolio of horizontal shared platform services—such as calendar, address book, invitations, geocoding, alerts, and policy engine—that are shared by all of the applications on our site. By leveraging these shared platform services, developers can focus on their core competencies and more quickly deliver new applications. For example, if a developer wants his application to notify the end user via SMS of schedule changes, that capability is already baked in and available for re-use. For their part, users benefit from a consistent experience as they traverse the different 'stores' on our site, from

 **Patrick Grady** is Founder, CEO, and Chairman of Rearden Commerce. A recognized pioneer in web services and on-demand technologies, Patrick Grady has guided Rearden Commerce to a commanding leadership position as the world's fastest growing commerce platform for goods, services, and applications. With more than 1,250 customers spanning the Fortune 50 to small/medium enterprises, leading distribution partners like American Express Business Travel, and more than 137,000 merchants and third-party application providers, the company is fundamentally transforming the way individuals and businesses buy and sell goods and services online.

Patrick founded Rearden Commerce with a singular vision—to provide the world with an online personal assistant for work and life that makes people wonder how they ever lived without it. With a single login and password, the Rearden Personal Assistant helps people find what they need based on who they are, what they like, where they are, and the context of what they are doing.

In addition to serving as CEO, Patrick is Rearden Commerce's strategic architect, guiding the company's product and technology vision. As an evangelist for the Web's next generation, he is a sought-after speaker with engagements including AjaxWorld, AlwaysOn, Burton Catalyst, CSFB Disruptive Technology Conference, InfoWorld Symposium, Internet World, PC Forum, the PhoCusWright Executive Conference, Red Herring, and Supernova. Prior to founding Rearden Commerce, Patrick spent 10 years in various venture capital and leadership roles in the technology sector.

travel to dining and entertainment to web/audio conferencing and package shipping."

These ideas mirror that of the larger service grid. While Rearden Commerce is initially focused on travel and employee business services, its underlying technology is deliberately general and can be applied to services and goods of all kinds. For those who are curious about how the service grid may develop, Rearden Commerce's approach is worth studying.

Less is More: A Minimalist Interaction Paradigm

Composing applications from services has to date been the province of business process modeling (BPM) software. The problem with this software, as Dr. Kürpick sees it, is the interaction paradigm. The software that has been built so far is too complex for end users. So, a new breed of products that are very intuitive, which are designed around the same line of thinking as the Apple iPhone, will emerge.

Streamlined BPM software, rather than the more complex traditional BPM products, could help empower users. "Any BPM product is a bunch of boxes and lines on a screen," Dr. Kürpick said. "One reason why we're stuck with this is the mouse only allows you to point out one place on the screen and act on this one place. Apple lets you act in two or three different places at the same time." Already, some vendors are offering intuitive desktops that let users dive into their business problems, aggregate solutions, put them together, and then drive processes, making them the end of an executable process, Dr. Kürpick said.

This poor interaction paradigm is hampering user-driven innovation. For example, Microsoft's BizTalk BPM package requires extensive training so people prefer to use Visio, Dr. Kürpick said.

Salesforce.com was designed the right way, because the designers asked themselves what they could leave out of the software, what functions they could eliminate, and still make the product marketable. That is the way BPM will go, Dr. Kürpick said, offering users just the minimum that they need and no more. That elegant simplicity of design will draw in the users, and then BPM can become progressively more complex. BPM has to be done up front, so that enterprises know what they want out of service grids.

It's important to be realistic about the possibilities of BPM and the service grid. Will end users build business applications themselves using services? The problem of semantics makes this unlikely, according to Ms. Manes. Users are unlikely to understand the semantic difficulties that exist between services. You can liken the problem to building sets. Legos don't work well with Lincoln Logs which don't work with K'nex. If you give someone a mixed box of such parts, their building won't cohere. In the same way, users will be more likely able to compose applications if provided with sets of services that are known to work together. This is one potential role for aggregators, enabling composition by end users by ensuring that semantic difficulties and other potential incompatibilities have been addressed.

How Will Composite Services Be Orchestrated through the Service Grid?

In the widespread setting of service grids, services are expected to innovatively derive functionality from existing services where possible, rather than starting from scratch. According to Dr. Alistair Barros, leader and entrepreneur of SAP Research's Internet of Services research field, the full potential of composed services will be reached when the whole gambit of service provisioning is leveraged—not only the applications exposed as web services, but also services addressing material resources and, ultimately human interactions.

Dr. Barros said that BPM technologies have matured to the point where they allow many artifacts of business processes to be coordinated, much beyond classical workflow management of 10 to 15 years ago. A significant development has been the expanse of process automation. Under classical workflow, process pipelines within organizations were coordinated. Recent developments, leveraging improvements in interoperability middleware, have seen cross-organizational processes between collaborating stakeholders of business-to-business value-chains supported through BPM technologies.

Web services can be said to be composed through business process descriptions because activities in the processes invoke operations on web services. The execution of the process, one activity after the next, leads to execution of web services, one after the next. This removes the need for users to know what service operation to execute next in a multi-step business task like the following: first check purchase orders for stock, then allocate stock, next assign resources for shipments, and finally schedule shipment and notify the customer about delivery. Control flow constructs such as sequences, decision points, parallel

Alistair Barros is research leader at SAP Research and an entrepreneur of its Internet of Services research field. He has a Ph.D. in Computer Science from the University of Queensland and 22 years of experience, having worked at CITEC and the Distributed Systems Technology Centre, before joining SAP in 2004. He has around 50 publications in refereed journals and international conferences, and his research has contributed to international standards (WS-CDL, BPMN, and UML Profile for EDOC) and references, including the widely cited workflow patterns in the BPM field. He has led technology transfer efforts at SAP involving BPM technologies. Dr. Barros has also led commercial projects featuring whole-of-enterprise service frameworks for Boeing, Queensland Government, and Australian Defence. His contributions to research funding acquisitions have included the Australian Cooperative Research Centre for Smart Services, the German National Lighthouse project, the European Union project SUPER, and various Australian Research Council projects. A number of these projects are aimed at developing a next-generation service delivery framework in the context of wide-scale service grids and ecosystems.

paths, synchronization, and looping are combined with message flows to orchestrate services across business boundaries.

Dr. Barros pointed to languages such as BPMN (Business Process Modelling Notation) and WS-BPEL (Web Services Business Process Execution Language) that figure prominently in the BPM products of SOA offerings. He observed that language consolidation through standards is an important development of industry adoption of BPM, yet agreed with Dr. Kürpick that modeling languages and tools, do not have the usability of applications such as Word, Excel, and Firefox that will help drive user adoption.

In addition to greater end user consumption, he identified a number of areas in which service orchestration capabilities need to be extended in the context of service grids.

Web-Savvy Service Orchestrations

Third-party web applications will provide new channels for service consumption in open service grids. Dr. Barros said that the way users interact on the Web offers important insights into how service orchestration needs to be extended in service grids.

Web applications operate with wide data sources, open markets, and community. They thrive on quick consumer satisfaction and convenience, for instance through effective search and low-risk trust for parties involved in Internet commerce. Single-consumer-to-service transactions—such as creating customer listings, doing basic look-ups and verification checks, and purchasing goods—are giving way to more distributed, multi-cast, pull-oriented, and data-streaming modes of interaction on the Web. Marketplace auctions, recommendations, and subscription-based RSS feeds are gaining participants and providing a large volume of data about preferences and interests. With the wider range of data available through the Web, semi-structured, audio, and video data is vying for integration in conventional transactions.

In considering these trends, if the value of service orchestration is to filter out to the "dotcom" world, flexibility and forecasting must be supported for a new generation of users who are not operating with predictable processes in dedicated roles. Dr. Barros cited, as an example, the value of regular forecasts on service grids to inform users of progress. He also observed that composed services would have to factor in negotiated terms and conditions for service fulfillment, proportional to alternative services being offered through the grid. As another example, he said service control would need to be extended for services implemented through long-running processes. Does the single point of payment still hold for long-running processes? Will one-off authentication still work? It is doubtful, according to Dr. Barros, considering the different paths that different service provisions could take through branching. Different payment points—indeed, pay-as-you-go—should be expected. Composed services could not be expected to execute in single sessions, and more systematic ways of handling authentication and access control need to be factored in. From a security perspective, longevity of processes leads to the issues of trust chains and delegated access. How critical security considerations can work seamlessly with BPM is still the subject of ongoing research.

At the same time, Dr. Barros pointed out that the Web is not the end of the story for consumption of composed services. Initiatives like digital communities, set on exploiting service grids, are pushing services to help drive the "Internet of Things." Motivating applications include vehicle guidance and remote access to public instruments and home devices (electricity meter readings) from utility service providers.

Will Processes in the Service Grid Be More Agile?

While the service grid and web-flavored interactions will extend the way services are orchestrated, Dr. Barros pointed out that the wide reach of services through the grid could overcome operational bottlenecks confronting today's business processes.

He observed that enterprise services are supplied as part of a vertical solution from a single supplier like SAP and its partner ecosystem and form the common software portfolio used by collaborating partners in the business-to-business production, supply, or value chain. Thus, today's business processes, managed through an architecture like SAP's enterprise SOA, have predictive behavior since they have well-defined structures and self-contained services.

However, just as external services have added value through third-party aggregators, marketplaces, and device channels, businesses are now embarking on mobilizing outside services to enhance their business processes without additional development costs. This is especially the case in industries featuring many partners, balancing regulatory operation and commercial efficiency, and geographically sparse coordination that inevitably breaks down operational dependencies.

Dr. Barros said that today's supply chains, as a pertinent example, range from analysis and collaborative forecasting of market and consumption patterns, contract planning and cyclic replenishments, logistics and transportation back to product merchandizing. Typically, these processes do not operate under the assumptions of linear process pipelines, but need to respond flexibly to asynchronous events generated through the distributed nature of collaborating partners.

He discussed two examples related to a supply chain and unforeseen exceptions that could be better managed through the use of third-party sensor services:

- Chemicals such as paint, having separate (component) suppliers that generally transport large quantities across national boundaries. The components have fixed times in which they can be combined and occupy scarce resources in sea containers and consolidation nodes. During delivery, a customer might cancel an order for certain stock because of factors like building construction delays. Transporting chemicals back to consolidation points or, worse, back to their origins, is extremely costly. The scarcity of containment resources means that in some cases containers need to be held in reserve, even after materials have moved on— should problems arise. This is extremely expensive for suppliers and limits growth in supply. An efficiency gain could be made through a service that "senses" demand from other customers for the same materials, in other regions. The logistics business process could use such a service from many different customers and referrals for new demand of cancelled orders. The process could then optimize transportation routes according to nodes adjacent to demand to ensure quick resupply in the event of cancellations.

- Minerals such as coal are transported through train and sea carriers. Variability of mining makes optimal shipment planning inefficient. In the event of surplus yield, rail transportation can be a bottleneck, delaying sea carriers for potentially long periods at pick-up ports. A sensing service could be used to determine alternatives for sea transport. Where sea carriers have spare capacity and transport paths compatible with a particular order, they could be targeted. Accordingly, a mining company could use the appropriate rail path to connect to an alternative sea carrier.

In these two examples, the business processes were able to respond to changing circumstances and adjust direction. Such agility is a crucial facet of high-process automation environments with time-critical and resource-scarce situations playing out along the critical path. The reality of current practice is that the sorts of exceptions just discussed are typically handled manually, leading to weeks of delay and sometimes loss of contracts.

Enterprise Service Bus is a technology solution that enables processes to be notified of remote occurrences and, accordingly, adapt to the new circumstances. It is a vital technology for agile business processes. It supports assessments of collaborating partners to adjust partnerships and operations dynamically as new event trends take shape. In order to exploit ESBs for agile business processes and dynamic trading networks, services must deftly address validation, exceptions, and other circumstances outside the capability of individual business processes and monitor them.

How Will the World of Computing Develop from the Current State toward a Fully Formed Service Grid?

Mr. Hagel, and Dr. Seely Brown, in their paper "Service Grids: The Missing Link in Web Services" point out a possible trajectory from the current state of the service grid to a fully formed service grid.

There will likely be three broad waves of development, beginning with bundling, then with providers going through a fragmentation phase, and ultimately culminating in a different form of bundling, Mr. Hagel and Dr. Seely Brown said.

In the early stages of the development of service grids, we are likely to see bundles of enabling services created by early aggregators or within large enterprises. Early aggregators will come from the ranks of the first generation of electronic marketplaces and industry collaboration hubs; both they and the large enterprises developed the enabling services for their own use and will begin offering them to business partners as a bundle.

They will likely tap the broader market because customers, limited by their aversion to risk and their inadequate skill sets, and concerned about the limited track record of more specialized service grid utilities, are more likely to look to larger, better-established aggregators than to smaller, newer ones.

Unbundling and fragmentation will come next, partly because even more specialized enabling services will be offered by both existing companies and new start-ups, to fill the gaps in the first-generation enabling service offerings. Increasing sophistication will lead many customers to seek out best-in-class utilities and create their own internal integration capability. More specialized enabling grid integrators will also emerge to help those sophisticated customers.

Meanwhile, the first generation of enabling service aggregators will begin spinning out some of their more specialized enabling services developed internally as independent businesses. They will have to focus heavily on investing in marketing, sales, and customer support rather than innovation, to cope with competition from more specialized aggregators who come in as start-ups. There will also be market pressures from independent grid service utilities providers, who will prefer to work with aggregators who do not own enabling services themselves.

So, two things will happen in parallel. More specialized aggregators offering new services that are not backwards integrated into enabling services will emerge. Meanwhile, more independent service grid utilities will appear, each highly specialized in a specific type of enabling services.

Eventually, there will be consolidation within the ranks of the aggregators as well as within certain segments of enabling services. Economies of scale and scope will lead to mergers and acquisitions between enabling service aggregators in the same customer or market segments on the one hand, and between enabling service providers of related services on the other. The latter will also be driven by similarities in functionalities and skill.

Ultimately, an industry structure designed to serve two needs will emerge—customer desire for convenience and access to world-class capability on one hand, and opportunities for innovation to accelerate performance improvement on the other.

So we will have highly specialized utility bundles and broad-based service aggregators. For the former, common skills and economics will see enabling services bundle together into clusters, with two or three very large providers surrounded by more highly specialized, niche providers in each cluster. Large enterprises may continue to operate their own highly specialized enabling services in certain areas with unique functionality requirements, with the services consisting of internally provided services federated with third-party service bundles.

For the latter, service aggregators will focus on specific target markets or customer segments. Within these, they will become highly concentrated, evolving as collaboration hubs to serve as orchestrators for a broad range of enterprises in their segment. They will create federations of service capability rather than own and operate the enabling services. These federations will consist of both third-party utility bundles and enabling services still owned and operated by their customers.

There will also be two tiers of service integrators, similar to the system integrators we are familiar with today. A few large, sophisticated enterprises will maintain their own integration capability, but the large services integration needs will be tackled by broad-based third-party integrators which will be large, concentrated businesses specializing in recruiting and developing deep service integration talent, rather like today's large system integrators. Then there will be smaller integration specialists serving niche markets who will operate as subcontractors to their larger colleagues.

Managing the operation of service grid utilities will become a highly focused and concentrated business. Companies operating in this area will have expertise in ensuring appropriate performance levels and owning and operating large, scale-intensive facilities. They will either serve enabling service utilities, service aggregators, or larger enterprises that own internal enabling services capabilities.

How Will the Service Grid Reshape the Environment for Enterprise Computing?

The service grid has the potential to impact markets in a significant way. Its most important function is to enable user-driven innovation, where users can compose applications using services.

Because the service grid will provide so many utility services that subsume complexity in much the same way that application frameworks like Java EE does, service grids offload technical complexity from IT departments, allowing such complexity to reside in the service grid itself rather than at the edge of the network.

What opportunities does the service grid present? Some large enterprises may expose their software as services. Citibank, for example, has begun to expose its payment processing engine that had previously been accessible only within its walls. Many larger companies like GM, Dell, and Merrill Lynch are deploying web services technology within their own enterprises and with business partners, Mr. Hagel and Dr. Seely Brown said. In many cases, they are creating enabling service capability internally and drawing upon more specialized third party utilities to put together their own service grids. Over time, they may offer other companies access to their service grids.

Meanwhile, Google and Amazon are already exposing applications as services. "You can actually use Amazon to deliver a service in terms of looking up the ISBN number of a book," Dr. Seely Brown said. While that sounds trivial, it means that Amazon's internal platform is now a complete web service platform, so it has hundreds of sub-services inside its walls that do all kinds of specialized things to do with retail, and more and more of them are being exposed externally.

What Role Will Vendors Have?

While technology vendors have moved aggressively to support SOA standards and protocols, they take an enterprise-centric view, Mr. Hagel and Dr. Seely Brown said. So, they have overlooked the role of the service grid in the adoption of SOA technology. Technology vendors need to decide what role to play in the deployment of service grid capabilities.

At the least, they can play the role of evangelist and facilitator for early service grid utilities and service aggregators, by educating customers about the service grid, investing in certifying the capability of the early service grid providers, and helping to introduce them to customers, Mr. Hagel and Dr. Seely Brown said.

In some cases, vendors may be able to function as aggregators, identifying essential service grid utilities and coupling them together into service grids targeted to their own customer bases. Vendors could add in specialized enabling services to support nonfunctional requirements. For example, a vendor could ask a service provider with expertise in security such as VeriSign to deliver public key infrastructure services, offer access management services, and issue SSL certificates to enhance the security of their services.

Emerging service grid capabilities could lead to commoditization of enterprise-centric technology platforms from vendors, undermining their customer base. Meanwhile, some vendors like SAP are looking to stay ahead of the curve by exposing their applications as services.

Will that be enough? Will users continue to work with their vendors once they expose their applications as services, or will they be looking for best-of-breed services to build their own applications no matter where the services come from and who the provider is? The latter is a difficult proposition, objects Ms. Manes. "There will always be an advantage associated with buying an integrated solution from a single vendor. Significant work is required to integrate best-of-breed systems." On the other hand, Salesforce.com has created a platform of its own on which smaller companies can base their own service offerings. While the service grid may not be a buffet where users can choose any service offering at all, the rise of new aggregators can only increase the choices available to companies.

The Role of IT

The role of IT will change dramatically once the service grid emerges. Currently, lines of business in a corporation, which are on the leading edge of developing business services, get stymied by IT because they cannot get the CIO's approval fast enough. "IT is the biggest obstacle to innovation," Dr. Seely Brown said. So, they go out on their own and try to get things done. For example, at General Motors, a small team of people was hired to develop services, and that developed into eGM, the company's online arm.

Or take QuickBase, the set of online workgroup applications from Intuit. These include project management, sales management, marketing, professional services, and Sarbanes-Oxley Act compliance. Users can customize their applications on the fly, and Quickbase will automatically create a web-based application based on users' data when they import it into Quickbase. This appeals to innovative lines of business within large corporations that want to go out and try something. "They use tools like Quickbase, to do the business modeling that they want and the accounting that they need, to actually get out there and build a small business inside the big mother ship," Dr. Seely Brown said.

These examples of "shadow IT," whereby business units bypass IT and all governance processes, are symptomatic of an underlying problem in the relationship between IT and the lines of business. According to Ms. Manes, "The business units bypass IT because IT is too mired to respond quickly to the needs of the business units. What that means is that IT must transform itself into a more agile and responsive service provider."

If instead IT becomes an enabler of the service grid by providing services that users can deploy to create mashups, the relationship between IT and business can improve. In this way, IT could facilitate change rather than hindering it.

As mentioned earlier, facilitating the service grid requires the provision of infrastructure services. By deploying effective intermediary platforms such as Amberpoint, IT can satisfy its desire for order and governance, ensuring policies are being enforced and protecting corporate data appropriately. At the same time, users can be empowered to experiment with service grid concepts and begin to build more dynamic relationships with partners.

But will partnerships ever be entirely dynamic? Will the issues of trust be overcome by technology? A disclaimer is in order, says Ms. Manes. Aggregators, in part, are necessary because they provide the vetting, as Li & Fung does in a business partner context. Dynamic business relationships are only possible if you have reason to trust the other partner. Although this may make these relationships somewhat less dynamic, it also opens a market opportunity for companies to serve in the capacity of aggregators for various industries and business contexts, providing the infrastructure and an essential element that that technology can't provide—trust—to realize the vision of the service grid. Within every company, IT also has a significant opportunity to enable the service gird for its users, empowering them to drive innovation, as described in Chapter 4.

Innovation is the Holy Grail of the competitive business world. Corporations constantly struggle to obtain an edge in increasingly crowded, fast-shifting, technology-driven markets. But until recently, users have not been recognized as a fertile source of ideas. Instead, engineers, scientists, and R&D teams were entrusted with innovation.

Now corporations are waking up to the realization that customers or internal users of products and technology can be valuable sources of innovation that can augment the traditional research and development process. Who knows better how to employ—or improve—a tool than its user? And who else wields so much potential influence on fellow users?

This process is termed User-Driven Innovation. The internationally acknowledged guru of this subject is Dr. Eric von Hippel of the Massachusetts Institute of Technology (MIT). He has spent more than 30 years researching user-driven innovation and is the author of the books *Democratizing Innovation* and *Sources of Innovation*. User-driven innovation means empowering people with do-it-yourself capability. It's a democratization of innovation, turning the masses of users into a virtual R&D team. It unites a diversity of expertise. Large numbers of people can engage in parallel problem solving so more options can be pursued and tested.

The changes wrought by the adoption of Enterprise 2.0 and the rise in maturity and scope of a public service grid will likely accelerate the trend toward user-driven innovation in the corporate world as it relates to information technology and new forms of business enabled by technology. Enterprise 2.0 technologies are increasing collaboration far beyond anything that could be done with traditional three-letter applications like ERP and CRM that are the systems of record. The Internet of Services applied as a service grid connects that collaborative space with information in the systems of record and with powerful collections of special purpose functionality. Taken together, all these elements create a massive playground in which users can do more for themselves than ever before. In short, the barriers to innovation have been substantially lowered. This functionality helps tremendously when the product that is the focus of the innovation is a computer system. Even when it isn't accelerated, communication and collaboration speed the innovation process.

Companies ignore these changes at their peril. Unfortunately, current corporate and government policies of concentrating innovation support resources are inefficient. Many companies cling to the old model of innovation as something that must be bred in captivity. Instead, they should look outside their own walls for ways to reap the benefits of the experimentation; similarly, they should tap into the expertise and innovation of their in-house users.

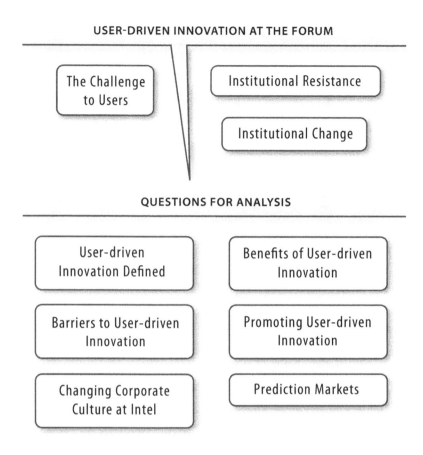

USER-DRIVEN INNOVATION AT THE FORUM

The Challenge to Users

Institutional Resistance

Institutional Change

QUESTIONS FOR ANALYSIS

User-driven Innovation Defined

Benefits of User-driven Innovation

Barriers to User-driven Innovation

Promoting User-driven Innovation

Changing Corporate Culture at Intel

Prediction Markets

Figure 4-1. User-Driven Innovation Chapter Map

Conference Proceedings

These pressing questions pushed user-driven innovation to the forefront at the International Research Forum 2007. This session examined the theory of user-driven innovation and the challenges that were emerging as that theory has increasingly become applied in the real world. The following questions were used as seeds for discussions:

- What are the conditions for successful user-driven innovation?

- What barriers prevent user-driven innovation?

- What are the lessons to be learned from Web 2.0 and Enterprise 2.0 about how to promote innovation?

- What are the strengths and weaknesses of introducing self-directed innovation time into an organization?

- How can ideas that emerge from community innovation be reconciled with a grand strategy?

- How can you determine the right tools for a given population of users?

The User's Challenge

Stephen Miles of MIT kicked off the discussion by describing his work with Radio Frequency Identification (RFID), a technology that uses "electronic labels" to store product data. It also happens to be an area where user-driven innovation has posed many challenges.

Mr. Miles leads MIT's Auto-ID Network Research Special Interest Group, an international research consortium that is exploring industry requirements for exchanging Electronic Product Code (EPC) Data between participants in a collaborative supply chain. He compared RFID to Web 2.0. "We've heard a lot about it, it sounds very exciting, but we're having some problems."

"Sometimes employees in a company get to see less about the data than the supply chain partners down the street. The latter have more access because there are no role-based security systems that are transferable today."
— Stephen Miles

Indeed, Mr. Miles' work in electronic product codes provides a glimpse into some of these complications. In the U.S., the industry faces new standards for sharing patient data safety and improving the security of the healthcare supply chain. The industry is struggling to organize, collaborate, and share information about validating the "E-pedigree" of drugs as they move through supply chains. The industry has established messaging standards and developed software specifications to allow all members to share this data. Documents are given a hash code and a unique stamp each time they're passed along. Originally, the system was designed to trace documents through the supply chain, so, for example, a federal inspector could follow the document trail back to the source.

But things change once users get involved. As Mr. Miles told the audience, "Now the supply chain guys are saying, 'You know, if we went to all the expense of tagging things and putting RFID readers into this regulatory compliance application, couldn't we also use this to optimize our supply chains?'"

In other words, users start to innovate—and that causes a whole slew of new problems. One major issue involves access to data. In an enterprise, people are assigned roles that limit their ability to see data in the company's ERP system. "Sometimes employees in a company get to see less about the data than the supply chain partners down the street," said Mr. Miles. "The latter have more access because there are no role-based security systems that are transferable today."

"Instead of having somebody dictate how they're going to optimize their supply chain, they'll get the information and be able to do it themselves."

—Dan Woods

There are more nettlesome questions. What about authentication models? Should registries be thick or thin? How much access should be given to third parties? And, given that the system must generate a certificate whenever all these people access the data, how should all this new information be managed?

Some new research efforts are addressing these matters. For example, Mr. Miles' lab at MIT is working with SAP Research in California to develop models on role-based security.

Mr. Miles offered one final example of user-driven innovation from his lab. The Aerospace Department at MIT developed a flying robot built from Lego parts. Mr. Miles' colleagues then added their own personal stamp. "Our guys have mounted an RFID reader on it and students are working on an algorithm that would make sure this robot would cover the complete airspace within a warehouse, so it could take inventory there," he said.

Forum moderator Dan Woods summed up: if standards are addressed, people could adapt solutions as they see fit to improve their performance and efficiency. "Instead of having somebody dictate how they're going to optimize their supply chain, they'll get the information and be able to do it themselves," said Mr. Woods. Echoing the same analogy made in the first session, Mr. Miles compared user-driven innovation to jazz music: once users master the basic form, they should be free to improvise.

Institutional Resistance

But the ability to improvise remains an elusive goal. The next speaker, Dr. Gautam Shroff of Tata Consultancy Services, placed much of the blame squarely on IT.

The reason: the intransigence of IT. "Innovation is critical and IT is always in the way," said Dr. Shroff. "It always changes too slowly. Secondly, we spent so much money on existing systems, there's no time left for new work."

In his presentation, Dr. Shroff recounted how his company and others have been applying Web 2.0 lessons in enterprise applications—an area referred to as "Development 2.0." He outlined a vision for this movement: It should allow business analysts rather than programmers to configure applications. It should allow syndication, mashups, and "drag and drop" reuse of application functionality. Instead of SOA, it should emphasize "software as a service" and take advantage of the rich capabilities of Web 2.0 to give a "web-like" feel to enterprise applications and allow for user personalization.

Some platforms already are available. JotSpot (recently acquired by Google) provides a simple way to design collaborative web applications. Nsite (recently acquired by Business Objects) enables creating custom applications in a browser without programming. Tata Consultancy Services has developed InstantAppstechnology, a "behind the firewall"

SaaS platform that enables custom applications within a browser. All these platforms, added Dr. Shroff, rest on two key technologies: dynamic model-driven architectures and multi-tenant architectures.

Even with all these technologies, lamented Dr. Shroff, user-driven innovation remains difficult to achieve in practice. Programmers often do not want to embrace it because they fear it reduces their own value. It requires a new class of employees—business analysts who are able to both understand and configure platforms—but it remains unclear whether such a group actually exists or where they should fall in the organization. It requires a new software development process in which design, configuration, and integration is done by analysts or, when necessary, farmed out to a pool of developers. User-driven innovation also requires a shift in the role of the software professional to become more focused on domain understanding and business innovation. Finally, Dr. Shroff concluded, computer science must focus on understanding domain models, rather than just programs.

"The most important thing that you have to do is create a sort of cocoon where users feel comfortable and have access to the things that enable them to talk, not about the thousand reasons why we can't do this but the thousand reasons why we can."
—Mary Murphy-Hoye

But is such a change really practical? Mr. Woods questioned whether some oft-cited examples of user innovation really offered useful models for businesses. Google Maps may help find toilets or crime trends, but they don't offer a valuable model for business enterprises. Even the examples that do offer useful business models, like Linux and Apache, are cases where the main innovations came from the founders. "In almost every open source project there is an individual who actually did most of the design and then relies on a bunch of other people to fix and refine it," said Mr. Woods.

"Is what you're talking about really possible?" asked Mr. Woods. "Is there really anything such as user-driven innovation, or is it something that you wish existed?"

Institutional Change

It was left to Mary Murphy-Hoye of Intel to begin tackling this question. She addressed two key issues: How do you enable innovation within a large company? And, if you succeed, what are the implications?

"If we create tools to enable innovation," she told the audience, "we also need mechanisms to support that innovation."

But that requires a change in the DNA of the organization, she added. Corporate culture often stifles innovation with its hierarchy, bureaucracy, and division of labor. "The most important thing that you have to do is create a sort of cocoon where users feel comfortable and have access to the things that enable them to talk, not about the thousand reasons why we can't do this but the thousand reasons why we can," she said.

And even if they can, they'll face many new hurdles. Say a company sets up a mechanism for user innovation. Now it has created an *expectation*—employees want to see that their suggestions don't just vanish into a black hole. How does the company keep employees engaged? How does the company avoid the trap of raising *false* expectations that only lead to disappointment? "How do you incentivize the user to tell me those ideas more than once?" asked Ms. Murphy-Hoye. "After all, the first time I don't do something about it, they'll never tell me again."

The short answer: create capabilities. Intel has set up environments to incubate innovation and encourage people to take risks without fear of failure.

But again, this leads to more potential problems. Say a company puts together a menu of services that allows users to assemble their own solutions. "The minute something goes wrong, you're responsible, you're liable," she said. "You just took on the risk of my enterprise because you enabled me to assemble these services."

There lies the dilemma of managing user innovation: How does the company create a safe haven for creativity while erecting structures to make sure it doesn't get out of control? Ms. Murphy-Hoye offered some solutions, at least in principal. "Manage it properly so that it gives users the ability to try these ideas and incubate them," she said. "But also provide a way to connect them so that you don't create a nightmare, either for the IT organization or for the enterprise solutions."

Continuing the Discussion

At this point, Forum participants broke into groups and delved deeper into more questions. One group identified the characteristics of successful innovation. "Users also need to be educated about the possibilities of IT," said Prof. Janet Wesson. "Without that awareness, users often are not able to contribute significantly to innovation."

More concerns followed. How should the company manage the design process and evaluate the final product? What kinds of tools best support the collaborative design process?

R&D, they concluded, needs clearer incentives. What are the business models for encouraging user involvement and managing collaborative design? Similarly, what are the models for managing the development process, all the way from initial idea to production?

Another group grappled with a fundamental question: Does user-driven innovation mean replacing the designer? "Who makes a profit?" asked Friedmann Mattern. "You have to reward not just the controller who has to manage all this, but you also want to give incentives to those who produce the ideas that you build on."

These questions only spawned more. What does this mean for intellectual property? Liability? When should users get involved, during the design phase or only during product refinement?

Where does user-driven innovation make sense and when is it inappropriate? Near the end of the discussion, Mr. Woods, the moderator, played devil's advocate by asking if user-driven innovation was just an overreaction to past failures. "Is this just an admission that we've done a bad job of including users in the process, and now we're trying to overcompensate for that?" he said.

Others also voiced skepticism. "I think user-driven innovation in many ways is like a hoax that the companies are playing on us to make it look like we're involved when we really are not," said Dr. Pradeep

Khosla. "Look at most of the disruptive technologies. There were no users involved in the Internet. The airplane was not invented by the user."

Others rose to the defense of user innovation. Maybe users didn't invent the Internet, said Ms. Murphy-Hoye, but they definitely changed it.

Prof. Michael Rosemann argued that great potential exists if users are sufficiently involved. The key, he argued, is to find the right balance between users and producers. Do you simply want to survey the opinions of passive users? Or do you want them to actively design the product? The answer depends on the particular situation. "There's a whole spectrum," he said, "and you have to find the right spot on this spectrum."

"There are many new business opportunities for creating new businesses around enabling users in a larger sense of the word to come up and build their own stuff. Telco companies pushed all the innovation to the edges. They just supplied the large, complex system and infrastructure that enabled the Web globally. It is extremely user-driven."

But, Prof. Rosemann added, user innovation has not realized its potential simply because people lacked tools that are easy to use. "As it stands today, open software is not something that the average user can easily use, so there's a lot of room for improvement there."

On that, everyone could agree. "We have these gorgeous success stories," said Prof. Rosemann, "but because users are not involved early on, 90% of the inventions do not turn into innovations. This is where we can make improvements."

By the end of the morning, the participants had identified many of the key issues that will continue to resonate for years as user-driven innovation moves from theory to practice. The discussion led the authors to draw up a list of fundamental questions that must be addressed in order to realize the full potential, and perhaps the limits, of user-driven innovation. What are the potential benefits? And what barriers stand in the way?

Analysis

The authors were quite satisfied with the energy and excitement that participants brought to the discussion of innovation. They decided that the best approach for this chapter would be to examine the same questions raised during the International Research Forum with the help of some of the leading experts in the field.

The authors performed further research interviews with some of the top experts in the field:

- Eric Von Hippel, Professor at MIT and the leading researcher on user-driven innovation

- Sonali Shah, Assistant Professor at the University of Washington, one of Dr. von Hippel's former students

- Mary Murphy-Hoye, a Senior Principal Engineer at Intel Corporation

- Professor Nikolaus Franke, Director of the Institute for Entrepreneurship and Innovation at the Vienna University of Economics and Business Administration.

Professor-driven innovation

Eric Von Hippel not only advocates open innovation, he practices it. Dr. Von Hippel has made his books, *Democratizing Innovation* and *Sources of Innovation,* available for free on his website. When contacted by the authors, he insisted that this book likewise be freely download-able. The authors were happy to agree for this book, as well as for the previous year's *International Research Forum 2006.*

What Is User-Driven Innovation?

As defined by Dr. von Hippel, user-driven innovation calls for putting the tools needed to build and configure products into the hands of those who use them. The goal is to eliminate the difficult and error-prone translation of users' requirements into engineering specs for products that will ostensibly satisfy those requirements. By giving users the right tools—ones that collapse this translation process through automation, for instance—they'll be able to directly design and develop products that meet their needs.

STEP 1:
The ability to modify and improve a product is put into the hands of those who use it

STEP 2:
Users now can do for themselves, and are not required to translate their needs into a form that others will use to change the product. They can change the products themselves

STEP 3:
Experimentation confirms which ideas for modifications are successful

STEP 4:
Usually dramatic product improves result

Figure 4-2. User-Driven Innovation: The Basic Process

Dr. von Hippel illustrates this concept with the example of a user-designed house. In the past, a person who wanted to build a house would come up with a wish list—say an eat-in kitchen with a view of the yard and south-facing windows—and then consult with an architect. The architect would translate these requests into detailed plans and take into account engineering requirements and building codes. Now imagine a user-driven process: with user-friendly software, the client could customize the design without an architect. The software would take care of the required structural engineering, adding new beams or reinforcing existing ones and so forth, and calculate the costs. "It's

Eric von Hippel is the T. Wilson Professor of Management and Professor of Engineering Systems at MIT. He is known for his research into the sources of innovation. He finds that product development is rapidly shifting away from product manufacturers to product "lead users" in the Internet Age. The rapid growth of user-centered innovation requires major changes in company business models and government policymaking. Dr. von Hippel's new book, *Democratizing Innovation* (2005), explains user-centered innovation and how companies can adapt and profit. This book is available free on the web at *http://mit.edu/evhippel/www/books.htm*

Dr. von Hippel has founded and participated in startup firms, and is a founder of the entrepreneurship program at MIT. He serves on numerous editorial advisory boards for academic journals and is an active researcher with numerous international collaborators.

about enabling people to use their own insights in their own language," says Dr. von Hippel. "The layperson just wants to push up the ceiling, and there's no need for an architect to get between that desire and the actual redesign of the building."

In his book *Democratizing Innovation*, Dr. von Hippel says that 10 to 40% of users modify the products they use. These "lead users" are ahead of market trends and their innovations are an early clue of what may be of interest to the overall market and what manufacturers may wish to commercialize. These lead users often have a more accurate model of their needs than manufacturers do. They engage in collaborative innovation and freely share intellectual property. More and more, says Dr. von Hippel, these lead users will complement manufacturer innovation or even displace it.

Lead users are the canaries in the coalmine, people who are particularly sensitive to the limits and possibilities of their favorite tools, from software to sports gear to kitchen appliances. A typical example is the journalist who, as an avid runner and father, devised the first jogging stroller. Lead users, Dr. von Hippel is quick to point out, are more than just early adopters. They recognize the need for some new product or feature well before any such item actually exists. They con-

"It's about enabling people to use their own insights in their own language. The layperson just wants to push up the ceiling, and there's no need for an architect to get between that desire and the actual redesign of the building."

—Eric von Hippel

ceive, design, build, test, and refine the item to solve their own problems. And they do this long before the manufacturer introduces anything similar to the market.

For years, Dr. von Hippel has been encouraging manufacturers to pay more attention to users' innovations. These inventions, Dr. von Hippel has discovered in one market after another, frequently address needs that may appear to have a limited audience today but eventually will grow into the demands of a larger one. By identifying these needs and proposed solutions early on, manufacturers gain competitive advantage.

Other forces also drive this movement. In the article "Creation Nets: Getting the Most from Open Innovation" Mr. John Hagel and Dr. John Seely Brown describe how the new economy has transformed the value of knowledge itself; it has become less something to be hoarded and more something to be shared. In times of stability, information is guarded because it holds lasting value; if others gain this information, they can undermine our competitive position. In times of rapid change, however, something unsettling happens: stocks of knowledge become *less* valuable and more quickly obsolete. Now the game is to maximize knowledge *flow*. These networks of like-minded people are termed "creation nets." "Rather than jealously protecting existing stocks of knowledge, institutions need to offer their own knowledge as a way to encourage others to share their knowledge and help accelerate new knowledge building," writes Mr. Hagel and Dr. Seely Brown.

Of course, user-driven innovation doesn't replace the expert. We still need our Thomas Edisons and Leonardo DaVincis. Users don't invent everything, but they almost invariably modify it.

What Are the Benefits of User-driven Innovation?

It has long been assumed that most products are innovated by manufacturers. This assumption is wrong. In fact, the first business computer, the LEO computer developed by the J. Lyons Catering Company in England, was a case study of user-driven innovation. The modern world of business technology is filled with examples of innovations created by users. Apache, the popular Web server software, was developed within the open source community. Firefox, the Internet browser that challenged the dominance of Microsoft's Explorer, depends on users to develop innovations. The Danish company Lego taps customers to help develop its Mindstorms NXT robotics kit. Even corporate behemoths like IBM are employing open source techniques in developing their own software.

Dr. Sonali Shah, Assistant Professor at the University of Washington who studies innovation communities, looked at innovations in industrial products: 20 to 70% of them were made by users.

Let's examine some of the benefits.

Harnessing the Best Ideas

User-driven innovation turns your users into a source of ideas. In theory, it's a meritocracy of ideas that allows the best ones to rise to the top. These ideas can be refined within the walls of the company. Dr. von Hippel argues that user ideas—and solutions—should be treated as a vital "feedstock of innovation" for companies

Lead users are the equivalent of what we call "opinion leaders" in the political world. They're at the leading edge of change, people who are engaged in the process and willing to offer opinions, applause, and criticism.

They are bellwethers of market trends: their innovations are an early clue to those that may be of interest to the overall market and that manufacturers may wish to commercialize. Dr. Shah examined the skateboarding, windsurfing, and snowboarding industry and found about 60% of innovations were developed by users. "Even the

Sonali K. Shah is Assistant Professor at the University of Washington, Seattle. Her research examines the creation and maintenance of innovation communities in fields ranging from open source software to sports equipment to medical imaging devices. She has extensively studied the inner-workings of innovation communities, that is the motives, coordination structures, and strategies that support community-based innovation and product development. This work has led her to theoretical and empirical work investigating the processes underlying the formation of new industries and product markets and issues related to knowledge, entrepreneurship, and the role of institutions in shaping entrepreneurial and innovative activity at the individual level. Dr. Shah has worked with technology clients at Morgan Stanley & Co. and at McKinsey & Co. She holds B.S.E degrees in Biomedical Engineering and Finance from the University of Pennsylvania and the Wharton School. She received her Ph.D. from the Massachusetts Institute of Technology.

first windsurfing board, the first skateboard, the first snowboard were all user-developed innovations," Dr. Shah says.

This is a reversal of the normal process. Typically, we conceptualize innovation as something that occurs in firms' R&D labs, or in a university—the experts create the basic innovation and users refine it. "Here it was the opposite, where the users created the basic product," says Dr. Shah, "then users created the incremental innovations around those products and streamlined them and made them better. Most of the innovations that the firms were doing were refinements, safety innovations and, obviously, production processes."

Recruiting the Best Talent

Bill Joy, one of the founders of Sun Microsystems, once said, "There are always more smart people outside your company than within it." User-driven innovation essentially recruits these smart people—no matter where they are.

Mr. Hagel and Dr. Seely Brown term communities of users "creation nets." These networks of like-minded people encourage trust and information flow and harness talent, which tends to be widely dispersed at times of rapid change. "These edges often experience change first and people on these edges are often the first to develop new knowledge in terms of how to deal with these changes."

Companies can connect with more people, no matter if they're in Asia, Europe, or the Americas. Large numbers of people engage in parallel problem solving, leading to more options that can be pursued and tested. Often this leads to specialization. One subset of people pursues one facet of the problem relevant to their particular interest or expertise; another subset does the same thing with a different facet, and so on and so on.

Let Them Build It and They Will Come

Encouraging innovation won't necessarily sacrifice business; in fact it may *generate* new opportunities. Dr. von Hippel offers the example of the innovations of auto enthusiasts who personalize their Mustangs. "When one of their modifications—a wing on the back, say—becomes a big thing, users will keep coming back to Ford," he says. Millions of people modify their cars, far more than the auto industry could ever employ in research and development. One example comes from Tom Wolfe's 1965 book, *The Kandy-Kolored Tangerine-Flake Streamline Baby.* Wolfe described how car buffs personalized tailfins, double headlights, and low-slung bodies—changes that were later adopted by Detroit automakers.

Consider the story of gate arrays. Gate arrays are programmable logic chips. Manufacturers like Intel produced chips customized for customers, an expensive process. Then a pair of chip designers—Carver Meade and Lynn Conway—figured out a way to separate the layer of circuitry that had to be customized for each client. This top layer was the gate-array, with all of the user's input in the top layer. This was the last layer to be created during fabrication and the easiest to manipulate and customize.

In short, Carver and Meade simplified the problem of building custom chips by separating the user's content from the rest of the fabrication process. Users could now design their own circuits using only Boolean algebra. This greatly simplified the process. Before, engineers had to translate technical needs into complex chip designs that could only be fabricated in hugely expensive factories. Now, users could buy what amounted to blank gate-arrays and customize them on their own premises, at extremely low cost. The middleman was removed from the process.

Established chip makers resisted giving away their design tools to protect their market share. But a startup called LSI Logic took a different approach. They *did* give away their tools—and customers responded in droves. Eventually other companies were forced to follow suit. Researchers have figured out how to progressively peel off layers and hand them over to the user.

"Something very similar is happening in software, too," says Dr. von Hippel. "There will always be the high end, where intermediaries are needed, but the low end is progressively more tractable for this kind of user toolkit approach."

Users Become More Engaged

People become more vested in the outcome if they feel they have a voice in the process. They become stakeholders. Dr. Shah cites Amazon.com as a classic example of this process. The site encourages users to rate books, write reviews, and even rate the reviews of other users. Essentially, customers are generating their own sales pitches. Pages with lots of reviews generate more sales. "When other people click on those pages the likelihood of buying goes up by about three percent," says Dr. Shah.

What Barriers Stand in the Way of User-Driven Innovation?

While user-driven innovation makes an appealing theory, it is harder to achieve than many of us would imagine. Powerful psychological and institutional forces stand in the way.

Corporate Turf

Corporations are naturally reluctant to surrender their secrets. "Companies that own a marketplace, or its core technology, don't necessarily want to give that up to their users," says Dr. von Hippel. "Their incentive is to continue charging the users for the role they play in translating user needs to finished product."

In software, he says, "It will be companies with a big market share that will not want to go along with user-driven innovation. They have this thing wrapped in an enigma in a mystery, and they do not want to give it away."

Resistance to Change

People naturally resist upsetting the status quo. Corporations can be powerful forces of inertia. They are based on hierarchy. They are responsible to shareholders, value stability, and often avoid excessive risk. In many cases, they might not even be aware that their own employees are already modifying products and participating in creation nets.

"People resist change," says Dr. von Hippel. "They have an intellectual investment in the way things are at present. So if someone suggests to the IT department, 'You know what, we really want the users to design and build their own IT,' the department managers will find thousands of reasons why it can't be done."

Companies often fear they will lose control of their own products or sacrifice potential revenue. As Mr. Hagel and Dr. Seely Brown observe, "A natural reaction to accelerating change is to turn inward and tighten control in an attempt to protect what already has value. Creation nets require a different mindset, one that flows knowledge across institutional boundaries rather than becoming more insular and attempting to protect or guard that knowledge. Such fluid knowledge transfers are key to creating new knowledge."

The Innovator Comes Under Fire

Institutions often resist change—even in matters of life and death. One case study comes from the gunnery tactics of the British and American navies at the turn of the 20th century.

As recounted in the book *Men, Machines, and Modern Times* by Elting E. Morison, a pair of naval officers developed methods to greatly increase the accuracy of cannon fire aboard ship. But the innovation itself was just half the battle; the second half was against the naval bureaucracy.

In the 1890s, naval gunnery was complicated by the constant motion of the battleship. Gunners turned a small wheel that operated the elevating gears to bring the barrel to the proper level. After fixing the elevation, the gunner peered through the open sights, waited until the roll of the ship aligned his sights onto the target and pressed the firing button. Some guns had telescope sights, but these were of limited use because they were fixed to the barrel and recoiled into the eyes of the gunners.

This system had several shortcomings. The rate of fire was limited by the rolling of the ship. Gunners had to compensate for the "firing interval"—the lag between the time the sight came onto the target and the moment when his finger pushed the button.

These limitations disturbed one British officer, Admiral Sir Percy Scott. In 1898, he was the captain of H.M.S. Scylla. One day, when the ship's gunners were engaging in target practice and making poor scores because of the violent pitching and rolling of the deck in rough seas. Scott paced the gun deck and noticed than one gunner performed significantly better than the rest. He studied the man and observed that he was unconsciously working his elevating gear back and forth to compensate for the roll of the vessel.

Admiral Scott decided to develop this technique into a science and teach it to the rest of his men. He ordered the gear ratio in the elevating wheels changed in all the guns of the Scylla to facilitate these continuous adjustments. Telescopes were mounted so they would not recoil when the gun was fired. He rigged rifles into the breeches of guns and had his men practice firing at moving targets every day. Within a year, the Scylla established remarkable records.

Thus was born "continuous aim firing," which greatly improved accuracy. In 1899, 5 ships of the North Atlantic Squadron fired 5 minutes each at a lightship hulk at the conventional range of 1600 yards. After 25 minutes, they scored only 2 hits on the sails of the target vessel. Six years later, one naval gunner using these new techniques made 15 hits in 1 minute at a target 75 by 25 feet at the same range.

Admiral Scott possessed a mechanical ingenuity. He also bore what Morison describes as "savage indignation directed ordinarily at the inelastic intelligence of all constituted authority, especially the British Admiralty."

In 1900, Admiral Scott shipped out to the China seas as commanding officer of H.M.S. Terrible. There he encountered a young American officer, Lieutenant William S. Sims, who shared his interest in the new firing methods and the same contempt for bureaucratic inertia. Lieutenant Sims learned all he could of continuous aim firing, ordered similar modifications to the guns of his ship, and drilled his crew in the technique with impressive results.

Over a period of two years, Lieutenant Sims wrote 13 reports to the Bureau of Ordnance and the Bureau of Navigation, urging the Navy to adopt these new methods, which he supported with data from his own experiments and Scott's. Not surprisingly, the service was unmoved by such unorthodox ideas from a young officer in a distant outpost. The Navy was flush with its recent victory in the Spanish-American war. How could its methods be inadequate?

First his reports were greeted with dead silence—some were later found in files partially eaten by cockroaches. The Navy defended its equipment as adequate, suggested that Sims had failed to properly train his gunners and dismissed continuous aim firing as impossible. When Sims persisted, he was labeled a crackpot, egotist, and falsifier of evidence.

The young lieutenant responded with indignation. He circulated his reports to other officers and deliberately used combative language to provoke his superiors.

"I am perfectly willing that those holding views differing from mine should continue to live," he said, "but with every fiber of my being I loathe indirection and shiftiness, and where it occurs in high place, and is used to save face at the expense of the vital interests of our great service (in which silly people place such a child-like trust), I want that man's blood and I will have it no matter what it costs me personally."

Finally, Lieutenant Sims took the audacious step of writing President Theodore Roosevelt. In 1902, Roosevelt called Lieutenant Sims back to Washington and appointed him Inspector of Target Practice, a post he held for 6 years. By the end of his term, he was acclaimed as "the man who taught us how to shoot."

Stickiness

User requirements are often "sticky," that is, hard to explain to manufacturers or technical people to whom users want to communicate their requirements. Dr. von Hippel refers to information as sticky if it is difficult to transfer from one person or group to another. The greater the difficulty in communicating the information, the more sticky the information is (note that this use of sticky is very different from the term's use for web sites, which measure stickiness by their ability to attract users and keep them coming back). The stickiness of user requirements leads to an asymmetry between users and manufacturers. Users generally have a more accurate model of their needs while manufacturers have a better model of potential solutions; each group has its own vocabulary, further complicating matters.

Dr. von Hippel illustrates with an example of a notoriously sticky substance—barbecue sauce.

Imagine a customer approaches International Flavors and Fragrances and says, "I want to create a barbecue sauce that has a smoky flavor, that has gusto." This is *not* the natural language of flavor chemists, who tend to think in terms of the chemical components of flavors like butyric acid. Of course, the customer could switch to the flavor chemist's language. The problem is that the customer doesn't speak this language and thus much is lost in translation. The same situation holds when businesspeople convey their needs to IT. To one degree or another, businesspeople have been required to describe their problems in computing and software terms, not in their own jargon. To the extent that these users have only a rudimentary grasp of the language of computing and software, their requests are likely to be clumsy, fail to capture the nuances, and perhaps be misinterpreted.

Also, users have all of their solutions encoded in a private terminology—their native language, so to speak. *Smoky flavor. Gusto.* By forcing them to change their language, they're being denied access to their own solutions that are encoded in their own user language. This, in short, is the stickiness problem. Asking them to change their language risks losing the subtleties of the solutions the users are trying to communicate.

"It's a vast impoverishment of the customer's ability to create," says Dr. von Hippel. "And therefore, it's no wonder that the customer resists."

The User Wants to Remain a User

End users don't want to become developers. They want to get their job done.

Although Web 2.0 has led to the emergence of mashups and other new tools, merely providing tools to users often fails to encourage innovation. Often the complexity of tools overwhelms the people it is supposed to help. On the other hand, if tools are oversimplified, innovation can be stifled.

Open software remains elusive. For years, users have been able to build and customize their own software using scripting and macros. But software 2.0 still isn't something that most users can manage themselves.

Even when it's made relatively easy, customization doesn't necessarily win many converts. In the late 1990s, there was lots of hype about personalizing portal pages, and sites like Yahoo! and Excite spent heavily to make that possible. The actual percentage of users who actually tweak or modify pages is very low, possibly as low as one percent.

IT Behind the Times

Traditionally, IT has seen its job as maintaining the enterprise's integrity and keeping it in compliance with various laws and regulations. It hasn't necessarily seen its task as being user-friendly. Some frustrated users think that IT might as well stand for InTransigence. IT must change to accommodate this new ethos or face a loss in productivity and employee revolt. This disconnect gives rise to significant risks for the enterprise in terms of governance, risk and compliance issues, and the security and integrity of the business.

Managers and others on the edges of the enterprises, who have been empowered by Enterprise 2.0 amplified by the beginnings of the service grid, have much more freedom, flexibility, and choice. They are no longer beholden to the edicts of the IT organization. They can take matters into their own hands to meet business objectives, which now center on driving revenue and growing the company. They will use whatever means are at their disposal—and to hell with the consequences, because ultimately they'll be rewarded for satisfying those revenue goals.

Today's Enterprise 2.0 technologies are more of a threat to IT precisely because they exist on the Net. This greatly increases their potential impact by reaching large numbers of people and interacting with the enterprise's core systems of record.

Someone with high-level access may take a large data set out of the ERP system, post it to a wiki, and begin sharing it with others. Even though this may be productive, it causes a loss of traceability for that data and raises serious issues for the IT department that's grappling with issues of governance, risk, and compliance.

Also making Enterprise 2.0 more of a challenge to IT is that most of today's knowledge workers are enthusiastic users of the Web. This significantly raises their expectations of how information technology should serve them—quickly, easily, and personally. Programmers sometime resist such innovation because they perceive it as an encroachment on their turf.

Corporate Culture

The corporate incentive system is biased against innovation. The corporate reward system is based on contributions. The problem is that most innovations fail. Thus, there's a built in disincentive.

Big manufacturers aim for large market segments and pay less attention to heterogeneous users. Yet it is precisely these "edge" users who often come up with innovations.

Many companies rely on internally-driven innovation. But this can sentence an idea to a morass of bureaucracy and hierarchy that kills the idea or slows it to a crawl. In the pharmaceutical industry it often takes 10 years to generate first revenues. Fewer than 6 in 100 projects are completed.

There's also the problem of corporate monoculture. "If you have people in a firm's R&D lab, they tend to be relatively homogenous in terms of their skill sets and educational background," says Dr. Shah. "...They're very, very skilled and they're very good at engineering. But that doesn't mean they're going to initiate really novel product ideas. That type of innovation often comes from outside the firm altogether, by the individuals who are out there experiencing new needs and willing to create a product that satisfies their needs."

How Can Companies Encourage User-Driven Innovation?

Taking advantage of user-driven innovation requires some basic changes to business culture. In short, organizations must do something that sounds oxymoronic: they must institutionalize innovation. And they must put in place structures that keep the institution from behaving too much like an institution.

Many businesses fail to achieve their full potential. As Mr. Hagel and Dr. Seely Brown recount, innovation tends to be episodic and marginal to overall performance of the organization. Open innovation requires a reformation of organizational mechanisms. These mechanisms, they argue, actually are the most powerful innovations of all because they spawn wave after wave of new ideas.

Make It Simple

"The way to promote user innovation is simple: make the tools easier," says Dr. von Hippel. "Users innovate when the benefit they obtain exceeds the cost of making modifications. Anything a company can do to lower the cost of user innovation tends to increase the amount of that innovation that takes place." End users need the flexibility to adapt and the ability to do it themselves with ease.

MIT researchers have developed mashup software called Chicken First, Pot Luck, and Piggy Bank. These schemes enable people to grab various data sets that they might have in CRM, ERP, HR, and perhaps other systems. Some companies have experimented with toolkits for user design and creation networks.

"But developments are ongoing and therefore a real 'best' practice does not yet exist," says Prof. Nikolaus Franke, Director of the

Nikolaus Franke is Director of the Institute for Entrepreneurship and Innovation at the Vienna University of Economics and Business Administration. He is also Director of the TU/WU Entrepreneurship Center, a joint technology transfer organization together with the Technical University Vienna, Academic Director of the MBA in Entrepreneurship and Innovation (Schumpeter Program), and leads the User Innovation Research Initiative Vienna.

Prof. Franke is a board member of the Electronic Commerce Competence Center (EC3) in Vienna and Scientific Director of the annual competition "Top 100—Germany's most innovative SME." He is a member of many juries and evaluation committees, for example of the Ernst & Young Austrian Entrepreneur of the Year Award, the Austrian National Innovation Award, and the Rudolf Sallinger Award. He has consulted with many firms from start-ups to leading multinationals, and served as an invited speaker on many occasions.

Institute for Entrepreneurship and Innovation at the Vienna University of Economics and Business Administration. "I would also encourage companies to pay attention to the academic discussion in this field."

Reform IT

Dr. Shroff says that user-driven innovation requires a new class of people—"business analysts" who can conceptualize needs as well as configure new platforms. But such a field hasn't emerged or found a place in the organization. Do they belong within IT? Or on the business side?

User-driven innovation technology—or in Dr. Shroff's lingo, Development 2.0—requires a different software development process. Design, configuration, and integration would be done by analysts without programming, with the latter sometimes farmed out to developers. He argues that software professionals must evolve from a technical role to one more focused on domain understanding and business innovation.

Finally, Dr. Shroff says, computer science needs to focus on formally understanding and reasoning about domain models rather than just programs.

Adapting to the Inevitable

How should IT enable this desire? By embracing it. Clearly, employees want ways of commenting on information that's stored in the structures of transactional applications. By enabling a link in those applications that points to appropriate wiki pages, this kind of unstructured collaboration can be encouraged without the data diverging from or losing its link to an authoritative source.

Adding wiki-like functionality to enterprise applications retains the ability to track and trace the usage of data records. Yet users get the flexibility that they're looking for.

Radical Collaboration via Design Thinking

User-driven innovation often relies on the synergy of teams and diverse points of view. Companies must create structures to support such collaboration. The Hasso Plattner Institute of Design at Stanford University teaches the principles of "design thinking" to create a culture of innovation. This collaborative methodology pulls in people from many disciplines to engage in what they call "radical collaboration." They interact with people from other disciplines, ask for help when stuck, assist each other even when inconvenient, defer criticism, and build on each other's ideas. They integrate all human, business, and technical factors from the outset. They deemphasize hierarchical status and place responsibility in whoever has expertise in a particular problem at hand. They aim for big ideas and use prototypes to discover new solutions. As the school's vision statement says, "We believe true innovation happens when strong multidisciplinary groups come together, build a collaborative culture, and explore the intersection of their different points of view."

Of course, this is easier said than done. Many companies lose patience before they can reap the benefits of this collaboration. The

Stanford approach tries to solve this problem by using the design thinking methodology as the glue that holds the process together and creates an environment conducive to innovation.

Create Structures for Collaboration

Companies also must provide other venues for collaboration. Ultimately, Enterprise 2.0 is an inevitability. The challenge is to somehow weave the best practices of, for instance, wikis, blogs, forums, and social networking into the fabric of the organization. This means surfacing these capabilities where appropriate and in context to the users, wherever they spend the bulk of their time.

Mr. Browne predicts "every single bit that changes on a disk or passes over a network is going to be tracked and traced, and it's going to be correlated, and evaluated, and assessed, and get algorithms run against it to say what's actually happening." Just as Google's search engine analyzes streams of search queries, corporations will be able to learn more about their internal activities—and how to improve them.

Listen to the Wisdom of Crowds

Sometimes the best source of advice is the customer. Some companies are creating forums to solicit feedback; sometimes this advice substantially shapes the product. Prof. Franke helped the Ski manufacturer Edelwiser develop a business model in which skiers exchanged ideas and helped design products. The company acted as the organizer, provider of the IT infrastructure, and manufacturer. The model was so innovative that it won the Austrian National Award for Multimedia and E-Business 2007.

Prediction Markets

How can one discern the wisdom of crowds? You don't need an applause meter. The growing field of "prediction markets" helps turn collective intelligence into quantifiable information. It also offers a valuable resource for capturing or evaluating user-driven innovation.

Prediction markets aggregate responses of many people to predict the likelihood of certain outcomes. These strategies are gaining traction in the business world. Google uses marketplaces to predict timing for launching products. Hewlett-Packard uses them for forecasting sales. Eli Lilly does so to forecast new drug applications. Several companies offer predictive market platforms such as Consensus Point and Inkling Markets, as do consumer sites like the Hollywood Stock Exchange.

SAP has begun using predictive markets to help with forecasting and decision making, according to Dr. Eric Kasper, who has overseen the design and implementation of the market at the Waldorf, Germany, headquarters.

"The prediction market is nothing other than a stock market about future company events," Dr. Kasper says. "Each stock is related to a particular event and has an expiration date when the actual outcome and payoff will be judged by the market administrators."

SAP employees serve as players in this internal market. Each buyer is initially given a certain amount of "play money" to allocate as they wish. There is no obligation to trade, but employees usually buy stocks in areas where they have particular knowledge or expertise. A ranking mechanism identifies the best stock pickers; another mechanism identifies people with certain areas of competence. As in a real stock market, those who invest unwisely end up losing their money and influence in the market. As a further incentive, SAP is exploring ways of rewarding success in the predictive market with real compensation.

The company uses these markets to analyze strategic questions (the topics remain confidential). Participants express their opinion by buying or selling "stocks" that represent answers. The company has created two types of stocks. Binary stocks can be answered with a simple yes or no (will a product attract a certain number of customers within a certain time period?). Scales stocks ask questions in terms of absolute numbers (how many customers will buy a certain product?).

Dr. Kasper says SAP also has been exploring the possibility of a two-market system. One market would gather as many ideas as

Eric Kasper has been working with SAP since 2005 as part of SAP Research/SAP INSPIRE —the corporate venturing unit of SAP—which is continuously looking for new business opportunities. Before coming to SAP, Dr. Kasper worked as a research associate at Ludwigshafen University of Applied Science, where he worked at the Research Center for Innovation and Management and conducted a series of research and consulting projects. Dr. Kasper has a bachelor's degree in Business Administration and a Ph.D. from Leeds Metropolitan University (Great Britain). His major research interests are innovation management and R&D management.

possible and rate them. A second market would be used to make predictions about a selected set of the most-promising ideas. SAP's COIN system, a web application described in the conclusion of this book, is an example of the first kind of market. It invites everyone in the company to post ideas for new products and to post their own comments about those ideas.

Predictive markets offer several advantages over traditional decision making and forecasting, says Dr. Kasper, who wrote his Ph.D. dissertation on the subject. Effective allocation of R&D resources is paramount in today's era of global competition and shorter product life cycles. Traditional hierarchical structures tend to be slow, discourage sharing of information, may lead to opportunism by subordinates, and are no longer up to the challenge of the dynamic marketplace. Dr. Kasper's research supports an integrated approach of both hierarchies and market mechanisms.

Other analysts suggest that prediction markets also provide a check and balance against human bias. If prediction markets consistently produce results contrary to management recommendations, it might indicate that the corporate culture is overly politicized or that managers are distorting the message.

These predictive markets often become more powerful as the number of participants grows. Dr. Kasper says predictive markets work particularly well for evaluating projects that are close to hitting the market. They are less reliable for projects on the more distant horizon because fewer people will have enough knowledge to make informed bets. "Market mechanisms are often very good for making evaluations for incremental innovations, but less so breakthrough innovations," he says.

> *"We believe that the collective intelligence within the company should be used for decision making and forecasting."*
> —Eric Kasper

Dr. Kasper sees strong potential for using predictive markets with user-generated ideas. A select set of "lead users" could be invited to submit their best ideas to be evaluated through an internal market mechanism.

What does the future hold for predictive markets? "We will see these markets as embedded solutions within the supply chain, for example," Dr. Kasper says. This will play to SAP's strength as it already has the underlying data models that can be combined with prediction markets to find answers to specific questions. "The whole concept is based on the wisdom of crowds," says Dr. Kasper. "We believe that the collective intelligence within the company should be used for decision making and forecasting."

Find Competitive Advantage

Companies can exploit user-driven innovation to gain an edge over those that aren't so nimble. Dr. von Hippel cites the example of IBM and Linux. "IBM does just fine supporting Linux, because they sell WebSphere on top of it, and they sell hardware, on which they mount Linux. And they sell services to help users make all of that work. IBM is selling what economists call complements—products and services that are used along with a product. The icing on the cake for IBM is that its openness to Linux enables it to attack Microsoft, which is to their competitive advantage. Eventually, Dr. von Hippel predicts, Microsoft will follow suit.

"Microsoft cannot clamp down on the alternatives," he says. "It can only clamp down on what it's selling."

Create a Creation Net

Corporations must share their intellectual property and look for connections with others. They must become interwoven in "creation nets" or a community of users. For example, Dell Computer launched Ideastorm, a web site inviting customers to share ideas for new products and trade tips for enhancing current ones. Squid Labs has created a do-it-yourself community web site called the Instructables ("The World's Biggest Show and Tell"), a collaboration platform where users exchange tips for reusing Thanksgiving leftovers or building an egg peeling machine. Organizers plan to offer software to help companies build communities of citizen product developers.

According to Mr. Hagel and Dr. Seely Brown, such creation nets don't appear out of nowhere. They are shaped by network organizers and require understanding of management techniques needed to deliver results.

Mr. Hagel and Dr. Seely Brown distinguish between two types of creation nets: practice networks and process networks. These two categories call for different approaches.

Practice networks, such as the open source software movement, bring people together in a common set of activities. These networks share a common sensibility, allowing them to remain loosely organized. After setting criteria for participation, orchestrators of the practice networks can play a less active role in recruitment and management. Organizers pay most attention to the integration stage of the creative process when everything must be brought together.

The second type, process networks, brings people with more diverse backgrounds and experiences together. Process networks mobilize specialists across an extended business process and thus require more active orchestration (although still less than most managers would consider acceptable). Organizers must vet participants, assign roles, and monitor performance. Examples of process networks include the

Original Design Manufacturers (ODMs) in Taiwan, networks of hundreds of business partners that bring together complementary capabilities to design new electronic and high tech products, or the production network created by Li & Fung in China, which employs a network of 10,000 specialized business partners to create customized supply chains for each apparel line. These networks are described in more detail in Chapter 2.

These two types require different management techniques. Western executives tend to focus either on a simplistic version of practice networks or view innovation in terms of the "big blockbuster" new product. This, argue Mr. Hagel and Dr. Seely Brown, is an oversight, because innovation usually comes from improvements to existing processes—the very thing that has generated huge competitive advantage for companies like Dell or Wal-Mart. "Ultimately, individual innovations may matter less than the institutional innovations that create the capacity to sustain a rapid series of improvements and the pace at which they are developed and disseminated throughout the network," they write.

Mr. Hagel and Dr Seely Brown predict that process networks will become the dominant form of production for the 21st century. This "unbundling the firm" creates a platform for rapid growth. Process networks promote flexibility and scalability. In fact, the authors recommend that western companies go overseas to emerging markets specifically to learn this essential technique.

Mr. Hagel and Dr. Seely Brown offer a few tips on mobilizing effective creation nets:

- Choose carefully. Not all areas benefit equally from creation nets. When initially engaging in such networks, they recommend picking an area with the highest potential payoff. Look for areas with uncertain demand, many specializations, and rapidly changing performance requirements in the marketplace.

- Choose whether to establish a network or participate in an existing one.

- Choose what activities to shed. You can't do everything.

- Choose an appropriate governance model. Will it be more of a practice network or a process network? As described above, the two models require different levels of organization.

- Establish the network in phases. Don't try to do everything at once. Let the network evolve.

- Establish internal mechanisms to ensure participation in creation nets. Managers must prevent their people from focusing internally. The goal is to have two way communication across the boundaries of the enterprise.

Changing Corporate Culture: The Intel Example

Craig Barrett, the head of Intel, says big corporations often have a "creosote bush effect" on innovation. Creosote bushes inhibit the growth of plants around them. Big companies are like that—they discourage new ideas from taking seed.

To correct this stifling effect, Intel has taken pains to cultivate creativity. An example of this is Mary Murphy-Hoye, Senior Principal Engineer, specializing in next-generation supply network integration, strategic planning processes, and research of disruptive technologies in emerging business models.

Ms. Murphy-Hoye described how Intel has tried opening its culture to new ideas—no easy task in a big company. "Most of the time, organizational incentives are counter to that type of innovation," she says. "Indeed, it's discouraged...The IT organizational incentives and structure can be very counterproductive when it's engaged."

She offered these tips:

Get out of your silo: Stop talking to yourself. Don't get so wrapped up in your normal duties that you forget to look around. That makes you stale. "We forget to look around us at everything that's happening, what's going on at the universities, what's happening down the street at some other company not like ours at all, what's in the news," says Ms.

Murphy-Hoye. "As you start to listen to the signals, you start to realize that things may be unfolding, or opportunities may be happening, that you can take advantage of."

Build networks of expertise: Assemble teams with diverse expertise. Ms. Murphy-Hoye likens this to a movie crew: people with all sorts of specialties—director, actors, gaffers, camera operators, and so on—come together to make a picture. For the next picture, they may assemble a different crew. "You want to give people, especially creative people, the ability to move from one thing to another," she says. "We call it redeployment at Intel…It's a way to get that flow of expertise into different parts and different combinations in the company to allow for moving the right group of people together to form around the kind of work that needs to be done at a certain time."

Incubate: Similarly, Intel creates "cocoons" for innovation—virtual communities that unite people from all over the organization. "We share insights," she says. "We're all working on trying to understand how to use a new technology. And it kind of was disbursed all over the company, because different parts of the company were finding that it was valuable for different things."

Build forums for unstructured collaboration: Creativity often happens when people step outside the normal way of doing things. Give people a chance to interact with each other around the proverbial water cooler—even if it's a virtual one.

Once Ms. Murphy-Hoye borrowed an idea from the MIT Media Lab. They had built a live video link between one lab in the USA and another in Europe. They put a couch, coffee table, and keyboard in front of the giant screen. But when installed as an experiment at Intel, corporate nature being what it is, they fell into old habits. They scheduled structured meetings.

"I said, 'No, no, no, no, no! That's not what it's for!'" recalls Ms. Murphy-Hoye with a laugh. "It was about instantaneous collaboration, walking by and having a chat, keeping track of what the other guy's doing, getting to know each other."

Mary Murphy-Hoye is a Senior Principal Engineer in Intel's Software Pathfinding and Innovation Division. An innovator in Information Technology and Supply Chain solutions, she applies a broader Predictive Enterprise vision based on emerging technologies to create and implement large-scale experiments in high volume production environments. She is a pioneer in multi-disciplinary solutions connecting emerging technologies and business practices for cross-enterprise supply networks. Ms. Murphy-Hoye's most recent focus has been the creation of Intel's RFID/Wireless Sensor Networks Lab for industry-scale proactive computing experimentation across businesses.

Ms. Murphy-Hoye formed Intel's IT Research Agenda and specialized in research of disruptive technologies as applied to emerging business models. Her academic collaborations with the MIT Media Lab and MIT Sloan School of Business as well as the Stanford Graduate School of Business drove multi-year R&D efforts in Supply Chain Visualization, Internal Markets for Trade-based Supply/Demand Planning, Demand Creation through Product Transition Dynamics, and Smart Objects for Intelligent Supply Networks. She is collaborating with Arizona State University building self-contained wireless sensor networks and investigating multi-modal (audio & visual) techniques for complex large-scale predictive analytics.

Coauthor of *Surviving Supply Chain Integration: Strategies for Small Manufacturers,* (National Academy Press 2000), Ms. Murphy-Hoye is also a creator of Intel's Business Computing Vision, working with end-users to identify and address the key challenges of new technology deployment.

Ms. Murphy-Hoye speaks frequently to academic and industry audiences, addressing emerging technology, Digital Business, and Supply Chain strategy.

The concept car: Sometimes an outlandish idea may open the door for a practical one. Murphy-Hoye refers to the "concept car" often seen at auto shows. These tricked-out cars are too impractical for the marketplace, but they spur thinking and creativity...and that DOES improve real products. Encouraged by Intel's CIO, her team followed this exercise and entertained outlandish ideas from universities and users within the company. "We would bring weird ideas out of the universities, weird ideas that anybody in the company had," says Murphy-Hoye. "They could get access through this website that was set up with them to people who could help them with their idea. They could post a weird idea. And then they could, with bubblegum and string and whatever, put these ideas together, make them real."

Imagine the end user: Look at how a product will be used. Get out into the real world. "Don't just play in the lab," says Ms. Murphy-Hoye. Her team spends time in factories and warehouses ("I make sure to work with the business folks instead of with the IT guys," she says). They've attached wireless sensor networks to railroad cars and descended into the holds of cargo ships. They've brought in anthropologists and ethnographers to help them understand how humans interact with products and production lines. She recalls: "I said, 'Go be the product—figure out exactly what happens to it, where it moves, where it sits, who interacts with it. Do they write things on their hands and tell the next guy about something? What's really going on with this stuff that's moving inside this factory that's been designed around equipment?' We were really trying to give ourselves a fresh way of looking at the same thing that we've been staring at for 20 years."

Make failure an option: If you create an environment that encourages people to always play it safe, you won't get the risk taking that is essential for generating new ideas. Sometimes this requires a fundamental change in thinking. It's okay to try an idea that doesn't pan out. A long-time Intel colleague calls these "noble failures."

"Make mistakes: it's okay," says Ms. Murphy-Hoye. "You're not going to get in trouble. Change the rules about experimentation."

Take risks: Says Ms. Murphy-Hoye, "If you're not trying something where at least one person is telling you it's impossible then you're not far enough out on the edge."

Turn ideas loose: See what happens as people pick it up, play with it, and offer suggestions. The idea may grow into something you never expected. Ms. Murphy-Hoye uses the analogy of floating ideas downriver. You never know which one will turn out to be the next Moses.

Create environments that nurture creative types...and tolerate them!: Creativity can be encouraged, but it isn't something that can be taught in a workshop. "You can't teach innovation," Ms. Murphy-Hoye says. "You have to create an environment *for* people to be creative, and you have to understand that certain kinds of people are like that...And they tend to be irritating and obnoxious, because they aren't following the rules and they're not proceeding down the normal path. But that's sort of the point."

Wrapping Up

Where is this all headed?

According to Prof. Franke, user-driven innovation is in an era of rapid development and experimentation. Companies and users are trying different business models, technologies, and organizational forms with varying success. Academic researchers are trying to analyze these developments. Many companies are waiting to see what dominant designs will emerge.

"In a few years, all this may be more clear and user-driven innovation will be a natural part of companies' innovation management, IT-infrastructure, and business models," Prof. Franke says. "This means that institutions, both producers and users, might adopt new roles, and new institutions may arise. Naturally, pioneers have the chance of first mover advantages—and laggards risk missing the train."

Business Model
Transformation

5

The effects of the Internet of Services as manifested by Enterprise 2.0, the service grid, and user-driven innovation all point to a world of business where many barriers to change drop and many more ideas for improvement are in play. The main question facing business would cease to be "How do we get to where we want to go?" and become "What do we want to be?"

Right now, most companies face so many barriers related to technology implementation and change management that a clear identity for their business is perhaps less important than a general sense of direction. If every quarter they get closer to where they want to go, then all seems well. If they can move faster than competitors, that's even better. But implementation moves so much slower than imagination that precision in identity is not as important now as it will be.

If the promise of Enterprise 2.0, the service grid, and user-driven innovation is even partially fulfilled, companies will be able to move much faster as the actions of ever larger groups of people are coordinated and aligned. The gap between imagination and implementation will close considerably. Companies will have to think more carefully about who they want to be because the transformation will become that much faster.

The question of who a company wants to be is answered to a large degree by the question of what business model or models it follows. Corporate identity has many other aspects: values of corporate citizenship, attitudes and policies toward employees and investors, and a sense of financial and social mission. But identity crystallizes in the business model, which is the way that a company defines the process to create value and its relationships with customers, employees, and suppliers. Business models transform a company's identity into a plan of action.

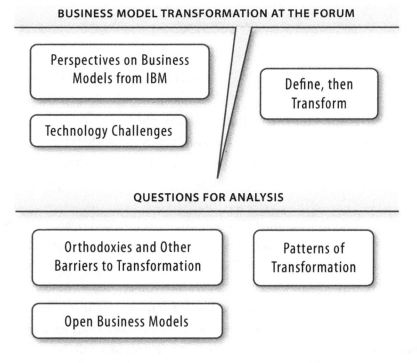

Figure 5-1. Business Model Transformation Chapter Map

It is in this context that we now turn to the last topic of the International Research Forum 2007: business model transformation.

Conference Proceedings

The session on business model transformation sought to illuminate the patterns and obstacles related to changing how a company does business. To spark thinking, the following questions were introduced before the conference began:

- How can business models evolve rapidly without confusing customers?

- How can business model experiments be performed in a way that doesn't introduce chaos?

- When does change and flexibility become too much of a novelty?

- Can making it easy to change business models do more harm than good?

- How do you run effective experiments with business models?

- Will customers' ability to accept new business models be the governing factor?

First up was Prof. Dr. Matthias Kaiserswerth of IBM, who laid out how business transformation has played out at Big Blue. During the early part of its history, IBM's research and development, manufacturing, and administrative functions were done mostly in the U.S. When the company expanded overseas, it replicated its U.S. organizational structures locally. Each subsidiary offered specialized products and services, and some did their own research. To make matters worse, because of local laws, some of these businesses had their own human resource policies, and some did their own marketing separately from headquarters.

In a globally integrated economy, IBM knew the way it traditionally ran its businesses no longer made sense. Big Blue now sees itself as

 **Matthias Kaiserswerth** leads the IBM Research Strategy in Systems Management and Compliance, coordinating the research work across IBM's eight global research laboratories. In addition in June 2006, he was reappointed Director of the IBM Zurich Research Laboratory. He is an honorary professor at Friedrich-Alexander University where he teaches applied computer science.

From 2002 until the end of 2005, Prof. Dr. Kaiserswerth was the Managing Director of an IBM Integrated Account, where he was responsible for the total global business between IBM and a large international power and automation company headquartered in Switzerland. In 2000 he became the director of IBM's Zurich Research Laboratory. He was responsible for researchers in the field of physical sciences, communications technology, and computer science. He also worked with the IBM Zurich Industry Solutions Lab where IBM hosts customers to meet with its researchers to discuss future technology and emerging business trends.

Most recently, he worked on smart cards and Java security, which led to the OpenCard industry standard for using smart cards in a Java environment and Visa's Java Card™ Price Breakthrough program based on the IBM Zurich Research JCOP platform.

a "globally integrated company" and is in the midst of moving business functions into geographic areas that make the most sense economically, Prof. Kaiserswerth said. IBM may end up with a single HR function, a single procurement function, and a single research function. None of this would be possible without advances in IT, such as service-oriented architecture (SOA) and low-cost telecommunications links. "The flat world is changing where and how business value is created, and its economics, expertise, and open business environments impact where companies locate their business functions," Prof. Kaiserswerth said.

Prof. Kaiserswerth explained how IBM is transforming its business model at three levels. In business strategy, IBM is organizing its portfolio of products and services to better meet the needs of the market. In a drive called optimized expertise, IBM is making itself more open to divesting certain businesses, acquiring others, and pushing into new technologies. The company is investing in growth markets such as China, India, and Brazil, as well as in Eastern Europe. IBM views improved access to resources at those locations as key to its global strategy. The company is also moving back-office functions into global regions—procurement in China, service delivery in India—and building shared service centers and centers of excellence as a way to improve efficiencies and develop new products and services. To do all this, IBM overhauled its management culture. It is creating what it calls a value-based management system to form decisions and build relationships because, Prof. Kaiserswerth said, "we all work along the same process."

"The flat world is changing where and how business value is created, and its economics, expertise, and open business environments impact where companies locate their business functions."
— Matthias Kaiserswerth

Prof. Kaiserswerth pointed out that Big Blue's clients are facing the same sort of challenges as the company.

Define the Business Model, then Transform

Dan Woods, one of the Forum moderators, suggested it's important for companies to first define their business model and then decide whether some or all of it needs to be transformed. The role that technology will play depends on what's being done.

Discussion continued on how HP reacted to Dell's rise in the PC market through its direct sales channel. HP, which used an indirect channel, needed to react to Dell's rise without alienating their business partners. Eventually, HP's strategy paid off and it now leads the PC market. Mr. Woods likened this to the rise of Craigslist, the Internet classified site that offers some ads for free, upending the business model newspapers have followed for decades. Craigslist is a case in which a competitor is willing to take less profit to take a higher market share. The same thing is happening with the telecom industry, which is now having difficulty adapting to new models as their businesses become commoditized. Mr. Woods seized on this point, arguing that now is the time to start knitting together ideas such as user-generated innovation and the service grid, creating a larger business model

Next, Mr. Woods raised the question about whether collaboration was brought up as a theme in any pods or discussions as a way to transform business models. Claudia Funke, Director of the Munich office of McKinsey & Co., replied that the discussion centered on business model transformation as an imperative. "Nobody does business model transformation willingly, right?" she joked. "We all talk about it, like wouldn't it be great if we could change things, but normally it happens because somebody's taking away your business, so you have to change." Sometimes, as is the case with the music business, companies have little choice but to change. Ms. Funke argued that companies don't often figure out how to change business models, or don't effectively communicate their changes in strategy, and wind up botching the execution. The problem, she argued, is that mature companies wind up fighting orthodoxies. (The authors found Ms. Funke's ideas on orthodoxies and other barriers compelling and analyze them further later in the chapter.)

In his remarks, Prof. Dr. Wolfgang Wahlster, CEO of the German Research Center for Artificial Intelligence, noted that business transformation is risky because there isn't any way to use technology to predict what will happen. At least with enterprise service grids, a company can test software before deploying it. A company gets only one chance to get business model transformation right, which makes changing a model dependent on IT highly risky, he said.

Carnegie Mellon's Dr. Pradeep Khosla argued that IT cannot transform a business model but is a useful tool to enable the process. Amazon, for example, has utilized technology to transform itself from a bookseller to a data collector, which has enabled the company to customize its sales experience in a way that's never been done before. "It's creating sales by showing you books and other items that you might also want to buy," he said. "Like the GRE exam, where new questions are tried out on students by sprinkling them among the graded questions that actually make up each exam, Amazon uses every opportunity to try out different combinations of items for cross-selling and even to try out new features on its site that may further engage its customers." Amazon is able to respond to customers so quickly that it can change business models over a two-day period.

The problem, as Dr. Khosla sees it, is that there are hardly any good models of business processes that can do automated reasoning, which is a pity because companies could use computer science techniques to uncover flaws in their business methods. They would be able to easily figure out if they were in compliance with laws such as Sarbanes-Oxley. SAP and Oracle would be able to deliver services that would enable companies to build and automate new business processes on the fly. "Then, one could imagine building virtual companies every six months, say, rapidly going into a customized situation for a product or through joint development, dismantling the company and going into partnership with another one."

At this point, Mr. Woods interjected that the discussion should focus on the relationships created by IT instead of just mechanics and process hierarchies. For instance, Amazon isn't only about IT. It's about the relationship that it has with each of its customers. As Mr. Woods noted, companies can execute their models perfectly yet still have horrible businesses. The central question, of course, is how you make customers happy. For instance, Threadless T-Shirts creates relationships by building a community of T-shirt designers. Scion at Toyota is creating a new experience of customizing a car to express your individuality.

IT serves two different purposes. In some businesses, such as manufacturers, it's a support function, and in others, such as financial

> *"Technologists still need to figure out how to translate into plain English what they can do for an enterprise and what they can't do. Talk to a businessperson about any IT concept and they look at you blankly, because it has nothing to do with their business. Translate it, though, and point out the benefits it offers them, and they will generate 100 ideas for it."*
>
> —Dan Woods

services firms, it is the business. "So when one deals with business model transformation, it's vital to distinguish between these two types of enterprises," Mr. Woods said.

A related area is continuous improvement, which can be learned from manufacturing and applied to the rest of the processes that enterprises deal with. Even small changes can be meaningful. For instance, IT found that profit margins at gas stations are huge between 12 and 2 p.m. so one company decided to enable operators to raise and lower prices during the day in order to maximize profits.

Prof. Maria Orlowska of the University of Queensland expanded on this point and raised the question of what triggers such major changes in business models. The reasons can be technological, such as when Kodak had to react to the advent of digital photography or globalization. Then Mr. Woods jumped in and asked whether IDS Scheer is trying to build a machine to model business processes. Prof. Orlowska replied that this is the "vision...but we will have to support how such a process is executed, what the bottom line is, and where the threads are. And, of course, semantics is still an issue." Prof. Michael Rosemann warned that, according to his research, such a tool may not be particularly interesting and warned against the proliferation of new terms for change management when established ways of doing things may be adequate.

Speaking the Same Language

Technologists still need to figure out how to translate into plain English what they can do for an enterprise and what they can't do, said Mr. Woods. "Talk to a businessperson about any IT concept and they look at you blankly, because it has nothing to do with their business. Translate it, though, and point out the benefits it offers them, and they will generate 100 ideas for it." People will only change their business models using IT if technologists can help them understand the value that can be created for both their management and customers. Not enough has been done to make technology relevant to the needs of business, said one participant. "We focus on building technologies.

We are technologists who want to build things rather than apply our science."

Since business models are changing more rapidly than ever, CEOs and CIOs need to speak the same language. The trick here is to show, not tell. CIOs can't throw terms around such as SOA and partner interfaces without explaining what they mean and how they can help drive a company's growth. CEOs also have to be sure that they have realistic expectations of their IT departments. As analysts such as Gartner have noted, most CEOs see their CIOs as operational people and not as business leaders.

One of the ways of making sure the partnership works is to have the CIO report directly to the CEO, because technology is becoming more of a strategic tool than a back-office function.

As Prof. Kaisersworth points out, the IT department is often consulted late in the process. As it is, most discussion is only about what he called "snippets of processes." IT can help figure out how to best implement policies and procedures so that companies can ensure alignment with their outsourcing partners on issues such as data governance—in other words, covering the whole business process, rather than just a snippet.

Some of the technology challenges that IT will need to deal with include:

- Process and policy discovery

- Treating compliance as an end-to-end problem

- Collaborative governance

IT needs to make sure that the company is getting the most bang for its buck by getting the best service with the lowest risk at the right price. CIOs need to be in the forefront of key issues such as how to best prioritize investments and figure out the best way for these resources and people to be deployed in an enterprise resource plan. By itself, IT can't transform a business model but it can assist in the transformation,

Dr. Khosla notes. There aren't any good models of business processes that can be used to do automated reasoning to find flaws in business models, methods, and processes.

Analysis

In the wake of these discussions, and some further research by the authors, it became clear that, although the topic is vast in scope and could be discussed on many different levels, patterns for success in business model transformation are emerging.

The authors then decided to explore more deeply the ideas of Claudia Funke, and also bring in thinking from two leading researchers, Navi Radjou of Forrester, and Henry Chesbrough, Adjunct Professor and Executive Director, Center for Open Innovation at the University of California, Berkeley, a pioneer in the analysis of open business models. Each of these thinkers' ideas are explored in the analysis of the following questions:

- What internal barriers will companies face as they attempt to change their business models?

- What patterns are emerging in the way companies are designing their business models?

- What forces will lead companies to pursue open business models?

What Internal Barriers Will Companies Face as They Attempt to Change Their Business Models?

Internal barriers are those barriers within a company or its culture that resist change to business models. Claudia Funke discussed how businesses identify orthodoxies and overcome them. Companies need to realize that those who can successfully transform their business models gain an enormous competitive advantage over those who just introduce a new product or technological innovation. Nonetheless, she concedes that transforming a business model is one of the most difficult things a company can do.

Claudia Funke is Director of the Munich Office of McKinsey & Company. She leads McKinsey's global enterprise ICT services practice as well as the German high-tech sector, which includes the software and services, datacom, consumer electronics, industrial manufacturing, and aerospace and defense industries, and is part of the leadership team of McKinsey's global high-tech sector.

Ms. Funke works primarily for industry leaders in software, IT services, and telecommunication in the enterprise customer segment. Her main areas of expertise include go-to-market approaches, strategy and executive counseling, and business model innovation. Ms. Funke is leading McKinsey's "Global leadership creation in High Tech" initiative, which deals with the question of how more European companies can become global high-tech leaders.

During an interview on this question, Ms. Funke reiterated her argument from the Forum that companies are held back by orthodoxies, that ingrained DNA that may have helped them get where they are, but may not help them get where they want to go. Many companies mistakenly believe that once technology is mastered, the business model will fall into place. That, according to Ms. Funke, is the wrong approach. While technology is an important part of transformation, it has limits, particularly when a company's orthodoxy makes it approach the same problems in the same way. Businesses often forget that conventional wisdom is exactly that...conventional. It's natural for people to resist change. Throughout history, many people have found this out the hard way. Galileo was placed under house arrest after he argued against the widely held view that the sun revolved around the earth. Later, he was forced to recant his views under duress. Though workers in the U.S. aren't going to be imprisoned for rocking their company's boat, many still could face harsh questions from colleagues and supervisors. For companies trying to transform themselves, it's vital to examine their internal barriers, Ms. Funke says.

Orthodoxies come in all shapes and sizes. Among the examples cited by Ms. Funke are companies that think that everything is about pricing, or that their actions in the market take place in a vacuum. In IT, many companies think that they can compete for business in other markets just because they are successful in one market. To successfully address new challenges requires "very open dialogue" between top and middle management, using what Ms. Funke and McKinsey & Co call "targeted interventions." She described "innovation at scale," which is a simple framework to highlight what companies need to work on. After a company has this framework, they need to make sure that, along with having the right technology in place to support business model change, they have the right processes and organization units across what she calls the "innovation engine." "If you think that you can just use technologies to enforce business model transformation, you're wrong," she said. "It's also wrong to think you can just reorganize a little bit and then change the processes, or just change the pricing scheme."

"If you think that you can just use technologies to enforce business model transformation, you're wrong. It's also wrong to think you can just reorganize a little bit and then change the processes, or just change the pricing scheme."
—Claudia Funke

These trends are playing out in the telecommunications industry. Many telecom companies have introduced IPTV services to compete against cable companies for telecom customers. IPTV requires telecom companies to employ a totally different business model than they have in the past. Now they need to rely on major partners such as Microsoft, because distributing video to the home is complex. Moreover, the companies are no longer selling just connectivity. They are in the content business, which has required them to strike deals with Hollywood movie producers. Also, this isn't a mass-market service such as telephony and requires a more targeted marketing approach to high-income customers. The typical telecom management structure, where people report on their progress every fourth week or so, will not work here, Ms. Funke said.

Instead, through the targeted intervention, the company must create a high-caliber cross-functional team that reports on its progress every week, to the CEO and the rest of the management team.

Business model innovation is more than just introducing a new product or going after a new customer segment. It usually means changing a company's go-to-market approach, everything from pricing to the deployment of resources. Given the amount of work involved, there are few examples of transformed companies such as Nokia and IBM. Both companies bear little resemblance to what they were 20 or even 10 years ago. They have, as Ms. Funke calls it, changed their DNA. Of course, the bigger the change a company needs to make to its business model, the bigger the challenge. However, the internal debate about its core value system can be healthy. Companies can decide what aspects of their culture and business model to save and which should be "creatively destroyed," she said.

Many of the biggest tech companies, such as SAP, have become successful by developing new business models. The more difficult task is figuring out the right approach. "Will you survive the next wave by creating a new business model along side your old business model," such as going after the mid-market segment along with the enterprise segment? Or, like Nokia, will you need to completely transform your business model? That, states Ms. Funke, is the challenge.

Many executives think they can transform their business models by introducing new products and services. As Ms. Funke says, it's not the same thing, even though product innovation obviously creates a competitive advantage. Transformation involves in-depth changes in major areas such as pricing and marketing. It also requires different types of skills. For example, companies that sell in no-frills retail cannot take the same approach if they want to attract luxury customers. Plus, companies need to change processes and underlying technological architecture to enable big changes such as moving from direct to indirect selling.

Ms. Funke also sees value in companies opening up their R&D processes, something that requires a process innovation to "capture the brains of many more people. Whether this leads to new business models remains to be seen," she said.

New business models continue to spring up even in pretty established businesses such as making T-shirts. Spreadshirt has created a new business model by incorporating design suggestions from users who can also vote for their favorites. Spreadshirt manufactures the T-shirts that get the most votes and sells them through its regular distribution channels. In another example, students from different universities along with designers from the automakers are jointly creating a new car. Ms. Funke expects to see more companies try and tap into the wisdom of the public or crowd-sourcing "where you need less brains but more creativity."

Remember the product with the best technology doesn't always win. Remember BetaMax? Back in the early 1980s, its proponents argued, with some justification, that it was technologically superior to VHS, but VHS won through marketing. Canon didn't beat Xerox in the copier market because its machines were better but because they were smaller. Technology can make a difference when one company is eons ahead of its competitors (Google's search engine or Apple's iPod), but this is the exception.

Consumers also don't make their purchasing decisions based on price alone. This doesn't just apply to luxury brands either. For example, she notes that customers of Starbucks pay top dollar for the Seattle-based company's products because they perceive it to be of higher quality than other coffee. Wine lovers are snapping up bottles of Charles Shaw wine—nicknamed "Two-Buck Chuck"—because, not only is it a good price, but it's a good wine as well. Also, people will pay higher prices for organic food.

But perhaps the biggest myth that Ms. Funke wants to debunk is that companies don't have to change their business processes to win over new customers. Think about the countless software companies that try to market enterprise solutions to mid-market companies. Often, the software providers seem to try to put a square peg into a round hole. The large tech firms approach them the same way they did enterprises—a huge mistake because their needs are vastly different.

Historically, she pointed out, many companies have failed not because they were run badly, but because they missed the business model transformations that disrupted their industries. And what held them back, Ms. Funke argued, were their own peculiar in-bred orthodoxies, their DNA. Technology isn't stopping companies from transforming their business models. IT consultants need to work with companies on identifying the orthodoxies to be overcome to transform their businesses.

McKinsey is undergoing the same process that it advocates for clients. That means that McKinsey is regularly assessing to what extent they should stick to or change their own orthodoxies. For instance, the consulting firm values its independence and has no interest in going public, according to Ms. Funke. This orthodoxy is considered crucial for the professional values of McKinsey, and will hence not be changed.

On the other hand, a debate at the firm about whether a client should be "owned" by one partner led to the conclusion to change that approach and have partner teams with complementary skills work together. McKinsey continues to debate the extent to which it should accept performance-based fees.

> "Historically, many companies have failed not because they were run badly, but because they missed the business model transformations that disrupted their industries. And what held them back were their own peculiar in-bred orthodoxies, their DNA."
>
> —Claudia Funke

What Patterns Are Emerging in the Way Companies Are Designing Their Business Models?

While everyone seems to agree that business models are changing rapidly, much of this discussion tends to be highly theoretical, which is why we found Navi Radjou's Theory of the Globally Adaptive Organization (GAO) to be so interesting. In a paper published in

Navi Radjou is a vice president at Forrester Research. He investigates how globalized innovation—with the rise of India and China as both a source and market for tech innovations—is driving new market structures and organizational models, which Forrester designates as "Global Innovation Networks." He advises senior executives worldwide on new organizational designs and business processes their firms must adopt to sustain global competitiveness through technology-enabled innovation. During his eight years at Forrester, Mr. Radjou has advised senior executives around the world on issues related to innovation, supply chain, and customer service. Mr. Radjou was named by *Supply & Demand Chain Executive* magazine as one of the "Pros to Know," honoring an elite group of professionals who have excelled in the innovative use of supply chain technologies and practices within user companies. Prior to joining Forrester, he was a technology consultant in Asia—working with both private and public-sector companies—and a development analyst at IBM's Toronto Software Lab. Trilingual, Mr. Radjou earned his M.S. degree in information systems at Ecole Centrale Paris and also attended the Yale School of Management.

December 2006, the Forrester Research analyst laid out a case for traditional multi-national corporations to transform themselves into GAOs so that they can rapidly adapt to changing market conditions.

To be sure, trade barriers are falling thanks to trade agreements such as NAFTA, which has opened the floodgates to goods, people, capital, and services moving from the developed to the developing world and back again. Further complicating the situation is the rise of the so-called BRIC countries (Brazil, Russia, India, and China) where Goldman Sachs predicts that the middle class will quadruple, contributing nearly 70% of global growth by 2010. These countries also boast a growing number of talented engineers, scientists, and other professionals, who do research and development at much lower costs than in the West. For instance, a new biotech drug costs $100 million to develop in India compared with an average of $1.2 billion in the West. Bolstering this trend is the global growth of Internet usage, which enables a small Indian farmer to trade on the New York Mercantile Exchange, and students in Romania and Argentina to solve scientific problems for Eli Lilly and P&G.

Though globalization's proponents often speak of how the economic upheaval that sometimes results will be sorted out by the market, Mr. Radjou cautions against such a simplistic approach. Market forces alone don't drive globalization. Other geopolitical and sociocultural concerns, such as the rise of a left wing political leader—Venezuela's Hugo Chavez for example—also play a role. "The result?" he asks. "Any momentum gained from flattening the world by dismantling existing barriers is bound to be matched by equivalent drag occasioned by the erection of new barriers that decelerate or reverse globalization."

For instance, government regulation continues to mushroom, increasing the cost of doing business. Large European banks are spending hundreds of millions of dollars to comply with Basel II. Sarbanes-Oxley compliance costs firms $4.3 million on average in the first year. Companies also face restrictive labor laws in India and France, stringent real-estate regulations in Japan, and a "convoluted" intellectual property governance in both China and Brazil, which cause huge headaches for Big Pharma. Rising costs in China are spurring companies such as Cargill, Target, and Hyundai to move manufacturing to lower cost areas such as Vietnam, Brazil, and India. Sometimes, though, as Mr. Radjou points out, that causes even more problems because of the "lamentable state of physical infrastructure in those regions—Africa, in particular."

In addition, free markets haven't made everyone happy. For instance, 59% of Latin American Internet users who benefit from the instant global access to information worry that globalization is altering their societal values, according to Mr. Radjou. People outside the U.S. also have channeled their opposition to the War in Iraq into a boycott of U.S. brands such as Coca-Cola and McDonalds.

"The 9/11 terrorist attacks exposed the soft underbelly of global trading networks as original equipment manufacturers (OEMs) like

Toyota and Dell were forced to nearly shut down their just-in-time U.S. factories when the cargo planes carrying their foreign-made parts were grounded," he writes. Even though U.S. companies continue to flock to India and China, these markets could begin to sputter from political tensions.

"Any momentum gained from flattening the world by dismantling existing barriers is bound to be matched by equivalent drag occasioned by the erection of new barriers that decelerate or reverse globalization."
—Navi Radjou

How can companies navigate through the often-treacherous waters of globalization? By being flexible, according to Mr. Radjou. Though there is no stopping globalization, it may, "contrary to the hockey stick projections of techno-capitalist pundits, evolve in a nonlinear, discontinuous, truly chaotic fashion," he says.

To tackle these challenges in what Mr. Radjou calls the third epoch of globalization, companies must seize new market opportunities worldwide and exploit the creativity of their employees, customers, and partners in product and business model innovations. They also need to have an adaptable workforce and, in order to compete internationally, effectively integrate their operations around the world. Almost as important as the process changes are the cultural ones. Mr. Radjou argues that companies should view corporate social responsibility as more than just a PR stunt. In addition, they should institute an open culture that seeks input from employees, partners, and other stakeholders in the setting of strategic direction.

Mr. Radjou also calls for sweeping changes to the structure of multinationals, including replacing hierarchical management structures with nimble entrepreneurial teams. He wants companies to tolerate risk-taking and respond to tactical risks with IT-enabled early-warning systems. He also believes companies need to realign the duties of their top management teams to meet this new global reality. His suggestions include:

- Having the chief strategy officer use forward-looking tools such as simulations and scenario analysis to forecast the future rather than just extrapolating old data

- Introducing a chief ethics, compliance, and risk officer to create a culture of transparency and allowing CFOs to build up the firm's social capital by funding corporate social responsibility initiatives

- Directing chief supply officers to build redundant supply chains that can withstand disasters such as bird flu or other geopolitical risks and telling CIOs not to put all of their eggs in one offshore basket

- Having human resources hire workers with strong interpersonal skills who are able to adapt to changing environments

Nowhere are the perils of globalization more evident than in the Chinese cell phone market, where demand for services continues to explode at rates much higher than in the U.S. or Europe. In fact, China's economy grew by 11.9% in the second quarter of 2007, the fastest pace in 12 years, according to the London *Times*. China Mobile, Asia's biggest mobile phone company, is opening offices in Europe, the latest sign of the company's growing clout. Sir Richard Branson's Virgin Group is also eager to enter the market, and countless U.S. and European companies want to expand their presence in the world's most populous country. China Mobile, which according to *Fortune* magazine has been aggressively expanding into the rural market, now offers coverage to 97% of China's citizens. Its signal comes in strong on the Beijing subway, inside Shanghai elevators, in Guangxi rice paddies, and even atop Mount Everest.

Nokia and Motorola, the world's biggest cell phone makers, have been in China for years and continue to be keen on the market. In the third quarter of 2007, Nokia delivered 29.5 million mobile devices in the Asia-Pacific region, up 41% from a year earlier. Meanwhile, Motorola announced it had signed a $394 million agreement with China Mobile Communications Corporation (CMCC) for GSM network expansion; both companies have taken vastly different approaches in China. Motorola has established a strong presence by selling sleek stylish gadgets like the

RAZR in big cities such as Beijing and Shanghai. One problem: that's not the growth area since market penetration for mobile phones is 92% in urban areas. In the rural areas of China, the penetration rate is 12%. The rural market, Mr. Radjou points out, is much different than the urban one. "What the rural villagers are looking for is trust," he said.

Selling to the 800 million rural people in China requires a much different business model, requiring relationships at the local level. Nokia gets that and Motorola doesn't, and that will likely create problems over the long term for the Illinois company. Mr. Radjou's research showed that new Motorola designs might take months to get to the Chinese market, since everything is remotely managed from the company's headquarters in Illinois. Nokia has taken the opposite approach, delegating decision-making power to its Chinese operations, even at the regional level. Nokia has "much more responsiveness to what's happening in rural regions in China," Mr. Radjou said. He predicts that within five years, Nokia will take over more and more market share from Motorola. Nokia's success in the Chinese rural markets won't come because it's building the perfect phone, but rather it's making "the right phone for the right customer," he said. Motorola's approach will struggle to succeed because it's trying to put a square peg into a round hole.

Amazon has also done it right. The Internet retailer is constantly fiddling with its business model. First it sold books, then added other items such as DVDs, clothing, jewelry, and apparel. Now, it's venturing into video downloads and rentals through its Unbox business. Amazon's business has evolved beyond selling goods and services. The company collects an enormous amount of data about its customers that users can find in the list of suggested items that the Amazon database thinks they might like. Few can customize sales like Amazon. The company always is experimenting and adding new services such as grocery delivery. None of this would be possible without the ability to change.

Latinos, Asians, and Baby Boomers

The financial services industry finds itself in a similar predicament in the U.S., as it tries to tap into the growing economic clout of Latinos and Asians. For example, Latinos eclipsed African Americans as the largest minority group a few years ago. The Pew Hispanic Center points out that the Latino population grew 14% between 2000 and 2004 while the non-Hispanic population rose 2% during that same time. Moreover, the number of Latino households earning at least $100,000 soared 137% between 1990 and 2000. The picture in the Asian community is similar. U.S. census data shows that Asians are the fastest-growing minority group and that their median income of $57,518 is the highest of any ethnic group. Companies such as Citigroup are now figuring out how to reach these consumers. "So they are looking at whether they should come up with a different type of online solution, like microcredit," Mr. Radjou said. "What if there is some kind of microlending program for entrepreneurs in the Latino community in the U.S., and if you offer microcredit to Hispanic Americans here, how do you do that online?" This is a question that affects many companies including appliance-maker Whirlpool and retailer Best Buy. Whirlpool, in particular, is strongly committed to diversity. Angela Roseboro, Whirlpool's director of global diversity, told Diversitycareers.com that the company cultivates a diverse work force because the company's goal is to be "in every home, everywhere."

Electronics retailer Best Buy, which is thinking about creating stores aimed at Latinos in some places such as Southern California, already cosponsors a scholarship for high school seniors with the National Council of La Raza. Best Buy also is increasing its advertising spending with Latino online media.

Let's not forget baby boomers. The first members of this post-war generation are already eligible for social security and are going to help lead the "second wave" of business model transformation, Mr. Radjou said. Lots of companies are already trying to target this demographic, which *USA Today* says will control 40% of the nation's disposable income and 77% of private investments. Among the more interesting products for Baby Boomers are shoes with vibrating soles to improve balance and touch-screen systems that allow people to open and close their doors, windows, and blinds from the comfort of their bedroom, the paper said.

Real Competition

Even industries that have faced global competition for years are starting to see it intensify. The Big Three automakers, which have been losing market share to their Japanese rivals for years, now have new low-cost competitors to fend off from India and China. India's Tata Motors is interested in buying Jaguar from cash-strapped Ford. The company recently introduced a $2,500 "People's Car," a low cost model that could compete with companies like Toyota, Volkswagen, Honda and Fiat. Meanwhile, China's Hunan Changfeng Motor Co. Ltd. is eyeing the U.S. market, and experts are predicting that Chinese-built cars will be on American roads by the end of the decade. U.S. airlines are starting to feel the pressure from Richard Branson's Virgin America. At a time when many carriers are skimping on the creature comforts, Virgin promotes them and brags that among other things that it's the first U.S. airline to offer "mood lighting" and customized in-flight entertainment. "I'm in San Francisco and I'm thanking God, because for the first time Virgin is going to be able to fly from San Francisco to New York," Mr. Radjou says. Competitors offering new products will increase the pressure for existing companies to adapt their business models.

What Forces Will Lead Companies to Pursue Open Business Models?

Some businesses have realized that it's not worth it to conceive, develop, and commercialize products by themselves. They are pursuing what Dr. Henry Chesbrough, Executive Director of the Center for Open Innovation at the Haas School of Business, calls "Open Business Models." In a paper published in MIT's *Sloan Management Review*, he argued that "open business models enable an organization to be more effective in creating as well as capturing value."

Developing products costs big money that enterprises do not necessarily have to spend all by themselves. Product development costs have been soaring over the past few years. Companies that opened up their research and development were soon getting results that were just as good if not better than previously.

For instance, Procter & Gamble bolstered its growth through a program called Connect and Develop, which licenses or acquires products from other companies and brings them into P&G brands such as CrestSpinBrush, Olay Regenerist, and Swiffer Dusters. Genzyme licenses technology and is one of the rare profitable biotech companies. Qualcomm quit making cell phones and now only sells chips and licenses, and Air Products, a chemical company, also scored big by licensing technology.

For P&G, there was little other choice. During 1999 and 2000, the consumer products giant was floundering. It missed several consecutive earnings forecasts, causing its stock price to plummet. Under CEO A.G. Lafley, the company was able to double its innovation capacity without increasing costs. A similar scenario played out at Air Products and Chemicals where the company now collaborates with others in developing products. An even more dramatic change came to IBM. During the 1990s, CEO Louis Gerstner overhauled Big Blue's antiquated corporate culture. Gerstner encouraged programmers to develop open software on Linux and began allowing its semiconductor business to be used by other companies. The change at IBM can also be found in how it handles patents. The tech giant used to jealously guard its treasure trove of intellectual property—it usually tops the list of companies with the most patents. Now, the company willingly licenses its patents and, in the case of open source software, even donates them.

Many companies, though, collect patents like kids collect baseball cards. This creates a booming business for patent attorneys and brokers but stifles innovation in the long run. According to an informal survey done by Dr. Chesbrough for his paper, 75%–95% of patented technologies simply lay dormant. Meanwhile, as companies amass patents, product lifecycles are getting shorter. For instance, during the early 1980s, hard disk drives would typically ship for 4–6 years before a better one became available. By the late 1980s, it was 2–3 years, and by the 1990s,

6–9 months. The expected shipping life of new drugs that enjoy patent protections has shortened because of longer testing procedures and the quicker entry to the market of generics, Dr. Chesbrough said.

Open business models, Dr. Chesbrough argues, address both rising manufacturing costs and shorter product life cycles. But instituting these changes is easier said than done. Companies need to be able to experiment with their business models and objectively review their results. One of the problems enterprises face is that the people entrusted with these sorts of decisions are business unit managers who may only be in their positions for two to three years. That means the business model is not a top priority. Moreover, many companies are understandably reluctant to conduct experiments that might hurt their reputations.

While building new business models, Dr. Chesbrough argues that companies need to figure out what to do with existing ones. For instance, praising a new model may somehow convey the impression that the old one is obsolete. Remember that scaling up a new model is never easy. Just because it worked well with a small number of highly trained workers does not mean it will work with larger numbers of employees. Sometimes, companies can spin too many plates at once. Former P&G CEO Durk Jager got into trouble by trying to push too many initiatives at once and "lost the operational discipline to deliver quarterly earnings investors expected." In addition, new business models must get the support of key contingents across the enterprise before they are rolled out companywide, which is why they can encounter tremendous internal opposition, according to Dr. Chesbrough.

Though opening business models can be a challenge, maintaining the status quo is no longer an option. Think about the U.S. auto industry, which has been in slow decline since the 1970s. Even after years of cost cutting, the companies still are in a weak financial condition and Toyota is poised to become the world's largest automaker in 2008. "Yet absent such experiments, companies could easily fall into a cycle of slowing revenues, leading to head count and expense reductions that trigger further business declines, resulting in still more cuts," Dr. Chesbrough said.

Conclusion

In today's global market, companies either must transform themselves or be transformed in ways that they may not like. Often it can be chaotic. During the 1990s, businesses that never heard of web sites found themselves not only running them but also hiring people to make them more engaging. Newspapers were and still are among the hardest hit by these changes. As soon as people discovered the Internet, advertisers fled papers in droves to follow them. Soon journalists were always on deadline, creating the 24-hour news cycle we have today. Most people under 25 never read printed newspapers and probably never will. They'll never use a travel agent because they book reservations themselves online. Many high school students probably never saw a roll of film or can imagine life without their cell phones and iPods.

Companies cannot change for the sake of changing either. They must undergo a rigorous self-examination of what Claudia Funke calls orthodoxies. Basically, they need to figure out where they have been and where they want to go. Whenever people think about business model transformation, they should remember the lesson of IBM, which needed to change its business model or face possible bankruptcy during the 1990s.

IBM's Irving Vladasky-Berger recently told the Collaborative Innovation Summit that IBM's near-death experience was an essential part of its transformation. "We used to think that we were the marketplace—the kind of hubris that the gods on Mount Olympus will absolutely punish," he said. "Having invented RISC microprocessors and relational databases in our research labs, as well as established the IBM PC as the leader in the marketplace, we let others reap the benefits of our work because we were making so much money from our proprietary mainframes, compared to the returns from these puny, emerging businesses. They don't call them tragic flaws for nothing."

Reading this book thus far may have invoked a feeling similar to that experienced by the attendees of the 2007 International Research Forum. At the end of the long day, minds were abuzz with new information and insights. The discussion and analysis of each of the four areas covered a monumental amount of ideas. The range of topics was breathtaking—everything was connected in an arc of thought that took flight with Enterprise 2.0, floated through the service grid, merged into user-driven innovation, and landed in business model transformation. For those who are involved in using Information Technology to improve the workings of their organizations one question remained: How can we do something about all the ideas we just heard?

The challenge for most participants was to select from the ideas discussed a handful that were the most promising and then to bring those back home and put them to work or use them as fodder for further research.

The authors, having attended the conference and then having spent several months talking to experts, enjoyed the benefits of time and perspective. They have chosen to take their own tour of each of these areas, presenting what they have learned and suggesting a program of incremental experimentation in each of the areas discussed at the Forum.

Enterprise 2.0: The New Chemistry of Information Technology

The user empowerment of Enterprise 2.0 suggests a new paradigm for Information Technology departments. The current paradigm might accurately be called Designed IT. The new paradigm could be thought of as Emergent IT. Both paradigms will continue side by side.

Designed IT is the practice of intermediated solution creation. This intermediation is needed when large complex systems are created. The IT department gathers requirements, designs a solution, and then delivers it to users. Most of what IT departments offer today arrives under this paradigm. A variety of methods, like iterative development or the use of roles like the business process exert, help improve the outcomes, but the fundamental creative force is the IT professional, not the user.

Emergent IT has been made possible by the introduction of an increasing amount of do-it-yourself tools, which have been greatly expanded in the world of Enterprise 2.0. Under the emergent IT paradigm, the IT department still plays a key role, but the creative force is the user, not the IT professional. Under this paradigm, the IT department provides a basic set of capabilities, a dial tone, if you will, for collaboration and creation of solutions by users.

The IT department observes the use of these tools the way a chemist might observe and monitor a chemical reaction. As the users create solutions, the IT department monitors which are being used and what impact the solutions have on the existing IT infrastructure. The IT department is also on the lookout for potential performance problems, security threats, or other governance problems that may arise in the user-created solutions. If a solution becomes popular, perhaps IT must step in and improve the design to improve efficiency. At times the emergent solutions will suggest improvements to the portfolio of designed IT. At other times, the emergent solutions will be good enough as they are. IT will also be on the lookout for patterns in user-created solutions that may be useful across the enterprise and will educate other users about user-created solutions that may benefit them.

Encouraging Emergent IT

Putting in a full suite of Enterprise 2.0 tools would be one way to encourage emergent IT. But few organizations could actually afford the time and money to put in a complete Enterprise 2.0 dial tone that includes blogs, wikis, social networking, search, tagging, services to connect everything to enterprise applications, environments for creating widgets and mashups, and so on.

Fortunately, a complete dial tone is not needed. Getting the enterprise environment to work as well as the Web would take a long time and is not a requirement. Most people have an intuitive feel for where the communication and collaboration gaps are in their organizations. Taking a small step like introducing a wiki or a blog infrastructure gets the ball rolling at a low cost. Experimenting with this technology will confirm if an appetite for improved collaborative tools exists.

Once users are working and the IT department notices patterns and encourages users through education and training where needed, targeted experiments can take place to create more complex solutions. Frequently these experiments involve increasing the convergence between the structured and unstructured worlds.

Collaborative Innovation at SAP Research

One such experiment in a collaborative solution based on Enterprise 2.0 technology was performed in 2007 by SAP Research. COIN, which stands for collaborative innovation, is a new communal effort within SAP, formally launched in Fall 2007, that solicits employees' ideas for new products and helps those ideas get evaluated, refined, and possibly implemented by potentially the entire company. Klaus Wriessnegger and Susanne Schmitt of SAP Research led the project.

In the past, explains Mr. Wriessnegger, there was no formal channel that employees with new product ideas could turn to. They might share ideas with colleagues or managers, but this didn't give the ideas much exposure and nothing prevented them from falling through the cracks. COIN institutes an explicit process by which all employees can easily both post their own ideas and suggestions and look at those of others.

"The entire SAP community, with whatever skills that they may have, is invited to add his or her point of view," Mr. Wriessnegger explains. Ideas that pass first muster may get further attention and eventually even win funding for formal development into marketable products.

COIN presents itself to SAP staff as a web application. The first step is to fill out a form that asks for a description of the idea; it can accept images, links to other Web pages, and attachments, and it offers the ability for users to tag their submissions as a way to categorize the ideas and help others to search for them. Once an idea is submitted, it shows up on COIN's Idea page, where others in the community can find it.

At this point, the community is welcome to publicly comment on the idea. Individuals from anywhere in the company are free to add their two cents, so to speak. They might endorse the proposed product as worthy of more attention or even development, explain why they think it won't work or sell, and add any suggestions that come to mind. In fact, the idea pages are wiki-like in that they are open to editing by the community and there is versioning to help with reviews of an idea's history.

Products that hold unusual potential or warrant special attention may be sponsored by a group within SAP. This means the products become subject to a private commenting process, conducted by the members of that group. The comments submitted by the sponsoring group are not visible to either the idea's originator or to the SAP community at large.

During a pilot project, the best COIN ideas were presented once a year to the SAP Board of Directors. The Board decided which ones were worth pushing forward through funding and assigning development resources. But this process will change, possibly with the addition of some kind of periodic harvesting of top-ranking ideas.

The ideas that have been submitted so far run the gamut, Mr. Wriessnegger says—from ideas about products for use in outer space to the positioning of buttons on current products' user-interface screens.

"We are looking for real product innovations, but also process innovation and product improvement," says Ms. Schmitt.

She emphasizes that she and Mr. Wriessnegger act only as moderators: "This is important; we are not owners. COIN is generic, it is cross-organizational, and it is open to everybody inside SAP." Groups nominate themselves for creation: anybody who is interested can say, "I would like to be a sponsor, so please create a group."

One aspect of COIN that seems to be contributing to its success is attractive design. "We designed a new application from scratch, more or less," says Ms. Schmitt. "The feedback we get is that it is completely different from what a developer at SAP sees on a daily basis. 'Wow, it looks cool,' people tell us. 'It's got all this Web 2.0 functionality.' This is what people like, that we have something at SAP with cutting-edge functionality."

COIN doesn't explicitly support social networking, but its discussion board has become the focal point for a fair amount of collaboration and community building, she adds.

The next step will be adding a prediction market to COIN, enabling individuals, in effect, to trade and bet on their future value. At a certain stage of development, a promising idea could be submitted to a market where community members could bid on it with a fictional currency. "Ideas would be similar to little start-ups, growing over time," Ms. Schmitt says. "Once they have reached a certain stage, they would go to the stock market."

As it turns out, the name COIN has paid off in unexpected ways. "After coining the name, we saw that it made sense to use coins as incentives to encourage people to participate in the system," says Mr. Wriessnegger. "After gathering 100 coins, they will get a baseball cap or some other small prize. The name is a synonym for these tokens."

The Story of Structured Wikis

Evolving the collaborative dial tone—gradually improving the collection of collaborative technologies—is one of the responsibilities of an IT department that is pursuing emergent IT. One proven way to augment the capabilities available to users involves promoting convergence of free-form and structured environments. Creating a suite of services that allows structured information to be brought into blogs and wikis amplifies the power of these environments. Increasing the ability to bring free-form information into enterprise applications by linking to wikis helps improve their power as well. For example, the free-form text field in a purchase order might include a link to a discussion on a wiki for further details.

Mr. Peter Thoeny is the inventor of the concept of the structured wiki, perhaps the most elegant merging of the free-form potential of Enterprise 2.0 with simple structural elements. This concept has led to the creation of similar structured wiki environments like JotSpot, which was acquired by Google, as well as a wide variety of enterprise wiki offerings from Socialtext, Atlassian, IBM, and other firms. As part of the research for the book, we interviewed Mr. Thoeny about the way he came up with and developed the idea for the structured wiki, a story that is instructive for anyone promoting the use of Enterprise 2.0 tools.

Says Mr. Thoeny: "Like it or not, the wiki is somewhat revolutionary. It can transform a company for the better. It provides a good deal more transparency within the organization. Since everything is under version control and there's a complete audit trail, there's accountability. And employees are empowered in new ways. People out in the field can make their own decisions."

"End-users would say the technology's key value is that it empowers them to help themselves by building structured applications fairly quickly and thereby making entire teams work more effectively," Mr. Thoeny says. "The IT Director sees value in getting Shadow IT under control. Instead of people experimenting totally on their own with IT, having no clue about what they are doing, IT is now maintaining the wiki. It's in control of the engine and updates and backup. With

Peter Thoeny is the founder of TWiki and has managed the open-sourced TWiki.org project for the last nine years. Mr. Thoeny invented the concept of structured wikis—where free form wiki content can be structured with tailored wiki applications.

He is a recognized thought-leader in wikis and social software, featured in numerous articles and technology conferences including *Linux World, BusinessWeek, The Wall Street Journal* and more. A software developer with over 20 years experience, Mr. Thoeny specializes in enterprise collaboration, software architecture, user interface design and web technology.

He graduated from the Swiss Federal Institute of Technology in Zurich, lived in Japan for 8 years working as an engineering manager for Denso building CASE tools, and managed the Knowledge Engineering group at Wind River for several years. He co-authored the *Wikis for Dummies* book, and is currently working on a *Wikis for the Workplace* book.

Mr. Thoeny co-founded TWIKI.NET (*http://www.twiki.net/*), a company offering TWiki solutions that help revolutionize collaboration and productivity in all organizations.

application logic delegated to different departments, IT has less work to do, yet still remains in control."

The structured wiki is hardly poised to replace full-blown ERP systems nor is it going to sweep away the traditional wiki and blog. But it represents a powerful new idea that could reshape enterprise software and enhance many traditional applications, including ERP.

The story of the invention of structured wikis started when Mr. Thoeny was given the job of creating tools for a technical support department that had to answer questions from developers about how to use a programming platform.

Mr. Thoeny was immediately attracted to wikis as a solution for collaboratively maintaining content for a team. His first instinct was to use a wiki as a foundation for a knowledge base for customer support. From the start, Mr. Thoeny considered the wiki not only as a single application but also as a platform upon which to build horizontal and vertical applications. The knowledge base application would just be one of those apps.

Commercial knowledge management solutions struck him as too cumbersome. Mr. Thoeny believes that, to be adopted, tools should be easy to use. Most knowledge management solutions have not been designed with usability in mind to accommodate the fact that people work in unstructured ways. Mr. Thoeny thought people wanted to put their notes down in an unstructured way yet still connect those notes to the structured world. Furthermore, knowledge management tools offer no way to add pages to the structure and make it difficult to link related content. The knowledge management solutions were designed by database administrators, who think in terms of rows, columns, and relations. That is fine for certain applications, but it is too much structure for a knowledge base.

The First Structured Wiki Application

Building on an existing wiki foundation, Mr. Thoeny called his structured wiki platform TWiki. The first application Mr. Thoeny created with TWiki was a forms-based application for technical support. When new knowledge was submitted, a page was created with a form attached. The unstructured part of the page has one section for the problem description and one section for the solution description. The form captures the software release that it applies to, a category (whether it's compile related, editing related, and the like), and offers pick lists for other types of metadata (such as whether the entry is for an external web site, external FAQ, or internal use only). Content stored in this way can be queried. You could ask a question like, "Show me all editor-related knowledge base entries related to release 2.0 that are for internal use only." This structure also makes it possible to construct a workflow. FAQs must be reviewed before they are published on the corporate web site, so these entries can be pushed to a staging server with a link sent to the reviewer. Once the reviewer approves the entry, she can publish it on the corporate web site. By making the content captured through the wiki available to customers, the company experienced a dramatic decrease in support calls.

The Anatomy of a Structured Wiki

Structured wikis also have at their core the functions of a publishing wiki, a wiki that allows pages to be created and published. By itself, a publishing wiki supplies strong, collaborative, organically maintained unstructured content. Publishing wikis have relatively little structure, just the cross-links between pages, namespaces for multiple webs in a wiki, categories to group related content, and tagging.

A structured wiki has all that, but it also offers a platform for creating structured, or wiki, applications. Instead of just putting text on a page or links to other pages or images, a structured wiki page can include one or more of the following elements:

Edit Table Plug-in: A component that inserts a table that looks like a small piece of a spreadsheet into a wiki page. When you click on the edit button, you can then add rows and change data in existing rows. You can also have cells with pick lists so that only certain values can be selected. So, instead of editing the whole wiki page to enter a new time and name and saving the page, you enter the values in the table and click Save.

Comment Plug-in: The comment plug-in enables the user to put a simple edit box on wiki page where users can type and click Add Comment to add their input to the page. The comment plug-in can incorporate custom input and output templates. Imagine someone wants to build a simple table with to-do items. A custom input template would describe what kind of task it is and to whom it should be assigned. Likewise, the output format puts the defined items into the template cells in that table row. Very quickly, content can be captured in a structured table.

Forms: If more structure is needed to enable queries against a large amount of data captured on wiki pages, a TWiki forms-based application may be necessary. This turns each page into a database record while also preserving its properties as a wiki page. The part of the page that is a form has data in fields, but the rest of the page can be edited as desired. A form has fields. Each field has a name and is a certain type, such as a pick list, radio button, or date field. Each field also has an initial value. Once a form is defined, it can be attached to a wiki page like a file can be attached to a page. In this way, a set of pages can be created that all share the same type of form. This produces a database table with each page of a certain form being a single record in that table.

The development community that has built up around TWiki.org has created dozens more plug-ins and other elements that add structured wiki pages.

Mr. Thoeny recommends to start unstructured when applying a wiki. He suggests that it is a mistake to apply the Designed IT paradigm and begin with too much structure or engineering. Instead, observe how users interact with the wiki. When you discover a pattern, capture it in a structured way and promote it.

These "wiki champions," who can create wiki applications and know how to apply best practices, are experimenting every day. Development of wiki applications doesn't follow the waterfall model, or top-down design. Typically, it's more like the flower model, cranking out a first version of the application, watching how people use it, and then modifying and improving it. Because wiki applications are so easy to create, this approach works well.

Semantic Wikis at SAP Research

Another way of adding structure to wikis is to focus on the meaning captured rather than the form of the wiki. SAP has begun experimenting with a Semantic MediaWiki (SMW), a wiki-based environment intended to make representing semantics as easy as possible. The SMW is a development of the FZI Karlsruhe, a research organization and SAP partner in applied semantic technology.

SMW is an extension of MediaWiki with semantic technology. Unlike the regular wiki, which uses plain text, the SMW allows navigation of the wiki according to the semantic connections between the pages. So far the project is seeking to represent knowledge used to gather requirements, design, support, test, and capture success stories about SAP solutions.

The project seeks to evaluate how semantics might be incorporated into SAP's own KM solutions, by addressing several important questions: Can semantic annotations, forms and automatic queries help the user quickly drill down to valuable information? Can they keep the overall information space consistent and up to date? Can semantic features be usable for authors and readers?

SAP has found many potential benefits to semantics in corporate wikis. SAP has simplified usability by hiding semantics in templates and forms. Even so, corporate users are not always well-prepared for the task, especially if asked to use more formal properties and relations such as RDF. Even the most user-friendly approaches require oversight by someone with information management skills, such as writing proper documents, structuring, and organizing information in the large.

While we are really only beginning to glimpse the world of Emergent IT, the experimentation represented by COIN and structured wikis shows the way that those in charge of the IT function can be stewards of progress.

The Service Grid: Building Skills While Waiting for Aggregation

Chapter 3, "Service Grid," makes a compelling case that the future of computing is likely to be dominated by an architecture that employs services as fundamental building blocks. But the analysis presented takes pains to avoid confusing a clear view for a short distance. Before we arrive in a promised land in which the Internet of Services used as a mature service grid meets all our needs, the analysis points out quite a few challenges to overcome.

On the other hand, significant portions of the service grid are in place now and more are emerging every year. It would be a mistake to ignore the potential of this functionality until everything is in place. Much can be done with the partial service grid. The authors suggest that three steps be considered in the near-term to maximize the benefits your organization can derive from the emergence of the service grid.

Use What You Can

Many of the services available now are fully productized and stable. Google Maps APIs are used by thousands of mashups and other forms of applications on the Web. Yahoo!, Amazon, eBay, all offer a variety of special purpose services. More and more companies are following suit and industry groups are promoting standards for web services that are increasingly being implemented. Large companies like Wal-Mart are encouraging the creation of services that solve problems for their supply chains or help implement business models like vendor-managed inventory. If you look around, you will find more potentially useful services than you might expect. Understanding what is available and promoting awareness is a great way to start.

It is also important to remember that products and higher level services are being constructed from the existing service grid. Almost every large software application is available now through the Software as a Service (SaaS) model. There are dozens of credible offers for email hosting. While using such applications is not a direct use of services, they do provide the benefits of the grid at an application level. Infrastructure as a Service (IaaS) also represents a significant second order benefit of the service grid. It is now possible to back up your computer or to use virtualized remote computing infrastructure for servers or databases in a reliable fashion over the network.

Finally, some providers of enterprise applications are now offering fully implemented collections of services that provide access to the data and functionality of their applications. It is possible to make these services available as part of a software upgrade to a new version. By using productized services or those from mature providers, you can get the benefit of services without having to solve the problems that will eventually become the job of service aggregators, according to Dr. John Seely Brown, an expert on the service grid who we interviewed for Chapter 3.

SAP is pursuing both the strategy of adding services through upgrades and creating new productized service grids as the foundation of new products. Every year SAP creates new collections of Enterprise Service Bundles, which add services to SAP's existing products through upgrades. SAP's new Business by Design product is one of the first comprehensive enterprise applications built with an architecture based on services. Instead of being an afterthought, services are available for use at the same time as the general release of the product. In essence, SAP Business By Design is an incarnation of a productized service grid, one that comes with tools and methodologies for designing and using services that allow customers and partners to build their own solutions. Each approach has proved popular with different customer segments based on their needs.

Build Skills and Services

Services on their own are not much good to anyone. Using services requires development tools and experience. The fastest way to put services to work is to use services to draw information into Enterprise 2.0 tools. If you have a set of services that can pull purchase orders, invoices, sales orders, and client information into blogs, wikis, and other environments, it is likely that the information in the systems of record will be available to more people and problems will be addressed faster and with more input. Of course, making such information available requires appropriate attention to controlling access to the information and adhering to privacy and security policies.

Providing users with the tools to create mashups on their own has sparked a flood of development of applications at most places that have introduced it. Providing developers with tools for development of advanced mashups or even more complicated composite applications opens up another outlet through which services can create value. Skills take time to develop at both the simple and complicated end of the development spectrum. But once value is demonstrated, skills can be quickly propagated and a thriving internal development community can come to life. Adding tools to create services is another way to increase the power of your internal development capacity.

Using one or two services is not really that difficult. But, as the use of services grows at a company and hundreds or even thousands of services come into use, it is impossible to ensure reliability and compliance with corporate rules without using a formal method of governance. A governance program helps determine which services should be created, how to find services available for use, and how to formally sign up to use them. Once services are being used at scale, operational skills must also be developed because running applications based on services presents a new type of challenge.

Become Your Own Aggregator

Developing skills for governance and operations of services is the beginning of addressing the tasks that will be performed by the so-called service aggregators envisioned by Dr. Seely Brown. Aggregators will assemble services from disparate sources and solve the problems of semantic consistency, reliability, governance, scalability, and other difficult issues that stand in the way of the emergence of a true service grid. If services pay off for you in the ways so far described, it could make sense then to take on the burden of becoming an aggregator to expand the pool of available services and ensure their quality. It is only the largest companies with the most complete IT infrastructure that will likely find becoming an aggregator an attractive proposition.

By following the steps just recommended, it is likely that both the smallest and largest organizations will find significant benefits from putting the current form of the service grid to work.

User-Driven Innovation: By Any Means Necessary

Chapter 4, "User-Driven Innovation," establishes that there are substantial benefits to be gained from putting the tools to create and modify products in the hands of those who use them. For the world of IT, Enterprise 2.0 and the service grid offer a concrete way to implement this vision. Users who have the tools empowered by services can create solutions for themselves to great effect.

Clearly, where innovation is important, it makes good sense to empower users as much as possible. But in many cases direct empowerment of users is not possible. Some products, especially software, can be modified only through the use of complicated configuration mechanisms and arcane development tools. Do such barriers mean there are sharp limits in the number of situations where the benefits of user-driven innovation can be harvested?

Happily, the answer is no. A variety of practices and methods can help achieve the aims of user-driven innovation without adhering to the strict rule that users must modify and improve products directly.

Before we delve into those methods, it is worth pointing out that user-driven innovation is a by-product of a culture that encourages it. Without a clear organizational value that encourages and rewards user-driven innovation, it is unlikely to happen. So if you want to get the benefits of user-driven innovation, you must get the word out.

To clearly understand the methods that the authors recommend, we first must revisit the analysis of why user-driven innovation works. One of the key reasons user-driven innovation works is that it is not intermediated. Users do not have to spend time explaining their requirements, which it turns out they are not able to do much of the time. The complex world of most workers is hard to explain. Dr. Eric von Hippel, a leader in the field of user-driven innovation, characterizes users' knowledge of their requirements as sticky, meaning it is hard to transfer to others who do not have the experience of the users. The techniques we recommend as alternatives to pure user-driven innovation work because they attack this problem.

The results of user-driven innovation can be obtained in an intermediated development process through prototyping. In this model, the designers of IT solutions do their best to understand what users want but instead of building the entire solution, create a prototype or simulation instead. Users can then interact with the prototype and deficiencies in the designers' understanding of the users' needs can be remedied.

The practice of iterative development has a similar effect. Iterative development methodologies like eXtreme programming, Scrum, or the Rational Unified Process seek to build a solution in a series of steps that create systems that are put into production and used. The requirements for the successive steps of the solution are improved based on the experience the users have with the results of the previous steps. This approach is also reflected in the "design thinking" methodology taught at the Hasso Plattner Institute of Design at Stanford University, which emphasizes collaborative innovation and experimentation with prototypes.

Another approach to increasing the voice of the user is to change the nature of the intermediary. The role of the Business Process Expert (BPX) aims to increase the transfer of sticky knowledge of requirements from the user and improve the crafting of technology by the developers and engineers. The BPX role is filled by people who have deep knowledge of the business and the processes that are used to run it and are also experts in understanding the capabilities of the technology. The BPX can communicate with users and understand requirements better than technologists usually do. The BPX can also help translate user requirements into a suggested technology design that will fulfill them. With one foot in the world of the user and one foot in the world of technology, the BPX improves the quality of communication, requirements, and the solutions created. (SAP has created a community to support people playing this role at *www.bpx.sap.com*.)

While prototyping, simulation, iterative development, and the BPX all increase the voice of the user in a process of intermediated development there is nonetheless a gap between these practices and true user-driven innovation. In intermediated development, the designers are the creative force who set the context and make many decisions about how a solution is created. In user-driven development, the user is the creative force and can experiment in any direction that feels right, following instinct and serendipity in new directions.

Business Model Transformation: Changing Before They Make You Run

Transforming your business model is made easier by all of the practices discussed in the first three chapters. If IT is more flexible and users are able to innovate and come up with new ways of adapting business processes and IT support for them, ideas for changing business models will no doubt occur at a faster rate and implementing them will be easier.

As the barriers to implementing changes to business models drop, the psychological barriers to change will become more important to recognize and overcome. As companies operate in more markets around the world and increase the niches markets being addressed with specialized products, the need for the same company to employ different business models will increase, which again may be more challenging as a cultural transformation than as a technological one.

Business model transformation is a highly idiosyncratic undertaking, depending on the capabilities and market situation of a company. Innovation in business models is quite possibly the most important type of innovation a company can perform. The rewards for successfully creating a new business model usually dwarf those gained by increasing efficiency.

Conclusion

Participating in the 2007 International Research Forum was an intense pleasure for the authors. Building on the ideas discussed at the Forum in a book by performing research with leading thinkers is a privilege. This year, based on the success of the *International Research Forum 2006* book, we were able to enlist the leaders in each field we discussed. Because of a suggestion by Prof. Eric von Hippel, this book and the 2006 version will also be available in electronic form to download over the Internet.

What became clear during the research is the key challenge facing those who struggle to make IT work. For Enterprise 2.0, the service grid, user-driven innovation, or business model transformation, it is clear that new ideas with substantially different characteristics have arrived. Those ideas are not replacing current practices; they complement them. The world of Emergent IT must be embraced while Designed IT stays in place and does the job it was intended to do. The service grid opens up new possibilities which must be pursued, at least in the short and medium term, while existing monolithic solutions stay in place. User-driven innovation doesn't solve every problem, but must exist along intermediated development. New business models in many cases must supplement new ones.

The key challenge facing companies is how to expand their thinking and capabilities so that multiple ways of doing business can be pursued at once. Companies that are able to expand their minds will be best positioned to benefit from the ideas described in this book.

Authors

Claudia Alsdorf has 10 years' experience in the executive management, development, licensing, and commercialization of new consumer electronic products and services across the domains of the Internet, online commerce exchanges, virtual reality, and wireless. For more than five years, she has served as Founder and CEO of a global provider of 3D and online exchange products and services called echtzeit AG. In the beginning of 2002 she joined SAP and became Vice President of Communications Development within Global Communications and is responsible for communication strategy and long-term plan development including the alignment of communications strategy with non corporate communication units. In this position, she spent one year in SAP's New York office working with the Global Marketing team. In 2004 she became the Head of SAP Inspire, the internal venturing group of SAP worldwide. Since 2006 she has also been responsible for SAP Research Communications.

Lutz Heuser, Vice President SAP Research and Chief Development Architect at SAP AG, is responsible for the overall research portfolio management and the corporate venturing organization. His areas of expertise include collaborative business processes, ubiquitous computing and its integration into business applications, blended learning as part of corporate and noncorporate training, and security in corporate applications. Prof. Heuser serves on the advisory boards of imedia, Providence, FhG-Fokus, Berlin, FhG-IPSI, Darmstadt and is a member of the e-Science-Kuratorium monitoring the D-Grid initiative. He is a Visiting Professor at the National University of Paraguay and an Adjunct Professor of the Queensland University of Technology in Brisbane. In 2004 he was awarded an Honorary Professorship at the Technical University Darmstadt and in 2006 he became a member of acatech, the "Council for Engineering Sciences at the Union of the German Academies of Science and Humanities."

Dan Woods, CTO and Editor of Evolved Media, has a background in technology and journalism. Dan has written 10 books about technology-related topics, including *Mashup Corporations, Wikis for Dummies, Open Source for the Enterprise,* and *Enterprise SOA: Designing IT for Business Innovation.* His technology experience began in 1982 with a B.A. in computer science from the University of Michigan. Dan served as CTO of TheStreet.com and CapitalThinking and has been a board member and adviser to many firms. Mid-career, in 1989, Dan earned an M.S. in journalism from the Columbia University Graduate School of Journalism. He then spent six years as a business journalist before returning to technology. Evolved Media, which Dan founded in 2002, creates books, wikis, white papers, training courses, and documentation to explain the value and workings of technology.

Participants

Witold Abramowicz chairs the Department of Management Information Systems at The Poznan University of Economics, Poland.

His areas of particular interest are information and services filtering and information and services in contexts. He has served as an editor or co-author of 19 books, 37 book chapters, and over 100 articles published in journals and conference proceedings. He is on the editorial board of eight international journals and has served as a keynote and invited speaker at numerous international conferences. Prof. Dr. Abramowicz is currently Vice President of the Association of Management Information Systems, Poland, and a member of ACM and GI. He also serves as Honorary Consul of the Republic of Hungary in Poznan. At present, Prof. Abramowicz is working on several projects for the European Union, including enIRaF (enhanced information retrieval and filtering-coordinator), SUPER (Semantics Utilized Process management within and between EnteRprises), TOWL (Time-determined Ontology-information system for real time stock market analysis), and EastWeb (building an integrated Euro-Asian higher education and research community in the field of the Semantic Web).

Serge Druais is an Ecole Polytechnique graduate with a doctorate in artificial intelligence. As an extension of the NESSI initiative, Dr. Druais successfully advocated the creation of Thales's own applied research facility to focus on the same technologies. ThereSIS (Thales European Research Centre for Security & Information Systems) was set up in 2006 on the Ecole Polytechnique campus near Paris. Today, Dr. Druais is spearheading the drive by the group's research and technology department to capitalize on this experience in Asian markets. In Singapore, the Thales Group and the Singaporean government are studying plans for a local ThereSIS facility to consolidate and expand Singapore's leadership in security, e-government, and e-health. Dr. Druais, with the backing of a major industrial group, is recognized as one of the leading specialists in e-government technologies. He is also closely involved in the work of the Club Informatique des Grandes Entreprises Françaises (CIGREF), the Institut des Hautes Etudes de la Défense Nationale (IHEDN), and the Institut d'Administration des Entreprises (IAE) in Paris, la Sorbonne University, particularly in the area of competitive intelligence, information systems security, and governance.

Jörg Eberspächer is one of the fathers of the ANSI FDDI-2 Hybrid Ring standard and one of the promoters of the ECMA standard Computer Supported Telecommunication Applications for the intelligent Host-PBX-interconnection. Prof. Dr. Eberspächer's research interests are network architectures for high-speed and mobile communication, multimedia services and applications, and interdisciplinary topics in telecommunications. He is co-author of the Wiley book *GSM Global System for Mobile Communication*, editor of several books on advanced topics in telecommunications, and has authored or co-authored many papers on telecommunication networks and services. He is editor for mobile networks of the journal *European Transactions on Telecommunications* (ETT) and has served as member of the scientific program committees of many international conferences. He is guest professor at the Tongji University in Shanghai, China and one of the scientific directors of the interdisciplinary Center for Digital Technology and Management (CDTM) München. Prof. Eberspächer is senior member of IEEE and member of ACM and VDE, and member of the "Deutsche Akademie der Naturforscher LEOPOLDINA."

Jose Encarnação was born in Portugal and has been living in the Federal Republic of Germany since 1959. Since 1975, he has been Professor for Computer Science at the Technical University Darmstadt and is head of Graphical-Interactive Systems (TUD-GRIS). Under Prof. Dr. Encarnação's leadership, the INI-GraphicsNet was established. This institutional network is one of the global key players in the area of visualization technologies, new media, and new forms of communications and interaction. He is author or co-author of more than 500 publications and articles, and is Editor-in-Chief of *Computers & Graphics*, published by Elsevier Science. Since July 2001, he has been chairman of the information and communication group of the Fraunhofer society.

Ulrich Finger is currently the director of the Institut Eurecom in Sophia-Antipolis, France. Prof. Dr. Finger's major research interests are in computer architecture and real-time operating systems. Prof. Finger is a member of IEEE, ACM, and IFIP working group 10.3. Since September 2000, he has been the Director of Institut Eurécom,

Graduate School and Research Center in Communication Systems located in the science park of Sophia Antipolis, France. Institut Eurecom is administered by a consortium and has partnerships with several international academic institutions and industrials (Swisscom, France Télécom, Thales Communications, SFR, Hitachi, Bouygues Télécom, STMicroelectronics, Sharp, CISCO, BMW Group Research & Technology, associated partner: SAP). Eurecom is particularly active in research in high performance communication and multimedia with a special emphasis on information security and wireless.

Elgar Fleisch is Professor of Information Management at the Department of Management, Technology, and Economics at ETH Zürich. He is also Professor for Technology Management and Director of the Institute of Technology Management at the University of St. Gallen (ITEM-HSG). Prof. Fleisch conducts research on information management issues in the ubiquitously networked world, including the dynamics of information systems in conjunction with business processes and real-world problems. Together with Prof. Friedemann Mattern of the Institute of Pervasive Computing at the ETH Zürich, he leads the M-Lab and co-chairs the Auto-ID labs, which specify the infrastructure for the "Internet of Things." Prof. Fleisch is also a co-founder of Intellion AG and a member of several steering committees in research, education, and industry.

Claudia Funke is Director of the Munich Office of McKinsey & Company. She leads McKinsey's global enterprise ICT services practice as well as the German high-tech sector, which includes the software and services, datacom, consumer electronics, industrial manufacturing, and aerospace and defense industries, and is part of the leadership team of McKinsey's global high-tech sector. Ms. Funke works primarily for industry leaders in software, IT services, and telecommunication in the enterprise customer segment. Her main areas of expertise include go-to-market approaches, strategy and executive counseling, and business model innovation. Ms. Funke is leading McKinsey's "Global Leadership Creation in High Tech" initiative, which deals with the question of how more European companies can become global high-tech leaders.

Tony Hey, Corporate Vice President for Technical Computing at Microsoft Corp., coordinates efforts across Microsoft Corp. to collaborate with the global scientific community. He is a well-known researcher in the field of parallel computing, and his experience in applying computing technologies to scientific research helps Microsoft work with researchers worldwide in various fields of science and engineering. Before joining Microsoft, Dr. Hey worked as head of the School of Electronics and Computer Science at the University of Southampton, where he helped build the department into one of the top five computer science research institutions in England. Since 2001, he has served as director of the United Kingdom's e-Science Initiative, managing the government's efforts to provide scientists and researchers with access to key computing technologies. Dr. Hey is a fellow of the U.K.'s Royal Academy of Engineering and has been a member of the European Union's Information Society Technology Advisory Group. He also has served on several national committees in the U.K., including committees of the U.K. Department of Trade and Industry and the Office of Science and Technology. Dr. Hey received the award of Commander of the Order of the British Empire honor for services to science in the 2005 U.K. New Year's Honours List. Dr. Hey is a graduate of Oxford University, with both an undergraduate degree in physics and a doctorate in theoretical physics.

Günter Honisch is Chief Technology Officer for EMEA and APAC at Symbol. He is a Symbol Fellow working on System Level Mobility and Emerging Technologies. From 1978–1994 he worked at Digital Equipment Corporation in the area of Systemlevel Postsales and Consulting covering Operating Systems, Servers, Storage, Networks, Management Design, and Troubleshooting of complex networked Computer Systems. In 1994 he joined Cisco Systems where he served as a Distinguished Engineer in the area of Consulting and Strategic Alliances, covering EMEA Trusted Advisor to large enterprises, government, and research organizations. In his work, his focus is on Campus, Storage & Datacenter Architectures.

Matthias Jarke is Professor for Information Systems and Databases at RWTH Aachen University and Director of the Fraunhofer FIT

Institute for Applied IT. His research area is information systems support for cooperative activities in business, engineering, and culture. Major results include the widely used logic-based metadata management system ConceptBase, frameworks for requirements engineering research, and contributions to BSCW, imergo, and InfoZoom—all Fraunhofer FIT research results that have been successfully commercialized through spin-off companies and other means. Prof. Jarke is currently involved in two DFG-funded Collaborative Research Centers and has served as coordinator of several European projects in the field of information systems engineering. Since 2004, Prof. Jarke has served as President of the German Informatics Society (GI) and he was scientific coordinator of "Informatics Year—Science Year 2006" for the German Federal Government.

Matthias Kaiserswerth leads the IBM Research Strategy in Systems Management and Compliance, coordinating the research work across IBM's eight global research laboratories. In 2000 he became the director of IBM's Zurich Research Laboratory, where he was responsible for researchers in the field of physical sciences, communications technology, and computer science. He also worked with the IBM Zurich Industry Solutions Lab where IBM hosts customers to meet with its researchers to discuss future technology and emerging business trends. From 2002 until the end of 2005, Prof. Dr. Kaiserswerth was the Managing Director of an IBM Integrated Account, where he was responsible for the total global business between IBM and a large international power and automation company headquartered in Switzerland. In addition, in June 2006 he was reappointed Director of the IBM Zurich Research Laboratory. Most recently, he worked on smart cards and Java security, which led to the OpenCard industry standard for using smart cards in a Java environment and Visa's Java Card™ Price Breakthrough program based on the IBM Zurich Research JCOP platform. He is an honorary professor at Friedrich-Alexander University where he teaches applied computer science.

Pradeep Khosla is Dean of the College of Engineering, Philip and Marsha Dowd Professor of Engineering, and Founding Director of

CyLab at Carnegie Mellon. Prof. Khosla's research interests are in the areas of reconfigurable and distributed collaborating autonomous systems, agent-based architectures, reconfigurable software and security for embedded systems, and distributed information systems. Prof. Khosla is Fellow of the Institute of Electrical and Electronics Engineers, the American Association of Artificial Intelligence, and the American Association for Advancement of Science. In 2006, he was elected to the National Academy of Engineering (NAE). Prof. Khosla currently serves on the editorial boards of IEEE Spectrum, and IEEE Security and Privacy, Oxford University Press Series in Electrical and Computer Engineering, and was appointed in 2003 to the National Research Council Board on Manufacturing and Engineering Design. Prof. Khosla's research has resulted in 3 books and more than 300 articles. He is a consultant to several companies and venture capitalists, has served on the technology advisory boards of many start-ups, and is a co-founder of Quantapoint Inc.—a high-tech company based in Pittsburgh.

Mathias Kirchmer has been Senior Executive at Accenture since January 2008. He focuses on the development and delivery of the firm's business process management services. For almost 18 years, before joining Accenture, Dr. Kirchmer was with IDS Scheer, the leading provider of business process excellence solutions, last as Chief Innovation and Marketing Officer. Before that he managed IDS Scheer's Americas operations and the Japanese operations. Dr. Kirchmer is an affiliated faculty member of the Program for Organizational Dynamics of the University of Pennsylvania as well as a faculty member of the Business School of Widener University, Philadelphia. Dr. Kirchmer often hosts presentations and lectures at leading universities and conferences around the world. In 2004 he won a research fellowship from the Japan Society for the Promotion of Science. Dr. Kirchmer is a member of the advisory board of the Business School of Widener University. He is the author of numerous publications.

John Manley is the Director of Utility Computing at HP Labs, Bristol. This program is a principal component of HP's Adaptive Infrastructure strategy and addresses how to intertwine Business Process Design with Application Design with Infrastructure Design, and how to adapt (automatically) to any class of change in the business process, application, or infrastructure. A particular focus is the Service Provider model of service delivery, whether internal, external, or public. For the last two years, Dr. Manley has led HP Labs' strategic collaboration with SAP Research on Adaptive SAP. This major program is coupling SAP's Business Process Platform systems with HP's Adaptive Infrastructure to enable rapid and flexible definition of Business Processes and the automatic design of the appropriate infrastructure, deployment, and lifecycle management of those Business Processes as a service. These services will run in enterprise data centers or on distributed, federated, shared Service Provider environments. Dr. Manly has served on the advisory boards of a number of UK Grid and Large-scale Complex Systems initiatives, as well as the CERN Grid OpenLab.

Friedemann Mattern has been a Full Professor of computer science at ETH Zurich since 1999. He heads the department's distributed systems research group and is the founding director of the Institute for Pervasive Computing. Prof. Mattern is a member of the editorial board of several scientific journals and book series, initiated and chaired a number of international conferences, published more than 150 research articles, edited several books, and is involved in various research projects, often in cooperation with industrial partners. He is a member of the German Academy of Sciences "Leopoldina," the Heidelberg Academy of Sciences, and of acatech, the German Academy of Technological Sciences. Prof. Mattern also acts as a scientific and strategic advisor to several research councils and international companies. His main fields of expertise are distributed systems and ubiquitous computing, and he is particularly interested in the upcoming Internet of Things.

Stephen Miles leads the Auto-ID Network Research Special Interest Group, a research consortium at the MIT Auto-ID Labs formed to address industry requirements for exchanging Electronic Product Code and Sensor Data in supply chains. He interacts extensively with the industry, including consulting in requirements for new shared business processes and netcentric services for improved cross-enterprise collaboration. Mr. Miles is the founder and co-chair of the RFID Academic Convocation. He participates in EPCglobal, W3C Semantic Web, and related standards organizations, is a frequent speaker at RFID Conferences, and chairs the MIT Enterprise Forum RFID SIG. Mr. Miles is co-editor of the upcoming Cambridge University Press book *RFID Technology and Applications*. He has served as President and Board Member for non profits including Beacon Hill Friends House, Cambridge Early Music Society, the Ipswich Historical Society, Ramallah Friends School, and the Green Garden School in Nairobi.

Max Mühlhäuser is a Full Professor of Computer Science at Technical University in Darmstadt, Germany and heads the Telecooperation Division and the Departmental Computing Center within the Informatics Department. Prof. Mühlhäuser has worked as either a professor or visiting professor at universities in Germany, Austria, France, Canada, and the U.S. since 1989. He has published approximately 200 articles and co-authored and edited several books on computer-aided authoring/learning and distributed/multimedia software engineering. His core research interest is development support for next-generation Internet applications, mainly in the areas of: ubiquitous, ambient, and mobile computing and commerce; eLearning; multimodal interaction, distributed multimedia, and continuous media; hypermedia and Semantic Web; cooperation; and pervasive security. The enabling technologies applied are comprised of distributed object-oriented programming, event-based and peer2peer infrastructures, hypertext, and audio/video processing.

Günter Müller is Founder Director of the Institute of Computer Science and Social Studies at the University of Freiburg, where he has been head of the Telematics chair since 1990. His line of research has won him numerous invitations, including NTT Tokio, Hitachi Laboratories, Japan, IBM, Harvard University, and ICSI Berkeley, where he acted as guest scientist doing work on security and/or human interface technology. Prof. Müller has served on many committees for industry, science, and politics, among them the Multi-Media Commission of the Baden-Wuerttemberg State Parliament and the Advisory Board to a similar task force of the German Parliament. He is a member of the Science and Technology Forum of the Ministry of Science and Technology in Japan. Today, Prof. Müller conducts research in Information and Network Security. He is co-editor of three computer science journals and one Information Systems journal (WI) and acts as consultant to several companies inside and outside Germany.

Mary Murphy-Hoye is a Senior Principal Engineer in Intel's Software Pathfinding and Innovation Division. An innovator in Information Technology and Supply Chain solutions, Ms. Murphy-Hoye applies a broader Predictive Enterprise vision based on emerging technologies to create and implement large-scale experiments in high-volume production environments. She is a pioneer in multi-disciplinary solutions connecting emerging technologies and business practices for cross-enterprise supply networks. Ms. Murphy-Hoye's most recent focus has been the creation of Intel's RFID /Wireless Sensor Networks Lab for industry-scale proactive computing experimentation across businesses. As Director of IT Research, Ms. Murphy-Hoye formed Intel's IT Research Agenda and specialized in research of disruptive technologies as applied to emerging business models. Her academic collaborations with the MIT Media Lab and MIT Sloan School of Business as well as the Stanford Graduate School of Business drove multi-year R&D efforts in: Supply Chain Visualization, Internal Markets for Trade-based Supply/Demand Planning, Demand Creation through Product Transition Dynamics, and Smart Objects for Intelligent Supply Networks. She is currently collaborating with Arizona State University building self-contained wireless sensor networks tuned for reliability and robustness and investigating multi-modal (audio & visual) techniques for complex large-scale predictive analytics. Co-author of *Surviving Supply Chain Integration: Strategies for Small Manufacturers*, National Research Council (National Academy Press, 2000) National Science Foundation, Ms. Murphy-Hoye is also a creator of Intel's Business Computing Vision and works with a wide variety of end-users to identify and address the key challenges of wide scale new technology deployment. Ms. Murphy-Hoye speaks frequently to academic and industry audiences, addressing emerging technology, Digital Business, and Supply Chain strategy, and has had numerous papers and articles published.

Andreas Neef is managing partner of Z_punkt The Foresight Company, a leading Think Tank and consultancy for all aspects of corporate future research and innovation strategies. Since the early 1990s, Mr. Neef has worked as an expert future scientist and innovation adviser. At Z_punkt, he is in charge of strategic innovation and foresight projects for well-known corporations like Siemens, Deutsche Telekom, BASF, Volkswagen, Mazda, Dresdner Bank, PriceWaterhouseCoopers, Wolters Kluwer, and Zeis. As a Foresight Researcher and Management Consultant with focus on ICT and the technology industries, Mr. Neef has many years' experience in projections and the corporate development of future use contexts and business options. Currently, his top priority is the paradigm shift towards innovation concepts modeled on biology. He expects the realization of a "bionic society." He has also written a number of articles and books on business futures and innovation topics, the most recent are *Corporate Foresight—Companies Shaping the Future*, "Web 2.0-Report," and "From the Personal Computer to the Personal Fabricator."

Ilhan Or has been a faculty member since 1976 at Boğaziçi University Industrial Engineering Department, Istanbul, Turkey; he has also held various administrative positions at Boğaziçi University, including the Directorship of the Graduate School of Science and Engineering (since 2005), Senatorship at the University's Senate (since 2005), and Chairmanship of the Industrial Engineering Department (between 1994 and 1998, and again between 2003 and 2006). Prof. Or's major fields of research and teaching interest are linear programming, simulations, risk analysis and management, and operations research applications in energy planning. He has published many articles and made numerous presentations in international scientific journals and meetings in these areas. He has also conducted continuing education and training seminars and worked as a consultant to industry in his fields of interest. Prof. Or served as an Associate Editor of the *Naval Research Logistics Journal* from 1993–2004. He is a founding member of the Energy Economics Association of Turkey and of the Solid Waste Turkish National Committee, and is a member of the Turkish Statistics Society and the Operations Research Society of Turkey.

Maria Orlowska is a Professor of Information Systems at the University of Queensland, School of Information Technology and Electrical Engineering in Brisbane, Australia, where she is currently the head of the research division of Data & Knowledge Engineering. Since August 2004, Dr. Orlowska has acted as Network Convenor for the ARC Research Network on Enterprise Information Infrastructure. International recognition for her work has been demonstrated by her election as a trustee of Very Large Databases Endowment (VLDB). In March 2003, she was elected a Fellow of the Australian Academy of Science and very recently appointed as a Full Professor at the Polish-Japanese Institute of Information Technology in Warsaw. Her research covers a diverse range of considerations, from pure theoretical and fundamental contributions to applied and experimental computing issues. Her research has had an impact on a number of areas in the IT field, including: Relational Database Theory, Distributed Database Systems, Integration of Database Systems into Multi-database Systems, Data Warehousing and Data Mining, and Business Process Management. Her contributions appear in over 290 published research papers in reviewed international journals and conferences.

Michael Rosemann is Professor for Information Systems and Co-Leader of the Business Process Management (BPM) Group at Queensland University of Technology, Brisbane, Australia. His areas of interest are process-based management, process modeling, ontologies, and Enterprise Systems (ES). He is the Chief Investigator of a number of applied research projects funded by the Australian Research Council and industry partners including SAP. Prof. Rosemann has been teaching SAP solutions at universities since 1992. On the educational side, he provided advice to a large number of universities about the design of an ES-related curriculum. He is the author/editor of 6 books, more than 130 refereed papers, and an Editorial Board member of 7 international journals. Prof. Rosemann chairs the Australian BPM Community of Practice (*www.bpm-roundtable.com*) and is a member of the ARC College of Experts. He was the Chair of the 5th International Business Process Management Conference in September 2007 (*http:// bpm07.fit.qut.edu.au*). Prof. Rosemann has intensive consulting experience and provided BPM-related advice to organizations from various industries including telecommunications, banking, insurance, utility, logistics, and film.

Joachim Schaper is Vice President EMEA at SAP Research. He oversees research sites throughout Europe (Darmstadt, Dresden, Belfast, Karlsruhe, Pretoria, St. Gallen, and Sophia Antipolis) and has overall responsibility for six research programs. His current focus is on aligning the SAP Research strategy with the European Research strategy of DG Information Society and Media regarding FP6 (2003–2006) and FP7 (2007–2010). Dr. Schaper is also closely involved with the definition of an industrial initiative (European Technology Platform) with several strategic research partners (Atos, BT, Nokia, IBM, Siemens, Thales, Telecom Italia, and Telefonica). From 2003–2005 he was part of the management of the SAP Research Center at Palo Alto and the group in Montreal. He oversaw the restructuring of the North American group and change management of the SAP INSPIRE team. He set up a new focus on Homeland Security in collaboration with SAP America (Public Sector and Public Affairs). Dr. Schaper also engineered the extension of the research partner eco-system (Intel Research Labs and HP Research Labs) and the re-alignment with major universities such as Stanford, UC Berkeley, CMU, and Rutgers. He pioneered regular scientific talks at the local SAP Labs, inviting thought leaders from the eco-system in Silicon Valley. Dr. Schaper is a member of the advisory board of DFKI and FZI, as well as a member of the advisory group for IST and of various small and mid-sized businesses. He is also Mini-Track chair of the HICSS conference regarding "Next Generation Learning Platforms."

Gautam Shroff heads TCS' Innovation Lab in Delhi, which conducts applied research in software architecture, natural language processing, multimedia, and graphics. Additionally, he is responsible for TCS' Co-Innovation Network, which works with emerging technology companies to create and take to market solutions that have disruptive innovation potential. As a member of TCS' CorporateTechnology Board, he is also involved in the process of recommending directions to existing R&D efforts, spawning new R&D efforts, sponsoring external research, and proliferating the resulting technology and intellectual property across TCS' businesses. Prior to joining TCS in 1998, Dr. Shroff had been on the faculty of the California Institute of Technology at Pasadena, after which he joined the Department of Computer Science and Engineering at Indian Institute of Technology, Delhi, India.

David Skellern is one of Australia's most successful ICT entrepreneurs, with a strong background in research, education, collaboration, and commercialization. Dr. Skellern became interim CEO of NICTA in May 2005 and in February 2006 confirmed a further three-year appointment as CEO. In 1989, Dr. Skellern took up the Chair of Electronics at Macquarie University. He spent significant time working in industry as a visiting researcher, including over two years at Hewlett Packard Laboratories. In 1997, he co-founded the Radiata group of companies in Australia and the United States, established to commercialize the results of the WLAN research project that he led at Macquarie University in collaboration with CSIRO. Radiata was acquired by Cisco Systems, Inc. in 2001, at which time Dr. Skellern joined Cisco and subsequently moved to the U.S. as Technology Director of the Wireless Networking Business Unit. Dr. Skellern was appointed to the NICTA board in 2003. Since 2007, he has been adjunct Professor at the University of Sydney.

Ralf Steinmetz is Professor at the Department of Electrical Engineering and Information Technology as well as at the Department of Computer Science at the Darmstadt University of Technology, Germany. He is in charge of a chair position as managing director of the "Multimedia Communications Lab." Prof. Steinmetz's research interests cover networked multimedia issues with the vision of "seamless multimedia communications," i.e., network dependability and security (e.g., gateways, firewalls), quality of service (e.g., network engineering), content distribution networks (e.g., streaming), context aware communications (e.g., peer-to-peer mechanisms), and media semantics (e.g., ontology enrichment, metadata). He has been the editor and co-author of a multimedia course, which reflects the major issues of the first in-depth technical book on multimedia technology. He has worked as an editor of various IEEE and ACM journals, as well as others. He is a member of the GI and VDE-ITG and was awarded as ICCC Governor, the honor of Fellow of both, the IEEE and the ACM. In 2005, Prof. Steinmetz became a member of the technology advisory board of the "Hessen Agentur" and was appointed as the advisor for information and communications technology by the Hessian government.

Wolfgang Wahlster is the Director and CEO of DFKI, the German Research Center for Artificial Intelligence and a Professor of Computer Science at Saarland University. In 2001, the President of the Federal Republic of Germany presented the German Future Prize to Prof. Wahlster for his work on language technology and intelligent user interfaces. He has also been elected to four international academies and learned societies. In 2002, Prof. Wahlster was elected full member of the German Academy of Sciences and Literature in Mainz. He was the first German computer scientist elected foreign member of the Royal Swedish Nobel Prize Academy of Sciences. In 2004, he was elected full member of the German Academy of Natural Scientists "Leopoldina," founded in 1652, and of acatech, the Council for Engineering Sciences at the Union of the German Academies of Science and Humanities. He has published more than 170 technical papers and 7 books on language technology and intelligent user interfaces. He serves on a number of international advisory boards, and is a member of the supervisory boards of various IT and VC companies. Prof. Wahlster is an AAAI Fellow, ECCAI Fellow, and GI Fellow.

Janet Wesson is Head of Department and Professor in the Department of Computer Science and Information Systems at the Nelson Mandela Metropolitan University (NMMU) in Port Elizabeth,

South Africa. She is also Head of the NMMU/Telkom Centre of Excellence in Distributed Multimedia Applications, which is funded by Telkom SA, Dimension Data, and the Technology for Human Resources in Industry Programme (THRIP). Prof. Wesson has published widely in local and international conferences and journals on user-centered design, user interface design, and usability evaluation. Her current research areas include information visualization, intelligent and adaptive interfaces, and mobile computing. Prof. Wesson is South Africa's national representative on IFIP TC.13 (Human-Computer Interaction), vice-chair of IFIP TC.13, and secretary of WG13.2 (User-centered Design Methodologies). She was a THRIP grant holder from 2003–2007 and was selected as a THRIP Excellence Awards Finalist for 2004. Her current THRIP project was initiated in 2006 and is entitled "An Investigation into Intelligent User Interfaces for Contact Centre Management." Prof. Wesson is currently a South African National Research Foundation (NRF) rated researcher and is acknowledged as an expert in HCI education and research.

Virtual Participants

Alistair Barros is research leader at SAP Research and entrepreneur of its Internet of Services research field. He has a PhD in Computer Science from the University of Queensland and 22 years experience, having worked at CITEC and the Distributed Systems Technology Centre, before joining SAP in 2004. He has around 50 publications in refereed journals and international conferences, and his research has contributed to international standards (WS-CDL, BPMN and UML Profile for EDOC) and references including the widely cited workflow patterns in the BPM field. He has led technology transfer efforts at SAP involving BPM technologies. He has also led commercial projects featuring whole-of-enterprise service frameworks for Boeing, Queensland Government and Australian Defence. His contributions to research funding acquisitions have included the Australian Cooperative Research Centre for Smart Services, the German National Lighthouse project, the European Union project SUPER and various Australian

Research Council projects. A number of these projects are aimed at developing a next-generation service delivery framework in the context of wide-scale service grids and ecosystems.

Denis Browne, Senior Vice President, Business User Imagineering at SAP, has over 17 years of experience in the enterprise software market. His team explores and develops emerging technologies and business models which provide SAP customers with new solutions to improve their performance in the global marketplace. With innovative concepts and tools like Enterprise 2.0 and widgets, Mr. Browne's team points to the future of SAP solutions and the enterprise software market. Currently, he also consults with early-stage startup companies in the bay area, providing professional advice and guidance. Before joining SAP, Mr. Browne spent eight years working with numerous startups as a founder, chief technology officer, and product manager. For example, he led product strategy for Software as a Service, a Web services platform company created by Marc Benioff, the Chairman and CEO of Salesforce.com. The solutions created by Software as a Service formed the basis of Salesforce.com's AppExchange offering. In addition, Mr. Browne spent several years at Oracle leading product development teams. Mr. Browne graduated with an MA from the Institute of Technology in Carlow, Ireland. He is an avid traveler and spent a year and a half in 2002 exploring over 30 countries across North, Central and South America, Africa, Europe, Asia, and the South Pacific.

Paul Butterworth is the Chief Technology Officer at AmberPoint, a leading provider of SOA runtime governance solutions. Prior to AmberPoint, he was the Chief Technology Officer for Forte Tools at Sun, where he was responsible for the technical strategy for the Sun developer tools products. As a founder of Forte Software, Mr. Butterworth was the Chief Architect and Senior Vice President of Engineering and Customer Services. Before founding Forte, he served as Chief Architect and Director of Product Engineering at Ingres Corporation. He holds a B.S. and M.S. in Information and Computer Science from the University of California at Irvine.

Nikolaus Franke is Director of the Institute for Entrepreneurship and Innovation at the Vienna University of Economics and Business Administration. He is also Director of the TU/WU Entrepreneurship Center, a joint technology transfer organization together with the Technical University Vienna, Academic Director of the MBA in Entrepreneurship and Innovation (Schumpeter Program), and leads the User Innovation Research Initiative Vienna. Prof. Franke is a board member of the Electronic Commerce Competence Center (EC3) in Vienna and Scientific Director of the annual competition "Top 100—Germany's most innovative SME." He is a member of many juries and evaluation committees, for example the Ernst & Young Austrian Entrepreneur of the Year Award, the Austrian National Innovation Award, and the Rudolf Sallinger Award. He has consulted with many firms from startups to leading multinationals and served as an invited speaker at many occasions.

Patrick Grady is Founder, CEO, and Chairman of Rearden Commerce. A recognized pioneer in Web Services and on-demand technologies, Patrick Grady has guided Rearden Commerce to a commanding leadership position as the world's fastest growing commerce platform for goods, services, and applications. With more than 1,250 customers spanning the Fortune 50 to small/medium enterprises, leading distribution partners like American Express Business Travel, and more than 137,000 merchants and third-party application providers, the company is fundamentally transforming the way individuals and businesses buy and sell goods and services online. Patrick founded Rearden Commerce with a singular vision—to provide the world with an online personal assistant for work and life that makes people wonder how they ever lived without it. With a single login and password, the Rearden Personal Assistant helps people find what they need based on who they are, what they like, where they are, and the context of what they are doing. In addition to serving as CEO, Patrick is Rearden Commerce's strategic architect, guiding the company's product and technology vision. As an evangelist for the Web's next generation, he is a sought-after speaker with engagements including AjaxWorld,

AlwaysOn, Burton Catalyst, CSFB Disruptive Technology Conference, InfoWorld Symposium, Internet World, PC Forum, the PhoCusWright Executive Conference, Red Herring, and Supernova. Prior to founding Rearden Commerce, Patrick spent 10 years in various venture capital and leadership roles in the technology sector.

Dion Hinchcliffe is Founder and Chief Technology Officer for the Enterprise Web 2.0 advisory and consulting firm Hinchcliffe & Company, based in Alexandria, Virginia. A veteran of software development, Dion has been working for two decades with leading-edge methods to accelerate project schedules and raise the bar for software quality. He has extensive practical experience with enterprise technologies and he consults, speaks, and writes prolifically on IT and software architecture. Dion still works in the trenches with enterprise IT clients in the federal government and Fortune 1000. He also is the creator of Web 2.0 University, which provides the world's leading educational solutions in Web 2.0, Enterprise 2.0, and Ajax for private corporations and for the general public. He also speaks and publishes about Web 2.0 and Enterprise 2.0 on a regular basis. Dion is working on a book about Web 2.0 for Addison-Wesley and is Editor-in-Chief of *Real World Ajax: Secrets of the Masters*. He is also currently Editor-in-Chief of the *Web 2.0 Journal* and *Social Computing* magazine.

Eric von Hippel is the T. Wilson Professor of Management and Professor of Engineering Systems at MIT. He is known for his research into the sources of innovation. He finds that product development is rapidly shifting away from product manufacturers to product "lead users" in the Internet Age. The rapid growth of user-centered innovation requires major changes in company business models and government policymaking. Dr. von Hippel's book, *Democratizing Innovation* (MIT Press, 2005), explains user-centered innovation and how companies can adapt and profit. This book is available free on the web at http://mit.edu/evhippel/www/books.htm. Dr. von Hippel has founded and participated in startup firms, and is a founder of the entrepreneurship program at MIT. He serves on numerous editorial advisory boards for academic journals and is an active researcher with numerous international collaborators.

Eric Kasper has been working with SAP since 2005 as part of SAP Research/SAP INSPIRE —the corporate venturing unit of SAP—which is continuously looking for new business opportunities. Before coming to SAP, Dr. Kasper worked as a research associate at Ludwigshafen University of Applied Science, where he worked at the Research Center for Innovation and Management and conducted a series of research and consulting projects. Dr. Kasper has a bachelor's degree in Business Administration and a Ph.D. from Leeds Metropolitan University (Great Britain). His major research interests are innovation management and R&D management.

Peter Kürpick is the Chief Product Officer (CPO) webMethods Business Division and Member of the Executive Board of Software AG. Dr. Kürpick joined Software AG in April 2005 and in his role is responsible for the company's webMethods business line, which holds all products related to Service-Oriented Architecture (SOA). Before coming to Software AG, he was Senior Vice President Server Technology at SAP and as such was responsible for major parts of the SAP NetWeaver stack, which is the foundation of all SAP applications. At the beginning of 2000, he acted as Executive Board Assistant, during which time he worked out of Palo Alto, New York, and Germany for Prof. Dr. Hasso Plattner, former CEO and co-founder of SAP. Dr. Kürpick started his career in IT in 1998, joining SAP as a software developer.

Anne Thomas Manes is a renowned technologist in service-oriented architecture with a 28-year industry background. In 2002, *Network World* named Ms. Manes one of the "50 Most Powerful People in Networking," and in 2001 she was one of *Enterprise Systems Journal*'s "Power 100 IT Leaders." Prior to coming to the Burton Group, Ms. Manes was CTO at Systinet, and Director of Market Innovation in Sun Microsystems's software group. Her industry background also includes field service and education at IBM Corporation, customer education at Cullinet Software, product management at Digital Equipment Corporation, chief architect at Open Environment Corporation, and research analyst with the Patricia Seybold Group. Ms. Manes' areas of technology expertise include service-oriented architecture, web services, XML, governance, superplatforms, application servers, Java, J2EE, .NET, application security, and data management. She is a frequent speaker at trade shows and at InfoWorld, JavaOne, and RSA conferences. A member of *Web Services Journal* editorial board, she authored *Web Services: A Manager's Guide* (Addison-Wesley, 2003) and has participated in web services standards development efforts at W3C, OASIS, WS-I, and JCP.

Andrew McAfee joined the faculty of the Technology and Operations Management Unit at Harvard Business School in 1998. His research investigates how managers can most effectively select, implement, and use Information Technology (IT) to achieve business goals. He was the recipient of a U.S. Department of Energy Integrated Manufacturing Fellowship for his doctoral research, which focused on the performance impact of enterprise information technologies such as SAP's R/3. His current research falls into three categories. The first is an exploration of how Web 2.0 technologies can be used within the enterprise, and what their impact is likely to be. The second is an exploration of when IT leads to increased use of market mechanisms for coordinating activity, and when it instead leads to greater use of hierarchies. The third is a study of IT's impact over time on the structure of US industries. He launched the first Harvard Business School faculty blog, which examines the impact of IT on businesses and their leaders. Dr. McAfee teaches an MBA course called "Managing in the Information Age" and an Executive Education course, "Delivering Information Services." He also teaches in the Owner/ President Manager Program, the General Manager Program, and the Senior Executive Program from the Middle East. He continues to consult, primarily on helping companies formulate and execute IT strategies. He speaks frequently to industry and trade groups.

Philip Nelson was an early innovator in search as the technical founder and CTO of Verity, the pioneering enterprise search company, from 1987 to 1997. Mr. Nelson also co-founded Impresse Corp., which offered a SaaS platform for marketing collaboration, and Anteros, which provides technology and services to enhance the user experience of enterprise software. He was also an Entrepreneur-In-Residence at Accel Partners, the CTO of Spark Networks (JDate), and has worked on diverse projects including gene sequencing, the design of artificial hip implants, XML file systems, and several DARPA efforts. He's currently working on the next generation of product search at thefind.com.

Navi Radjou is a vice president at Forrester Research. He investigates how globalized innovation—with the rise of India and China as both a source and market for tech innovations—is driving new market structures and organizational models, which Forrester designates as "Global Innovation Networks." He advises senior executives worldwide on new organizational designs and business processes their firms must adopt to sustain global competitiveness through technology-enabled innovation. During his eight years at Forrester, Mr. Radjou has advised senior executives around the world on issues related to innovation, supply chain, and customer service. Mr. Radjou was named by *Supply & Demand Chain Executive* magazine as one of the "Pros to Know," honoring an elite group of professionals who have excelled in the innovative use of supply chain technologies and practices within user companies. Prior to joining Forrester, he was a technology consultant in Asia—working with both private and public-sector companies—and a development analyst at IBM's Toronto Software Lab. Trilingual, Mr. Radjou earned his M.S. degree in information systems at Ecole Centrale Paris and also attended the Yale School of Management.

John Seely Brown is the independent co-chair of Deloitte's new Center for Edge Innovation, a visiting scholar at USC, and advisor to the Provost. Prior to that he was the Chief Scientist of Xerox Corporation and the director of its Palo Alto Research Center (PARC). While head of PARC, Dr. Seely Brown expanded the role of corporate research to include such topics as organizational learning, knowledge management, complex adaptive systems, and nano/mems technologies. He was a co-founder of the Institute for Research on Learning (IRL). His personal research interests include the management of radical innovation, digital youth culture, digital media, and new forms of communication and learning. Dr. Seely Brown—or, as he is often called JSB—is a member of the National Academy of Education, a Fellow of the American Association for Artificial Intelligence and of AAAS, and a Trustee of Brown University and the MacArthur Foundation. He has published over 100 papers in scientific journals and was awarded the Harvard Business Review's 1991 McKinsey Award for his article, "Research that Reinvents the Corporation" and again in 2002 for his article "Your Next IT Strategy." In 2004 he was inducted in the Industry Hall of Fame. With Paul Duguid, he coauthored the acclaimed book *The Social Life of Information* (HBS Press, 2000), and with John Hagel he coauthored *The Only Sustainable Edge* (HBS Press, 2005) a book about new forms of collaborative innovation. This book also provides a novel framework for understanding what is really happening in off-shoring in India and China and how each country is inventing powerful new ways to innovate, learn, and accelerate capability building.

Sonali K. Shah is Assistant Professor at the University of Washington, Seattle. Her research examines the creation and maintenance of innovation communities in fields ranging from open source software to sports equipment to medical imaging devices. She has extensively studied the inner-workings of innovation communities, that is the motives, coordination structures, and strategies that support community-based innovation and product development. This work has led her to theoretical and empirical work investigating the processes underlying the formation of new industries and product markets and issues related to knowledge, entrepreneurship, and the role of institutions in shaping entrepreneurial and innovative activity at the individual level. She has worked with technology clients at Morgan Stanley & Co. and McKinsey & Co. She holds B.S.E degrees in Biomedical Engineering and Finance from the University of Pennsylvania and the Wharton School. She received her Ph.D. from the Massachusetts Institute of Technology.

Peter Thoeny is the founder of TWiki and has managed the open-sourced TWiki.org project for the last nine years. Mr. Thoeny invented the concept of structured wikis—where free-form wiki content can be structured with tailored wiki applications. He is a recognized thought-leader in wikis and social software, featured in numerous articles and technology conferences including *Linux World, BusinessWeek, The Wall Street Journal,* and more. A software developer with over 20 years' experience, Mr. Thoeny specializes in enterprise collaboration, software architecture, user interface design, and web technology. He graduated from the Swiss Federal Institute of Technology in Zurich, lived in Japan for 8 years working as an engineering manager for Denso building CASE tools, and managed the Knowledge Engineering group at Wind River for several years. He co-authored the book *Wikis for Dummies,* and is currently working on *Wikis for the Workplace.* Mr. Thoeny co-founded TWIKI.NET *(http://www.twiki.net/),* a company offering TWiki solutions that help revolutionize collaboration and productivity in all organizations.